WITHDRAWN

D0717752

CA

101429

U0 DEC 1996

Coll. of Ripon & York St John

3 8025 00246364 7

BEYOND SUFFRAGE

CRPYK

Beyond Suffrage

Feminists in War and Peace, 1914–28

Johanna Alberti

MACMILLAN

© Johanna Alberti 1989

All rights reserved. No reproduction, copy or transmission
of this publication may be made without written permission.

No paragraph of this publication may be reproduced, copied
or transmitted save with written permission or in accordance
with the provisions of the Copyright Act 1956 (as amended),
or under the terms of any licence permitting limited copying
issued by the Copyright Licensing Agency, 33–4 Alfred Place,
London WC1E 7DP.

Any person who does any unauthorised act in relation to
this publication may be liable to criminal prosecution and
civil claims for damages.

First published 1989

Published by
THE MACMILLAN PRESS LTD
Houndmills, Basingstoke, Hampshire RG21 2XS
and London
Companies and representatives
throughout the world

Printed in the People's Republic of China

British Library Cataloguing in Publication Data
Alberti, Johanna
Beyond suffrage: feminists in war and
peace, 1914 – 28.
1. Great Britain, feminism, 1900 – 1920
I. Title
305.4′2′0941
ISBN 0–333–45435–9 (hardcover)
ISBN 0–333–45436–7 (paperback)

COLLEGE OF RIPON AND
YORK ST JOHN YORK CAMPUS

CLASS No.	ACCESSION No.
305 . 4094 AL6	2463647
CHECKED	DATE
AW	9/12/91

Contents

Acknowledgements

The author would like to thank the following for their assistance in preparing this book:
Nick and Pat Abbott; Ben and George Alberti; Linda Anderson; David Bowcock, Cumbria Record Office; Juliette Bright; Mary Clapinson, the Bodleian Library; Wilfred Congleton; David Doughan, the Fawcett Library; Irene Dunn, Newcastle University Library; Frances Evans; Sheila Fletcher; Neil Hamilton; Brian Harrison; Catherine Ireland, the Fawcett Library; Di Lansdown; Jane Lewis; Irene Maneylaws; Trustees of the National Library of Scotland; Colin Platt; Angela Raspin, the Library of Political and Economic Science; Liz Stanley; Margaret Wilkinson, and most of all, Cynthia Fuller.

The author and publishers would like to thank the following for permission to reproduce material quoted in this book:

Dr. Michael Ashby, for the papers of Margery Corbett Ashby.
Helen Blackstone, for the papers of Maude Royden.
The British Library, for the Marie Stopes Collection.
Tony Cooper of *The Townswoman* for 'The Woman's Leader'.
Frances Don of the International Alliance of Women, for 'Jus Suffragii'.
Major Furlong, on behalf of Miss E. Furlong, for the papers of Kathleen Courtney.
Mrs Barbara Halpern for the papers of Ray Strachey.
George Marshall for the papers of Catherine Marshall.
Margot Miller for the papers of the Women's International League for Peace and Freedom.
Naomi Mitchison.
Ann Patterson and Helen Stocks for the papers of Mary Stocks.
Sandra Shulman of the Fawcett Society, for the papers of the London Society for Women's Service.
Trinity College Library for the Pethick Lawrence Papers.

JOHANNA ALBERTI

To Aylwin Clark
in gratitude and affection

1 Introduction

On the evening of 6 February 1918 Evelyn Sharp walked up Whitehall with friends and fellow suffragists to celebrate the giving of the Royal Assent to the Representation of the People Act. By this Act eight-and-a-half million women over the age of 30 were given the vote. She recalled later that it had been 'almost the happiest day of my life.' She felt that she had lived 'to see the triumph of a "lost cause"', for which she had 'suffered much and would have sacrificed everything.'

> memories crowded into my mind, of women who had been insulted and rolled in the mud, just there, for attempting to enter the House of Commons and present their petition; memories of years of effort diverted from other causes and other interests, of friends lost by the way and friends gained in the struggle, of horrid disillusionment and transfiguring revelation; memories that hurt so much that they had to be buried out of sight and memories so illumined by fine behaviour and delicious humour that they would remain a precious possession until the end of life.[1]

Other suffragists were less elated about the culmination of their struggle. In France Cicely Hamilton was working in a hospital within sound of gunfire directed at an enemy plane.

> at this moment of official enfranchisement, what really interested me was not the thought of voting at the next election, but the puffs of smoke that the Archies sent after the escaping plane. Truth to tell, at that moment I didn't care a button for my vote; and, rightly or wrongly, I have always imagined that the Government gave it me in much the same mood as I received it.[2]

Ray Strachey knew that the Government had given women the vote after a final year of intense effort. She went to Westminster and found

> the occasion was really a great one in its way and we were all moved by it . . . when the moment actually came we all

1

caught our breath and looked at each other. And such a great
handshaking took place – after all we've had a good stiff year of
it together.[3]

A celebration service was held on 12 February. It was attended by
many suffragists, including Evelyn Sharp, but there were also many
who could not be there. Catherine Marshall, who was recovering
from a total breakdown in health and spirit, heard of the service
through a letter from a friend.[4] The celebration was also muted by
the limitations in the franchise which was granted: only women over
30 years of age could vote, and the qualification was occupation (or
marriage to an occupier), rather than residential as in the case of men.
Yet this partial enfranchisement was for many women the significant
result of a long political struggle:

> the possession of the vote . . . is a finer weapon than we have
> ever possessed; even before we actually held it in our hands we
> were made to feel its power, and at the moment our consciousness
> of that power is almost overwhelming.

Feminist activity for many women had been focused on the
vote in the Edwardian period, and there were dangers in this
which suffragists recognised:

> It compelled us to concentrate all our force, all our hope,
> all our enthusiasm, upon a single, narrow tenet. *It immensely
> simplified the women's movement.* And for those of us who grew
> up under the stimulus of that intense concentration, the ideals of
> the woman's movement seemed to be summed up in the three
> words of our battle cry, 'Votes for Women'.

Partial enfranchisement was not the end of the struggle but the
gaining of a 'brilliant strategic position'. From this position, with
its challenge and its opportunities, feminists recognised the danger
that the women's movement might fail through the diversity of its
objects.[5]

From the perspective of the 1970s it appeared that the women's
movement did falter and fail between the wars: in the late 1980s
we are more inclined to question this apparent discontinuity. In
the early 1980s Dale Spender, feminist and writer of a postwar
generation, interviewed Mary Stott, a journalist who has been a
feminist since 1929. 'And tell me, Mary, what did you do during
the time when there was no women's movement?' The indignant

response was: 'What do you mean, when there was no women's movement? THERE'S ALWAYS BEEN A WOMEN'S MOVEMENT THIS CENTURY.' Mary's confident statement became the title of Dale's book in which she offered a 'fragment of our past' in the lives of five women who were active feminists from the 1920s to the 1980s.[6]

There are histories of the women's movement in the nineteenth century and early twentieth century, and of the suffrage struggle in particular: Ray Strachey wrote one of the first of these – *The Cause* – in the 1920s.[7] For the period which followed the war there are still only fragments: this book is another. The question which lies behind it is what women who had been active suffragists did with their energy and their commitment once limited suffrage had been gained in 1918. In seeking answers to this question I found that the experience of the war was so crucial that I must begin my search in 1914. When the war broke out, hopes for enfranchisement were high: when limited suffrage was achieved three-and-a-half years later, the shape of the suffrage movement, as of the political context, had changed.

I have adopted a biographical approach to explore the experience of fourteen women who had been active suffragists before 1918 and whose political activities continued after the war. In order to understand why women made certain choices it is necessary to understand something of their personal lives and their relationships. The recreation of their lives is only possible in a limited way since there is, as there always is, a limit to the knowledge we can glean from the letters and papers available to us. The choice of women has been to some extent dictated by their decision to preserve their papers or to write autobiographies. There are those who have done neither: Chrystal Macmillan is one whose life and work was closely bound up with the women who are central to this study, yet she will remain a shadowy figure because she has left so little behind her. Her name appears often in the papers of the organisations in which she was active, especially the National Union of Women's Suffrage Societies (NUWSS), which became the National Union of Societies for Equal Citizenship (NUSEC) after the war, and the International Woman Suffrage Alliance (IWSA). The papers of organisations such as these will be used extensively in this study, together with feminist newspapers, in particular *The Woman's Leader* and *Time & Tide*. Interwoven with the reports and views presented in such sources will be letters which give us glimpses of the experiences and feelings behind expressions of opinion and choices of action. Some of these letters exist because below the institutional framework of feminism lay a network of friendship. Liz Stanley followed the lead given by Ray Strachey in *The Cause* and has traced a web of feminist friendship which existed between 1825 and 1938.[8] This book owes a debt to Liz Stanley's approach and to her emphasis on what united rather than divided feminists. In tracing the lives of a group of women, I have also been heedful to her warning that traditional biography, where the spotlight falls on one woman, tends to reduce and belittle the part played by other people in her life.

There are published autobiographies of six of the women in this study and three more have left unpublished fragments.[9] If one looks at the reasons they give for writing about their lives, there is a hesitation and ambivalence about placing themselves at the centre of the stage which Linda Anderson has suggested indicates a desire to deflect attention from themselves. Anderson finds in Helena Swanwick's introduction to her autobiography an apparent desire to reassure herself and her reader that 'she knows her place even though in the work itself she will go on to challenge the male for his territory, as both writer and public figure.'[10] Justification for writing could be found in the cause itself, whose singularity and immediacy vindicated its proponents. The most confident placing of her identity in an historical context is made by Emmeline Pethick Lawrence. She wrote mainly of her part in the militant suffrage movement which she understood as 'the final stage of the greatest bloodless revolution that has taken place since history began.' She believed that it had been 'given to me to prove in my own experience that "the Idea" is the strongest thing in the world and can overcome all obstacles.'[11]

Evelyn Sharp was also aware of the significance of the suffrage movement as a revolutionary force in society as well as in the lives of individual women, yet she belittled the struggle as an 'adventure' in her autobiography. Sharp portrayed herself as an eccentric spinster with a love of travelling and apologised for 'talking about myself'. Elizabeth Robins wrote mainly of her experiences on the stage, and filled pages with memories of famous names.[12] Margaret Rhondda's autobiography was originally intended only as a description of her schooldays, written to express how much her 'House-mistress' had meant to her: 'Gradually, I do not quite know how, the idea of making a whole book grew.' Rhondda sees herself as in no way exceptional, a typical Edwardian young woman who was 'set free by chance.' Writing in the early 1930s, she found that she could not write about the 1920s because those years

> have not yet arranged themselves into any pattern. They are still tangled up. If I delved into them I should, it seems, be dipping at random, not picking out the already patterned scenes from the surrounding mist . . .

She then identified the problem of perspective which haunts the writing of autobiography: 'The me of twenty years ago is so little me that I can talk of that creature with freedom. The me of ten years ago is so much me that I find it difficult to say a word about her.'[13] We have always to remember that the autobiographies used in this book offer yet another perspective on the events, and that this perspective is shadowed by the years which passed between, by the changes in political context and in personal experience. Mary Stocks did not write about her own life until she was in her late seventies, so that her reflections on the period covered by this book are crucially separated by the experiences of fifty years. In 1970 she was a well-known and respected broadcaster, a self-styled 'statutory woman' and a different woman from the feminist and socialist we shall meet on these pages. She wrote because her publisher demanded that she should, and apologised before she began for the possibility that her book might be 'inexpressively banal.'[14]

In writing letters and diaries, in writing at all, we are creating a fiction about ourselves, either for our own contemplation or that of our friends and relatives. Writing defined as fiction is also a source which will be used occasionally in this study. The link between such writing and the lives of the author is often ambiguous and always complex, but I have referred briefly to the novels of Evelyn Sharp and Elizabeth Robins, whose fictional writing was crucial in their lives. The perspective of contemporary letters and diaries is immediate and comparatively direct and honest, although this honesty is inevitably tempered by the writer's relationship with the recipient. Ray Strachey's letters to her mother are a rich source, but we have to remember that Mary Berenson did not necessarily approve of all her daughter's activities and views, so that Ray's description of them is modified by that knowledge. Perhaps the most vivid and truthful are the letters between friends, and I have read many of these in the surviving papers of Catherine Marshall and Evelyn Sharp. Evelyn Sharp has also left diaries, although they only cover scattered periods. Letters between Maude Royden and Kathleen

Courtney survive, although most of them were written before the war. Courtney had left a few letters to her family written in the period covered here, as has Margery Corbett Ashby. For two of the women there are extant biographies: Mary Stocks wrote lovingly of the life of her friend Eleanor Rathbone, and surviving letters were used together with her daughter's memories for a biography of Eva Hubback. It is the existence of this material which has guided the choice of the women in this book.

The common denominator is that they were all active suffragists, and at some period of their lives, they were feminists. The definition of feminist has been that their activities were informed by an understanding of the role and position of women in society which saw them as oppressed. They were all middle-class and there are perhaps three reasons for this. One is that it was largely, although certainly not exclusively, middle-class women who left the kind of writing which I wanted to use as sources for this study. The network of friendship which is so important to feminism is also relevant, in that friendships could cross class-barriers, but did not often do so. Finally my own social background meant that I find it easier to understand and write about the preoccupations of women who were faced with similar pressures, limitations and opportunities.

The fourteen women whose experience of these fourteen years is explored on these pages came from similar backgrounds: all were suffragists; they knew each other, and some were close friends. Yet within this coherence there are diversities which help to elucidate the direction of women's political activities both within the suffrage movement and beyond it. The oldest of them – Elizabeth Robins – was 50 in 1914 and the youngest – Mary Stocks – was 23. Most of them were members of the largest suffrage federation, the National Union of Women's Suffrage Societies, and four joined the more militant Women's Social and Political Union. For two of them – Evelyn Sharp and Maude Royden – feminist activity was an interruption of their life's work; for others it was seen as central from the beginning, or became so as a result of their involvement. They made choices which led them into different organisations and activities after the war. The focus of this study will move back and forth from their personal responses to the actions and statements of those organisations and the papers with which they were connected. From this double perspective we can begin to answer questions about the women's movement and its apparent decline in the interwar period.

The second chapter of this book introduces the fourteen women on whom it is based and places them at the outbreak of the First World War. In Chapter 3 their experience during the war is explored, and the implications of both war and the franchise for the suffragists are traced in some detail in Chapter 4. In Chapter 5 the chronology is interrupted for a consideration of the impact on feminists of ideas on women's sexuality which were current in the 1920s. Books by Marie Stopes linked women's sexuality with the need for birth-control and expressed an 'ideology of motherhood' which seemed to many to undermine the arguments for equality. In the first two turbulent years after the war the wave of hope for social change broke with a suddenness which left many suffragists gasping. Feminist activity continued in the face of increasing resistance to demands for equality, and the persistent efforts of two organisations and two newspapers with which many of the fourteen feminists were connected are described in Chapter 6. The cause of birth control and for family allowances – known at first and significantly as the 'endowment of motherhood' – were adopted by some feminists and rejected by others who could not accept the validity of such demands within the context of a belief in equality between the sexes. The stress placed both on feminist organisations and on individuals by this dissension is described in Chapter 7. The last chapter moves on to the international stage, where many former suffragists found a focus for their activities. Here similar pressures led to a consideration of the meaning and nature of feminism, particularly in its relation to pacifism.

The activity and achievements of the group of women whose lives are central to this study took place in a specific historical context, a period of both national and international uncertainty. For women as well as for men the veneer of Edwardian confidence was replaced by scepticism and a search for a path which would avoid the horrors of a world war and ameliorate its social and economic consequences. These women did not doubt the importance of continuing the struggle against society's failure to recognise women's political identity, but they did not always see this struggle as their first priority. They knew that the exhilaration of the height of the suffrage struggle could not be recreated. They sought, tentatively and thoughtfully, with shared knowledge and experience of the suffrage movement but with differing political perspectives, for ways in which they could contribute.

2 Coming Together

CATHERINE MARSHALL (1880–1964)

On the west shore of Lake Derwentwater in Cumbria, under the ridge of hills known as Cat Bells, a confident, Victorian house stands alone, its angular contours softened by sycamore and larch. In 1908 it was the home of Catherine Marshall and her parents and on a rainy day in July a group of Cambridge University students was given shelter there. They were touring the country speaking for suffrage, and on arrival in Keswick, at the head of the lake they were met in the rain by 'swarms of suffragists'.[1] One of the students was Ray Costelloe, and this was the first time she had met Catherine: their paths would cross again for they both became increasingly involved in the suffrage movement as it reached its climax in the years before the war.

Catherine had spent much of her childhood and youth in the security of public schools. Her father was a housemaster at Harrow, and in 1896 she was sent to St Leonard's School in St Andrews, the first public school for girls. Catherine survived her early problems with the tight discipline and mysterious rhythms of the school. She was fortunate to enjoy cricket, and Frank Marshall sent her enthusiastic advice on batting style. She was much involved in school drama productions, and her only mention in a history of the school compiled in the 1920s, is her performance as Sir Joseph Porter in *HMS Pinafore*.[2] She became a 'monitor', an achievement marked by the 'putting up' of her hair. She also edited the house magazine. Leaving school and moving from its structured days, firmly delineated successes and close friendships, was not easy for Catherine and her contemporaries. Five years after she left, Catherine wrote to her headmistress, Julia Grant:

> I can never thank you enough for all that you – and school – did for me. I realise ever more and more how valuable your help was from the frequency with which I long for it again.[3]

For one of Catherine's closest friends, Margaret McKerrow, parting from Miss Grant was 'dreadful' and made all the more

8

so in that it was necessary to disguise how much the parting meant to her. Describing her life at home Margaret wrote to Catherine:

> It's like having two natures – one that goes about at home and is called me, and another that has been put away in a box, and knows nobody here, and is even odder than the other.[4]

Catherine and Margaret had experienced living and working with close friends in a protected, yet emotionally and intellectually stimulating environment. One of the results of the strong and lasting appeal of such an experience was that Catherine Marshall would be at her happiest and most effective when working closely with other women for a cause. Margaret went on to University but Catherine remained at home: writing poetry; studying languages; reading widely; singing. She was so busy that her father wrote: 'take half your irons out of the fire at once please, and let them cool.' He was concerned about her health, because she was sleeping badly and during the day was tormented by headaches. She was showing signs of a characteristic and ultimately self-destructive tendency to try to fit too much into her life. It was also the case that for Catherine and her friends, as for so many unmarried middle-class women at this time, the constant demands of their parents, made more binding because they were loving and supportive, was a tie from which only school, then University, could free them. Margaret McKerrow wrote to Catherine: 'One's friends say – "Be not in bondage to your family" – but one cannot always help it.'[5] Women of this generation were able to see this tie as bondage, and one or two, among them Evelyn Sharp, had the courage and determination to leave. Others found in suffrage a cause which justified their departure.

In 1906 the Women's Social and Political Union (WSPU) began to appear regularly in press headlines as members demonstrated in the Ladies' Gallery in the House of Commons or, displaying flags, rang the bell of No. 10, Downing Street, resisting when the police attempted to remove them physically. Catherine and Margaret were restless, with energies and ambitions whose nature was not clear to them, except in that they were not fulfilled. Catherine had moved to Keswick when her father retired: Margaret had come down from Cambridge and had taught for a while, leaving the job because of illness. She was not needed at home because her sister was there, and wondered whether 'an ostrich farm in S. Africa or a ranch in Canada would be suitable. These are the usual refuge of the ne'er do well, I believe.'[6]

Margaret McKerrrow became engaged to be married in the summer of 1906. In a letter to Catherine earlier in the year she had written that she was 'sorry to hear that your political career is ended. I was hoping some day to hear you address a mass meeting . . . '[7] Catherine's political career was, on the contrary, about to begin as she found in the suffrage movement an outlet for her energy, a cause to which she could offer her immense abilities as an organiser, and a group of friends with whom she would share an intense experience. In 1908 Catherine Marshall and her mother, Caroline, founded the Keswick Women's Suffrage Society. Catherine's feminism had its roots in the commitment of her family, rather than growing from her experience within a family as was the case with other suffragists whom we shall meet.

Catherine later became Regional Organiser and then Parliamentary Secretary of the National Union of Suffrage Societies. While she found fulfilment in this work, she also experienced the tension of difficult political choices. Possibly the most risky of these choices was made in the summer of 1912 when the NUWSS had been deeply disappointed by the defeat in the House of Commons of a suffrage measure, a defeat which damaged suffragist faith in the Liberal Government. In June Frank Marshall had written to Catherine about rumours that the NUWSS was going to give money to Labour candidates: he hoped that the rumours were not true, as such an arrangement would represent 'a distinct declaration of war on the Government'.[8]

The rumours were based on truth. The Labour Party had been moving gradually and reluctantly towards support for suffrage. In January the party conference had passed a resolution in favour of franchise for women, and every Labour MP present had voted for the Bill on suffrage which came before Parliament in 1912. On 30 April the officers of the NUWSS met with Arthur Henderson, the party secretary, to discuss a plan for the establishment of a fund to help Labour candidates fight Liberal anti-suffragists in by-elections. There was reluctance on both sides of this proposed alliance. The Labour Party was far from united in its support for suffrage: it was desperately short of funds, but some members were suspicious that the NUWSS might try to influence party decisions. There was opposition to the scheme from a vocal minority on the executive committee of the Union, and Eleanor Rathbone was later to resign over the issue. After negotiations between the two organisations, the Labour Party finally accepted the NUWSS proposal in July, and the Election Fighting Fund was established.[9] When Frank Marshall found out about the EFF he was unenthusiastic about the prospect of Catherine becoming secretary to the committee which administered it. But, characteristically, she was unable to refuse this new challenge.[10]

The NUWSS ceased to concentrate its hopes on a policy of persuading the House of Commons to pass a private member's suffrage bill, and turned its attention to achieving electoral support for suffrage. Marshall and her new staff of paid organisers soon impressed the Labour Party with their energy and effectiveness. The organisers included Selina Cooper, Ada Nield Chew and Ellen Wilkinson, who all worked in the North West. Constituency committees and local suffrage societies began to hold joint meetings. All was not plain sailing, and Marshall's tact and perseverance in keeping the lines of communication open, and her ability to develop warm personal relationships with a variety of people, helped to keep the two sides working well together.[11]

While increasingly committed to the new alliance with Labour, Catherine was at the same time involved in negotiations between the NUWSS and the Conservative Party, the main purpose of which was to put pressure on the Liberal Government. She was also at the centre of activities designed to build up support in the Liberal Party. The conduct of these negotiations, together with her EFF work, took an enormous toll of her emotional energy and political integrity. Even when on holiday she found time to write to the Liberal MP Charles Trevelyan, to defend her political activities, which he had called 'parliamentary intrigue and badgering MPs and Ministers.'[12] Total absorption in suffrage work meant that the outbreak of war came to Marshall, as it did to so many suffragists, as a sudden and almost incomprehensible shock.

HELENA SWANWICK (1864–1939)

Catherine Marshall was sustained in her suffrage work by her friendship with Helena Swanwick. The two women may well have met originally on the slopes of Cat Bells, behind Hawse

End. Swanwick had spent her honeymoon at a farmhouse on the slope of the hill and returned there for walking holidays from her home in Manchester. Swanwick was described by Ethel Snowden, a fellow suffragist, as

> one of the most commanding personalities of the women's movement . . . She is a person of quite extraordinary intellectual power, a little lacking in tenderness to those of lesser calibre. She finds it extremely difficult to obey the scriptural injunction to 'suffer fools gladly.' . . . Her courage, both physical and moral, is of the very first order and beyond all praise . . . She is full of artistic appreciation, hates cant and humbug, and is devoted to practical things and persons.

Snowden worked with Helena Swanwick during the war, and may have become aware then of her 'lack of tenderness', although the way Swanwick put it was that she was 'worn out by the effort of ladling out appreciation and apology. I cannot refrain from something very like contempt for people who, in the face of all there is to be done, nurse their little feelings and complain when they are not appreciated.'[13]

Helena Swanwick had a sense of purpose and direction which carried her through the arduous work and difficult choices of the suffrage movement, although she is believed to have committed suicide in despair at the outbreak of the Second World War. This strength lay partly in her maturity – she was 40 when she became an active suffragist – but she also believed that its roots lay in her childhood experiences. She was born in Munich where her father, Oswald Sickert, earned a little money as an illustrator. The family depended, both financially and emotionally, on Helena's English-born mother, who had a small private income from her natural father. They lived in two rooms, one of which was a study for Sickert; the other a living-room for his wife and four children, of whom Helena was the youngest, and in her own opinion, the least loved. The family then moved to England, settling eventually in Notting Hill, where two more boys were born. When she was six, Helena fell dangerously ill with scarlet fever. The doctor recommended sea air to save her life, and she was sent to a boarding-school in Dieppe. There she grew strong and healthy, but was intensely unhappy: 'it was an inoculation of grief which took the poison from all subsequent griefs.'[14]

When Helena was twelve the school collapsed, and she returned to a family where she felt a total outsider. Moreover she found it hard to accept that she should be treated differently from her five brothers:

> I resented the assumption that, whereas education was of importance for my brothers, it was of no account for me. I resented also that I was required to render them personal services which they need not reciprocate . . . When I grew in my 'teens I resented the idea that I could not be allowed out after dark, even in frequented thoroughfares. When it was explained to me that a young girl by herself was liable to be insulted by men, I became incoherent with rage at a society which, as a consequence, shut up the girls instead of the men.[15]

Helena thought of herself as clumsy and was bored by talk of clothes. She believed she had no good features except the red hair which her mother hated. From this misery she was rescued by a quite different experience of a school at Notting Hill High School for Girls. Helena spent four years there, 'in an almost constant state of bliss.' She was 'ravenous for discipline, teaching, books, friends and leaders. The simple commonplaces of an orderly education were a delight to me, and I was gluttonous for friends after my own heart.' Thanks to a school scholarship and a generous grandmother, and despite her mother's doubts, Helena went to Girton in the autumn of 1882 to read Moral Sciences. She was intoxicated by college life. In her first summer in Cambridge, she met Frederick Swanwick, a lecturer at Manchester University. They began a correspondence which was interrupted two years later when Helena's mother discovered that Swanwick had not yet proposed marriage. Her mother's interference hardened Helena's determination to leave home as soon as she could, and earn her own living. She did earn her own living, lecturing and teaching, when she graduated, but she did not as yet leave home. Her father died at the end of 1885, and inevitably it was the only daughter who cared for a mother who could not bear to be left alone, even at night. In the evenings Helena had to bring her work into the sitting room, with its incessant interruptions, to prevent her mother weeping constantly. She was only conceded her personal privacy and her mother's respect when she married in the spring of 1888.

Before he met Helena Sickert, Fred Swanwick had 'resolved not to marry', and she 'had been prepared to remain his friend for life.' Having discovered the obstacles to such a relationship in late Victorian England, they married, and for Helena 'it was little short of heaven to share life with a man who was the most libertarian and unegotistic imaginable.' Fred Swanwick was 'self-poised, neither leaning nor wishing to be leaned on.' In Manchester, Helena found part-time teaching jobs again, and she contributed occasional articles and stories to magazines. She also helped to start and to run two social clubs for men and women, and helped at a working girl's club, which she found 'exhausting but fun'. She took the girls to the countryside for holidays. Through Margaret Llewelyn Davies, a contemporary at Cambridge, she became a lecturer for the Women's Co-operative Guild. These experiences 'gradually whittled away' her liberalism, although, like Catherine Marshall, she 'did not consciously become a socialist until after the Suffrage movement proved that the Socialist was the only party willing to stand or fall by the political freedom of women.'[16]

In between bouts of activity of this sort – which she accomplished on a bicycle – Helena Swanwick had regular periods when she was laid out by 'flu or bronchitis, and crippled, like Marshall, by back problems. When Fred's father died in 1900, the Swanwicks moved to Knutsford where she was content to 'vegetate', cultivating her garden and writing articles and a book on gardening; 'to feel health returning'. she followed the political scene closely, but, as a disenfranchised person, felt 'no call to take any share in party work'. Then in October 1905 she read of the actions of Christabel Pankhurst and Annie Kenney who interrupted an election meeting in the Manchester Free Trade Hall with demands for the Liberal Party to pledge its support for women's suffrage. They were roughly evicted from the hall and then arrested and imprisoned for obstructing the police and causing a disturbance in the street. Together with thousands of other women, Swanwick's 'heart rose in support of their revolt.' Despite her admiration for the WSPU action in 1905 she joined the North of England Society, which was affiliated to the NUWSS, because she knew a great deal about the Pankhursts and felt that she could not work with them. But, as for most suffragists, it was partly a matter of chance as to which union they joined.[17]

Until the outbreak of war Helena Swanwick devoted her energy and talents entirely to the cause. She spoke at meetings up and down the country, in public and in private. She hated the advertising of meetings by billboard, the bell-ringing and chalking of pavements, as she hated standing to collect signatures for petitions, but she enjoyed the challenge of writing an article for a paper at speed. Her experience as a journalist led her to take on the job of editing *The Common Cause*, the NUWSS paper. At first Swanwick worked from Manchester, but in 1911 moved to London where she worked 12 hours a day and seven days a week until her resignation in the summer of 1912. She was by then 'unutterably weary . . . both of the Liberal Government and the WSPU': her resignation was the result of her frustration in the policy of restraint imposed on her when she wanted to criticise the militant tactics of the other Union. After her resignation, Swanwick continued to write for the suffrage cause, and spoke at meetings from Gloucester to Whitley Bay[18] in Northumberland. She also wrote a book, *The Future of the Women's Movement*, in which she put forward her ideas about the origins and nature of the movement. In August 1914, she was back in London.

KATHLEEN COURTNEY (1878–1974)
MAUDE ROYDEN (1876–1956)

In the suffrage movement in Manchester, Swanwick had worked closely with Kathleen Courtney. Courtney arrived there from Oxford with a 'big reputation as an office organizer' and was recommended by Hudson Shaw. Courtney had met Hudson Shaw, a radical Church of England minister, through her close friend, Maude Royden. Kathleen Courtney and Maude Royden met at Lady Margaret Hall, Oxford. Kathleen had gone to university because her family 'did not know what to do with me'.[19] Neither young woman needed to earn her living after university, and they seemed not to have shared Swanwick's determination to do so. Both of them returned to their parents' homes and became involved in voluntary social work, of the sort which Swanwick had done in Manchester. Royden worked in the Victoria Women's Settlement in her home town of Liverpool, and Courtney at the Lambeth Girl's Club. Neither young woman had felt the personal sense of oppression that had fired Swanwick's feminism. Courtney was one of five girls, which is probably significant, and Royden later recalled that she was treated in the same way as her brothers. Courtney found that the lives of the girls she met in Lambeth made her aware 'that there was something terribly wrong in our society that must be changed.' From this 'passionate feeling about the wrongs of women' sprang her commitment to suffrage.[20]

Their settlement work did not satisfy the two women. In 1902 Royden wrote to her friend: 'Kathleen, mavoourneen, I am feeling rather unhappy about you. Are you really well in body? . . . I feel that you are unhappy – perhaps I should rather say dissatisfied.'[21] She advised Kathleen to move away from her parents' home, where she was not needed but stayed on because of her 'desire to acquire those most desirable virtues which home life makes for'. Neither of them was well suited to the work they had chosen. Kathleen was having difficulty in persuading the girls at the club to behave in an orderly way. Maude did not have that problem, but she felt that the girls did not like her. She longed to throw herself completely into some work: 'I am in such a terror of my besetting sin of laziness and self-indulgence, that I feel the hardest life would be the safest.'[22] In 1902 she moved to Rutland to live with Hudson Shaw and his wife, and help in his parish. This still did not prove to be sufficiently absorbing, and Shaw suggested that she begin speaking and preaching. He put her in contact with a sympathetic rector and she began to preach at services on Sunday evenings, becoming a remarkable and memorable speaker.

Meanwhile Kathleen Courtney had moved to Oxford where she did administrative work for the University Extension Delegacy which gave her the experience she was later to use in running the suffrage office in Manchester. The two women spent some time together in Oxford before Courtney moved to Manchester, and in 1906 Courtney offered to look after Royden when she was ill that year. Royden's response was that it would be wrong for Courtney 'to make even a part of your life mine, in a sense which really means that what you would do independently is of less importance than what I would do'.[23] Active Edwardian men had wives to organise their domestic comfort; for active women the domestic part of their lives was often a problem. Royden's supportive companion in these years was Ida O'Malley, another active suffragist

In the North of England Suffrage Society in Manchester, Courtney found the challenge and fulfilment she had sought since she left university. She then moved to work at the central office of the NUWSS in London where one of her many tasks was the organisation of meetings. Her skill filled Helena Swanwick with gratitude and admiration:

> thanks to Miss Courtney's excellent organization, our meetings were now co-ordinated, so that one had a whole series for ten

days or so in one area, and did not waste strength and time in dashing from one end of the country to another.[24]

Maude Royden had almost been 'seduced by the dramatic and heroic methods of my militant sisters' but she too joined the NUWSS; 'The suffrage struggle absorbed and widened my life.' When Helena Swanwick resigned as editor of *Common Cause* , she took on that task and continued until the spring of 1915. In June 1914, Royden and Courtney went on holiday together to Italy, where Catherine Marshall was delighted to hear they were getting much-needed rest, sleeping for twelve hours each night, and spending the days in the open air.[25]

ELEANOR RATHBONE (1878–1946)

London and Westminster served as a magnet for active suffragists when hopes of a Suffrage Bill were at their prewar peak. In the last years before the war Catherine Marshall, Helena Swanwick and Kathleen Courtney moved to London from the North West. From Liverpool came another suffragist, Eleanor Rathbone.[26] The Rathbone family were wealthy shipowners, and Eleanor's father was a Liberal MP. Her childhood was therefore spent partly in London and partly in Liverpool, where the family were well-known for their philanthropy. Eleanor's political and social education in this large and busy family made more impression on her than her schooling. She was also aware of her need to spend time away from the demands of her family life, and university was the obvious solution. She went to read Classics at Somerville four years before Kathleen Courtney began her degree in Oxford. Among her college contemporaries Eleanor became known as 'The Philosopher': her absent-mindedness and her capacity for cogent argument were lifelong characteristics.

After graduating, Eleanor returned to Liverpool and to a life influenced, like Catherine Marshall's, by her much-loved father. She became a visitor for the Liverpool Central Relief Society, and a manager of a Council School. Later she was on the committee of the Victoria Women's Settlement where Maude Royden worked as a volunteer. Elizabeth Macadam was appointed Warden of that settlement in 1902: she became Eleanor's closest friend and lifelong companion. Rathbone was remembered by her contemporaries as a fierce feminist, and she was an early convert to the suffrage cause. In

1897 she became Parliamentary Secretary to the Liverpool Women's Suffrage Society, and lobbied Members, spoke at meetings, wrote articles and organised other suffragists for the next twenty years. She was politically active beyond the suffrage movement, and in 1909 was elected as the first woman councillor for Liverpool. In 1913 she helped to launch, and became the first president of the Liverpool Women Citizens Association whose aim was to educate women as citizens and electors.

Rathbone's political stance was then, and alway remained, emphatically independent. Her opposition to alignment by suffragists with any political party led to her resignation from the executive of the NUWSS. The last two years before the war were for her, as she later confessed to Catherine Marshall, an 'unhappy time, one of the unhappiest times of my life'. She and Catherine were to maintain contact despite their disagreements at that time, and in the early years of the war. Rathbone wanted women to retain what she saw as a tradition of 'English political life', the possibility for 'political opponents who quarrel on platforms or deal each other hard blows, to maintain their personal friendly relations unchanged'.[27]

MARY SHEEPSHANKS (1878–1958)

In the year of Eleanor Rathbone's birth another future suffragist was born into a large Liverpool family. There the resemblance ceases, for Mary Sheepshanks's family was poor, and her childhood unhappy.[28] Although Mary too admired her father, he gave her little love or encouragement in return. Mary was the eldest of seventeen children, and she was like Helena Swanwick in her anger at the preferential treatment given to her brothers. Again like Swanwick, Mary Sheepshanks found school a place of refuge where she found friends and intellectual excitement. After leaving school, she went to Germany for a year where she learned the language, and, for the first time in her life, visited theatres, concert halls and art galleries. She enjoyed herself immensely. She returned to England and to Newnham College, Cambridge. Many of the friends she made there were men, and they included Bertrand Russell and Theodore Llewelyn Davies.

In Germany and Cambridge Mary Sheepshanks developed a capacity to enjoy life, but she was deeply imbued with a sense of social responsibility, and from the comforts and the intellectual stimulation of university she moved to Southwark, to work in the University Women's Settlement. Southwark was probably the poorest borough in London at the time, and there Mary taught at the Workhouse school, collected rents, took children to hospital for treatment, organised evening clubs and helped to run a fund which offered city children a holiday in the countryside. Unlike Rathbone, Royden or Courtney, Mary had no private income and she was supported financially at first by a scholarship. Mary developed a great respect for the working class among whom she lived and worked. From Southwark she moved to Stepney where she continued to work, living in dingy lodgings. However, she had made friends at Cambridge which made it possible for her to spend evenings in quite a different milieu, keeping in touch with Theodore Llewelyn Davies and meeting Helena Swanwick's brother, Walter Sickert, who was making a name for himself as a painter. She also escaped from London to take bicycling holidays in France and Italy.

In 1897 Mary Sheepshanks became Vice-Principal of Morley College for Working Men and Women. Mary was only 25, but had always given people the impression of being older than her years. She was only asked three questions by the interviewing committee: whether she had any sisters who could nurse her parents if necessary (the answer was five!); whether she could tell when a lecturer on 'The Care of Horses' was drunk; and whether she could stop a glove fight which got out of control in the gym. To these last two questions, Mary, who was six-foot tall, answered a firm: 'Yes'. She was paid £100 per year, which was considered to be a 'semi-voluntary' stipend.

In 1905 Theodore Llewelyn Davies was drowned in somewhat mysterious circumstances. Mary's love for Theodore, and her intense unhappiness after his death were private feelings she shared only with Bertrand Russell, although her friends may have guessed what made her so 'bitter and sour and unamiable' at this time.[29] Despite her unhappiness, she was an energetic and innovative teacher and administrator, introducing 'At Homes' for women only, to give them space for debate and discussion after classes while the men played billiards or smoked.

Mary became an active suffragist through her friendship with Hilda Clark, whose older sister, Alice, was on the executive of the NUWSS, and was a friend of Catherine Marshall.[30] Mary travelled to Lincolnshire and Oxfordshire with Philippa Strachey to speak on suffrage. In 1908 she attended the International Woman Suffrage

Alliance (IWSA) Meeting in Holland. Her knowledge of languages led her to be invited by the IWSA in 1913 to undertake a lecture tour in Europe, starting in Brussels, and ending in Budapest, where another IWSA Congress took place. At the Congress Mary was asked to become Secretary of the IWSA in London, and to edit its monthly paper, *Jus Suffragii* (The Right of Suffrage).

Mary had for many years leased a house near Westminster, where she let rooms to other suffragists, including Catherine Marshall. The two women were very different in their habits: Mary liked a quiet, regular life; perhaps because of her experience of living close to working-class women, she was thoughtful about the demands she made on her one domestic servant, and took her meals at regular times. Catherine liked to have visitors, sat up late at night, talking or working, and was notoriously unpunctual. However, in the hot summer of 1914, the two women were living together in apparent amity at 1 Barton Street. In late July, as the political situation in Europe deteriorated, Marshall suggested that the women's suffrage organisations organise a public meeting to bring pressure on the British Government to remain neutral and to become a mediator between Austria-Hungary and Serbia. The Women's Peace Meeting took place on 4 August 1914.[31]

EVELYN SHARP (1869–1955)

Evelyn Sharp was on holiday in the last week in July 1914. When her close friend Henry Nevinson, a journalist, came to say goodbye to her before he left for Berlin, he warned her that the situation in Europe was so serious that war involving Britain was almost inevitable. She found his prophecy difficult to accept. For her, as for so many others, the war came with catastrophic suddenness. Her involvement in the suffrage cause had helped to distract her from international politics.

Sharp is the first suffragist of the fourteen who was a member of the WSPU: in other ways, the pattern of her life was strikingly similar to theirs. Like the Sickerts and the Courtneys, the Sharps were a middle-class family living in London. Her father retired early from the family slate business, and buried himself in his study with his books, leaving the running of the household and the upbringing of a family of ten children to Jane Sharp. Evelyn was the eighth child to survive infancy, and the main source of love and support in her childhood was Nurse Brown, of whom Evelyn wrote:

> She was the most faithful friend life has given me, and I have not been without friends. Her loyalty was unassailable . . . she had the gift of loving as few know it . . . When she died in February, 1921, she left a gap in my life that no one else could fill.[32]

The size of her family prevented Evelyn, like Mary Sheepshanks, from developing a close relationship with either of her parents. Many years later she came close to her mother for a few years before Jane Sharp died in 1915. There was a firm line between 'the others' as the older half of the family were known and the younger ones whom they tyrannised. Temporary relief came when Evelyn was sent to boarding school. Not yet fully aware that she was a 'misfit' in her own family, she thought it odd that her contemporaries did not share her desire that the school term should last for ever. She discovered to her surprise that she was not stupid, and that it was not necessary to be musical to justify one's existence. She also encountered new codes of behaviour. In her family she had learned that girls 'possessed neither courage nor a sense of honour, and further, that treasons, stratagems and spoils, whatever these may be, are too good a fate for all who have not music in their souls'. She did not form intimate relationships with schoolfriends, however, partly because a visit by a friend to Sharp's home meant an 'agony of spirit watching her inability to reach the perfection required of her by my own critical family'. She was passionately devoted to the headgirl who 'was always too sensible to take advantage of my emotional attitude towards her'. The atmosphere of the school was not conducive to intimacy. According to Evelyn the Miss Sparks who ran it helped their pupils to avoid 'the hysteria and other adolescent troubles that I gather from books was sometimes the case with the cloistered Victorian girl'. For the rest of her life, Evelyn Sharp was wary of intimacy. There were very few people who had what she called 'the horrid power to sweep me off my feet and plunge me into heaven or hell to my utter undoing as a useful member of the community'.[33]

Although the school may have increased Evelyn Sharp's reserve, it gave her a 'vision of a wider world' from which she found herself excluded when she left. Her parents had retired to a country village, and they would not agree with her plan to go to university. Her resentment was intense. She continued to study on her own and started evening classes for village boys much her own age. She began to send the short stories she wrote to magazines: she called the pile of rejected manuscripts her 'Mount of Humiliations'.

One of her motives for writing was that no one else in the family showed any inclination to do so, and she thus felt secure from comparison. She wrote her first novel in the mulberry tree in the garden. Thirty years later she revisited the village and recorded in her diary the recollections of a couple who had been the Sharps' neighbours and who had first seen her

> coming down from the mulberry tree with a book under my arm, and staring dreamily at them without seeing them till some members of the family jerked me awake and introduced us – 'You were the most beautiful thing I had ever seen,' said Mr Cooke with a reminiscent smile. — Such a waste! I thought, to hear that 30 years too late.[34]

In these 'desert years' there was one bright interlude when she went to Paris for four months with her two sisters. They went to lectures and to concerts; gave hot-chocolate parties and explored the city. Then it was back to the stultifying existence of a Victorian spinster in an English village, where she was expected to have no other ambition in life than 'to sit at home and wait for a problematic husband, performing meanwhile such ornamental household tasks as were left over when a mother, elder sisters and competent servants had all had a hand in them'. For Sharp there was no possibility of breaking free unless she actually left home, and we have had a glimpse of how difficult this was from Swanwick's experience, and to a lesser extent, from those of Courtney and Marshall. It took Evelyn Sharp six years to accomplish her growing resolve to go to London and earn her own living. Her decision to go was greeted with 'consternation' by her family, although her departure was beneficial to the declining family income which was still supporting four unmarried daughters. Jane Sharp, who was in any case ignorant of the financial situation, 'saw nothing but original sin in my revolt'. Thirty years later, Evelyn Sharp wrote of her 'revolt'.

> Some force was driving me out from home that I could not define, and I knew only that, had this been less impelling than it was, I must have yielded to the pull of old loyalties and abandoned my bid for independence. For it is family affection, not the want of it, that enslaves man and woman in the home.[35]

She needed all her strength of will during the first months in London. During the day she taught a private pupil and at schools. Each evening she returned to her Bloomsbury hostel to write in a cubicle, using her bed as a table, and writing by candlelight once the gas was turned off at 11 o'clock. Within a year she had had a short story published and a novel accepted by The Bodley Head. The effect on her life was dramatic. Although she still had to teach to earn a living and write in the evenings, she now had an active social life and was able to move to the Victoria Club where she had a bedroom to herself. It was a small room in an attic, at the top of a long, twisting staircase, lit at night only by candles, but Evelyn was able to use the club writing room. Her social life sprang from the literary circle which surrounded John Lane, the sole owner of The Bodley Head publishing company. In this sophisticated society Evelyn Sharp was an innocent in whom, in her own words, there was 'still a good deal of the young prig left'. She seems to have suffered from an emotional upheaval in this circle of friends, an experience which led her to write to John Lane:

I can't write anything but fairy stories just now; real things have gone so badly for me that I am too sore at heart to attempt a real story. Oh, I do wish I hadn't got a heart at all. I think if you are born a woman your heart ought to be left out to put you on an equality with men. How can there be equality of the sexes as long as women are given hearts? What rot I am writing to you, where is my sense of humour?[36]

It was clearly expected in her circle that one retain one's sense of humour, and Evelyn Sharp tried all her life to make serious criticisms of society through the use of irony and humour. She also retained her image of love as a place where there were no rules, a sort of fairyland. She contained her pain in hard work, and wrote of her experiences in her novels.

By 1906 Evelyn Sharp was a well-established novelist and journalist. In the autumn of that year she was sent by the *Manchester Guardian*, for which she was by now writing regular articles, to Tunbridge Wells to report on the annual conference of the National Union of Women Workers among Women and Children.[37] The customary session on women's suffrage at this conference was filled to capacity because of press reports that day on the appearance of Emmeline Pethick Lawrence and others on charges of obstruction outside the House of Commons. Millicent Garrett Fawcett, president of the NUWSS, made a speech in which she defended the actions of the suffragettes. In the discussion that followed, the first speaker was Elizabeth Robins, an American actress and writer. Robins had never spoken on a suffrage platform before, but the impact on Evelyn Sharp was so great that it was to alter the direction of her life.:

> The impression she made on me was disastrous. From that moment I was not to know again for twelve years, if indeed ever again, what it meant to cease from mental strife; I soon came to see with a horrible clarity why I had hitherto shunned causes.[38]

She joined the local branch of the NUWSS, but then followed Elizabeth Robins into the WSPU, believing 'that the militant movement aimed at winning social and economic freedom for women as well as political equality with men'.[39] Other women believed that these aims were those of the NUWSS: they were certainly the aims of most dedicated suffragists. Sharp was immediately involved as a speaker, and addressed many audiences, although she never lost her distaste for the platform. A letter written by an admiring listener suggests that this distaste was well hidden. The letter also reveals something of the ambivalence towards the suffrage movement which was felt even by men who professed sympathy with 'the Cause':

> When you were sitting down you did not look remarkable, but when you spoke you were downright charming. Your face was of the Italian Madonna type, and your voice was exceedingly pleasant . . . As long as you were speaking of your objects, I thought you were perfect . . . But when you dealt with the suffragette methods, I got suspicious. Your sense of humour, which before had seemed part of your sanity, now became alarming. You represented yourself as a simple, earnest, meek little lamb who was cruelly ill-used by men . . . but all the time one could have sworn that you were a demure little imp of mischief who made the teasing of cabinet ministers a fine art, and hugely enjoyed the rows you raised.[40]

The transformation of meek little lambs into militant suffragists was a shock to hundreds of Edwardian families, and those lambs were often fired by a private rebellion which was now given public expression. In Sharp's own family we only learn of the reaction of her mother, and of Nurse Brown. Nurse wrote to Evelyn in January, 1908:

> I shall be pleased to come to hear the speeches and sincerely hope you all will gain the day it will be a grand thing for the

labouring class. I often think the aposite (sic) sex get a little too much their own way. It will be a hard battle to fight and knowing you are a very determined charricture (sic) and just the one to help in just cause. I hope you will not get knocked about at any time with the roughs dear that would almost break my heart to see my dear child unkindly treated who is always trying to do good.[41]

Jane Sharp was at first shocked when Evelyn joined the militants, and made her promise not to do anything which would lead to imprisonment. Their correspondence on the suffrage issue brought them close together for the first time. When Evelyn wrote to say that she felt that her mother had never approved of anything she had done, Jane Sharp responded with amazement that Evelyn had yet been

> such a devoted unselfish child to me. I am more sorry than I can express that all these years, instead of cheering you & helping as a mother should I have utterly failed . . . You do know now don't you that in all you do – except being arrested – I am with you entirely.[42]

The desire to be with friends in the risks they took, the urge towards solidarity, was a powerful force in the suffrage movement. Evelyn received this letter from her mother:

> I am writing to exonerate you from the promise you made me – as regards being arrested – although I hope you will never go to prison . . . I have been thinking so much about you, I feel sure what a grief it has been that you could not accompany your friends: I cannot write more but you will be happy now, won't you?[43]

On 11 November 1911, Evelyn Sharp threw a brick through the window of the War Office: because she was a pacifist, the choice of target gave her particular satisfaction. Prison came as a shock. She found that it required all her self-control not to scream and batter at her cell-door when she heard other prisoners – not suffragettes, she assumed – do the same. She went to prison again in July 1913, and took part in a hunger strike:

> Only the sense of fighting for a cause for which one is prepared to die would give anybody the strength of will to go on with it after the first day or two.[44]

Outside Holloway, Sharp's talents as a journalist were made full use of when she took over the editing of the WSPU paper, *Votes for Women* after the Pethick Lawrences were sentenced to nine months' imprisonment. When both the Pethick Lawrences and their paper were cut adrift from the WSPU by the Pankhursts, Evelyn Sharp joined them in forming the United Suffragists, together with Henry Nevinson and the Ayrton family.[45] In June 1914, Sharp and Nevinson marched with Sylvia Pankhurst and a deputation of working-class women from the East End. Nevinson was thrown to the ground when a mounted policeman seized and arrested Sylvia. It was the last time they would take part in a suffrage demonstration before war was declared.

ELIZABETH ROBINS (1862–1952)

The woman who inspired Evelyn Sharp's commitment to the cause was an actor, and her power to move people had been apparent in her roles in Ibsen's plays in the 1890s.[46] Her decision to act had been a revolt against her family. Her father had wanted her to be a doctor, and her grandmother, who had to a large extent brought her up, was deeply shocked that she should work for money. The family wealth became a thing of the past when her father went bankrupt, and Robins earned her own living from her twenties. Money was the apparent cause of the suicide of her husband, also an actor. They had been married only a short time when George Richmond Parks jumped into the Charles River in Boston, wearing chainmail, and leaving Elizabeth a note that read: 'Bills, bills, bills.' The young widow went to Norway with friends, and from there to London where she determined to make her way in the theatre. She succeeded, first as an actor and then as a playwright and producer, in partnership with Lady Florence Bell at the New Century Theatre. She also wrote novels, and a description of the journey she took in 1900 to find her beloved brother in the Arctic.

When Robins spoke at the NUWW meeting in Tunbridge Wells, she was already passionately feminist, but had taken no part in the suffrage movement. After that meeting, she was called upon again and again to speak. At first she refused, and concentrated her efforts on writing a play, *Votes for Women*, which she later transformed into a novel, *The Convert*.[47] Later she agreed to speak, and also continued to write articles, short stories and letters to the press. She became a member of the WSPU executive, together with Emmeline Pethick Lawrence, although this body rarely if ever met. She helped to organise the Actresses' Franchise League and the Writers' Suffrage League. She established a home at Backsettown in Sussex, which served as a sanctuary for exhausted suffragists. On an individual basis she gave financial support to a young neighbour from Sussex, Octavia Wilberforce, who defied her family by training to become a doctor. Later, the two women lived together at Backsettown and in Brighton where Wilberforce established a practice.

Although in some ways a shadowy figure, Robins was influential in the women's movement before and after the war. *Votes for Women* was a commercial success, as was *The Convert*. She inspired other suffragists by what she wrote, by what she said and how she said it. She had the capacity to stir people through the power of her own commitment. Like Helena Swanwick the strength of her own conviction meant that others turned to her to restore their own faith. These two women, born in the 1860s, were mother-figures to the suffrage movement. They both knew that the achievement of the vote would not be the end of that struggle. We shall see later that Robins' trenchant analysis of women's oppression was sustained into the 1920s.

EMMELINE PETHICK LAWRENCE (1867–1954)

Helena Swanwick's criticism of the WSPU was that it appealed to the heart rather than to the mind. She wrote of Emmeline Pethick Lawrence that she had 'in her a strong vein of poetry and mysticism' which she used to 'attract young women to daring and sacrifice by methods that seemed to me hypnotic . . . Had she moved my mind as she moved my heart, I should have come over.'[48]

Although they were very different in temperament, there were strong similarities in the experiences of the two women: both of them came from large families; both were sent at an early age to boarding schools where they were very unhappy; they both had supportive husbands (called Fred!), and they remained childless, devoting themselves to similar social and political causes over a long period. Where they differed was in their experience as adolescents. Emmeline Pethick felt that she was loved by her family, and was indeed removed from the school that she hated. As the eldest in the family she developed a close relationship with her father. Harry

Pethick was an ebullient man, a tolerant and companionable father – once his children had reached 'the age of reason'. Emmeline believed that the driving force behind her father was his hatred of injustice, and that she inherited this passion from him. He was proud of her involvement in the suffrage movement, and she was grieved that he did not live long enough to see women obtain the vote. Her mother, although normally calm and serene, was shocked by Emmeline's activities: it was bad enough, in her view, to have daughters who were considered by the neighbours to be 'much too advanced'. Emmeline was sent to finishing schools in France and Germany, but on her return home, she suffered, like Evelyn Sharp, from the sense of being imprisoned in her loving family. She too longed to earn her own living, but was told that to do so would 'only be increasing competition and taking bread out of the mouth of a woman less fortunate than myself'. The thought of marriage and settling down in Weston-super-Mare appalled her. At the age of 23 she wrote to an acquaintance, a woman who had set up a mission 'where she had gathered round herself a band of educated girls whom she was initiating into social work'. According to the familiar pattern that we have seen in the experiences of Swanwick, Courtney, Royden and Sheepshanks, she was immediately placed in charge of a working-class girls club. The members were mostly engaged in the clothing trade at very low wages, and they 'had the high-spirits of the young and the recklessness of the oppressed'. What she saw of the lives of these girls, and of their families, led her to 'accept the gospel of socialism'.[49]

Emmeline Pethick lived in the mission house, and there she 'experienced the joys of community-living which gave me the opportunity of forming deep and intimate friendships'. Mission-life offered her what other women had found at school or at university. However, the restrictions of such a life meant that after five years the urge to be independent remained unsatisfied, as did the desire to move closer to the 'problems and experiences common to working people'. Emmeline and her friend Mary Neal resigned from the mission; each of them had a small private income which made it possible to break away. They set up the Esperance Social Guild which aimed to offer regular employment in dressmaking at decent wages.[50]

For five years Emmeline Pathick devoted herself contentedly to working for the Guild. Then in 1899, Emmeline met a young 'poor man's lawyer' who was helping at the Canning Town Settlement: they married two years later at Canning Town Hall. Emmeline kept her own name (adding Lawrence), but not her way of life. Frederick Lawrence had a house in Dorking, designed by Lutyens, and a service flat in London. For her first wedding anniversary Emmeline's husband gave her a smaller south-facing flat in the same building. Here she was later able to take refuge from the demands of running the WSPU, whose headquarters were the larger flat. In the early years of her married life she used her husband's wealth to enlarge and improve the country home of the Guild. She wrote later: 'all this loveliness had fallen into my lap and I rejoiced in it.'[51]

In 1906 the Pethick Lawrences had just returned from a visit to South Africa when the General Election was held. They greeted the Liberal victory and the increased representation for the Labour Party with enthusiasm, confident that the government would introduce votes for women. Emmeline believed, as did Evelyn Sharp, that the justification for the franchise lay in the need for social reform, and that reform planned only by men 'would not touch some of the worst evils'. It was the working-class girl from Lancashire, Annie Kenney, who persuaded her to become treasurer of the WSPU and, once committed, she never wavered in her loyalty to the WSPU. Her friend, Mary Neal, joined her on the inactive National Committee. In 1907 she and Fred launched and then edited *Votes for Women*. She was imprisoned three times, finding, unlike Sharp, that 'the locked cell could become as conducive to meditation as the mountain can to the ascetic'. The third occasion followed the trial of both the Pethick Lawrences for conspiracy, a charge arising from their involvement in the WSPU. They refused on principle to pay the expenses of the case, and their property was confiscated. When they came out of prison, Emmeline Pankhurst expelled them from the WSPU, believing that their property would be a focus of attacks by the government and that it would be a source of weakness rather than strength to the organisation. The severance was total: 'From that time forward I never saw or heard from Mrs Pankhurst again, and Christabel, who had shared our family life, became a complete stranger.'[52]

It was not the end of the Pethick Lawrences' commitment to the suffrage movement. *Votes for Women* continued to be issued, and its scope was widened to include the exposure of the social disadvantages of women beyond their votelessness. In July 1914 they announced that the newspaper was to be handed over to the United Suffragists, and Evelyn Sharp (who had been assistant editor) became editor when she returned from her holiday.[53]

MARGARET HAIG, LADY RHONDDA (1883–1958)

Evelyn Sharp, Emmeline Pethick Lawrence, and to a lesser extent
Elizabeth Robins, were part of what has been seen as the heart of the
WSPU, the inner friendship circle of women who worked in London.
But the WSPU was not as centralised as they were made to appear by
the press at the time, and by historians since.[54] Margaret Mackworth,
as she then was, moved on the periphery, and was none the less
militant. This militancy is perhaps surprising in a woman who leaves
the impression of reflection rather than passion in her writing. Yet she
herself judged that her involvement in the militant movement 'was a
temperamental, not in any sense an intellectual, conversion . . . My
intellectual assent was complete, but it came second, not first.' In her
autobiography she offers a picture of a young woman carried away by
events and circumstances. She believed that she was set free largely
by chance, and not by her own efforts, from the environment which
had moulded her life and character. Yet the reader has the impression
of a woman in control. Conscious of growing up in a transitional
period, 'with one foot in the Victoria epoch and the other in the
modern world', she believed that women of her generation had to
adapt to a transformed society.[55] Her own adaptation did not involve
a direct challenge to her family: she seems rather to have carried her
inheritance with her into a changed world.

   Margaret Thomas was an only child born to wealthy parents. Her
father was a mine-owner and a Liberal MP. He was disappointed that
his only child was a girl, but he treated her as he would have a son,
talking business with her from the time she was eleven or twelve.
Because of his attention to her and because she had many cousins.
Margaret did not suffer from loneliness. She must have been aware
of the restrictions of her Victorian upbringing, for it was she who
asked to be sent away to school when she heard of one where girls
were allowed to go for walks without mistresses in attendance. The
school was St Leonards, and Margaret arrived in St Andrews just
as Catherine Marshall left in 1898. Margaret was 'gloriously happy'
there and when she came to leave, found 'intolerable the idea of
giving up that very perfect present'. Yet she had no idea that she was
'in any way unfitted by character and training for the role which for
the first few years of my grown-up life I must try to play'. St Lenoards
had taught her a 'freedom of initiative' which made it impossible for
her to become 'the young lady at home . . . One might as well have
tried to put a carthorse into a drawingroom.'[56]

She planned to go to university, but first 'came out' in London, which meant going nightly to dances with her mother. However unsuited to this life, she did not reject its basic premise, which was that she was destined to fall in love and marry. By the time she went to Oxford, she was already 'half in love', and rejected what the university had to offer:

> I could not bear the cloisterishness of the place . . . the air of forced brightness and virtue than hung about the cocoa-cum-missionary-party-hymnsinging girls and still more the self-conscious would-be naughtiness of those who reacted from this into smoking cigarettes and feeling wicked.[57]

She returned to Monmouthshire; to marriage with the son of neighbours and to live in an old house in the country. And marriage for her, as for Helena Swanwick, brought a 'freedom I had never known before, and the status of an adult human being – I was happy – often exultantly happy'. Later she came to understand that her happiness arose from her activities: within four months of her marriage, she had joined the WSPU. Her husband did not interfere, he 'asked only to be left in peace to potter round the kennels'. She rejected the acceptable occupations such as teaching 'village women something about household and child management,' on the grounds that they knew far more about such things than she did. She regarded 'doing good to the poor' as 'an intolerable and unpardonable impertinence'. The suffrage movement offered Margaret Mackworth that 'sense of being some use in the scheme of things' which an earlier generation had found in 'doing good to the poor'. Suffrage activity gave her 'release of energy', and she enjoyed 'speaking at rowdy meetings, selling papers in the gutter, walking clad in sandwich boards in processions'. She also went to prison: like Evelyn Sharp she hated it, describing the experience as 'sheer taut misery'.[58]

Margaret's activities did not destroy the support she had, and would always have, within her family. Her father was essentially unconventional. Her mother's sympathy with the social purity movement of the 1880s had led her to pray passionately that her baby daughter might become a feminist. Four of her aunts went to prison for suffrage activities, followed, reluctantly, by Margaret's mother. The compulsion to bear witness to commitment to the cause was very strong. Even Humphrey Mackworth and his parents accepted Margaret's militant suffrage activities. She did promise him that she would not do anything which would result in imprisonment, a promise she kept to the letter, if not the spirit. Her imprisonment, came after she had set fire to a letter box, feeling that her chances of being arrested for the action were slim.

Margaret Mackworth conducted a double life in the years before the war. While acting as secretary to a WSPU branch, breaking the law and disturbing the peace, she was also working for her father as his 'right-hand man'. She went to an office in the Cardiff Docks where 'the only women in the entire place were two telephone girls tucked away on the top storey'. She credited her success in this unusual environment to her father's confidence in her, and to her schooling: 'At St Leonard's we were taught that what we undertook we had to perform: being a girl was no excuse for failure.'[59]

MARGERY CORBETT ASHBY (1882–1981)

Margaret Mackworth's feminism was fostered by an older generation of feminists: Margery Corbett was inspired by her mother, an ardent feminist. Margery felt that she had been given an equal status with men as

> my birthright, for in all my youth I have shared every advantage with my brother equally – from love and affection to the best possible education and opportunities, and the critical but unstinted encouragement which to the young is like sunshine to a plant.

An external sign of her mother's feminism was said to be the fact that in the country 'she regularly wore the breeches she had taken to when bicycling came in, at least a decade before wartime made them permissible'. Maric Corbett was active in local political affairs; a practical, busy and forceful woman. Margery, the eldest child, was close to her father. Like the other fathers who had a strong influence on their daughters – David Thomas, Lord Rhonnda, and William Rathbone – he was a Liberal MP, although only for a brief spell. Margery was encouraged to go to university by both her parents, and read Classics because her mother believed that 'women must measure up to the hard schools'.[60] Margery did not do well, and Newnham did not make as much of an impression on her as it did on many of her contemporaries. She viewed marriage in the same way as Margaret Thomas, as a natural and not unwelcome prospect.

Margery Corbett was active in the suffrage movement as a student and at one meeting became friendly with Helena Swanwick, who was on holiday in her old college in Cambridge.[61] Like Swanwick, she found the personality of some members of the WSPU very attractive, but joined the NUWSS of which she was briefly secretary and for a longer period a member of the executive. She travelled extensively in Europe in the years before the war, and became involved in the International Woman Suffrage Alliance from the time of its inception in 1904. The scope of her political activities was wide from the time when she helped in her father's campaigns until she was in her nineties. Her commitment to suffrage was part of her analysis of society, based on liberal principles of freedom and individual rights. It would become part of her understanding of society that only the state could finance social reconstruction, and she came to this con-clusion, as did other suffragists, from her experience of social work. In 1913 she was elected a Poor Law Guardian for Putney. By this time she and Brian Ashby were married and living in Upper Richmond Road in Putney.

Just before the war Margery Corbett Ashby resigned from the NUWSS executive together with Rathbone over the issue of the Election Fighting Fund. They were thus somewhat distanced from events in the opening months of the war.

RAY STRACHEY (1887–1940)

Women who became 'constitutional' suffragists were often attracted by the militant approach. Ray Costelloe was captivated by the way one of the militant suffragettes managed an audience of rowdy medical students, and was for a time tempted to join the WSPU.[62] However, on leaving Cambridge, she followed her friend Ellie Rendel, together with most of the women of the Rendel Family and their cousins the Stracheys, into the NUWSS. She organised volunteers and arranged meetings, hating the work much of the time, but moved by a 'beastly conscience'. Her ambivalence about political activity remained with her, although once involved she was always stimulated and often enthusiastic.

Ray's political conscience had first been prodded by her aunt, Alys Russell, before she went up to Cambridge. At Newnham support for suffrage was growing and spreading. Jane Harrison, who inspired generations of students of the college, was converted to suffrage at this time.[63] Ray's grandmother lamented her own inability to take part in suffrage processions, but her mother was convinced that politics would 'bore thee to death'. Aunt, mother and grandmother were all forceful women. The grandmother, an American Quaker, had brought Ray up when her mother ran away to Italy with Bernard Berenson.[64] Childhood for Ray and her sister Karin was divided between a sober and industrious life with their grandmother, and wild summer trips to visit their mother and tour Europe. On one of these trips Ray learned to drive a car, and to her mother's distress was happier driving the car or lying in the mud trying to get it to work again after it had broken down, than looking at pictures or flirting with young men. Her interest in cars sparked off an interest in engineering at Cambridge where she was supposed to be reading Mathematics. This fascination would lead her to play an active part in facilitating the training and employment of women in engineering during the war.

After leaving Cambridge, Ray's life was divided between writing, suffrage activities, and developing her friendships with the intellectual circle which included the Stephen and Strachey families. The two Costelloe sisters married into these families: Karin married Adrian Stephen soon after the outbreak of war; Ray had proposed to Oliver Strachey in April 1911. He had recently returned from India, was thirteen years older than Ray, divorced and with a ten-year-old daughter in his care. He had no job and very little income. Ray's mother dreamed of a white wedding, but Oliver wrote to her:

> How you could have visualized her in a wedding dress beats me. I have tried for hours but in vain. I can conjure up the whole scene – me in a frock coat and lavender gloves, Karin and Ellie as bridesmaids . . . everything except the figure of my Ray in a wedding dress and orange blossoms. That won't come.[65]

They went secretly to Cambridge and married by special licence with only Karin and Lytton Strachey as witnesses. After a honeymoon in India Ray and Oliver lived on her income, which included an allowance from Berenson, and began to write a book on Indian history together. In July 1912, their daughter Barbara was born. Ray was throughout her life to protest that she would prefer to cultivate her garden – later, she meant this literally – than to be politically active. According to a friend from later life she expressed the cynicism of the Stracheys in words, and her own faith and optimism in her actions.

In the early summer of 1914 she witnessed an accident and the shock led to the loss of the child she was carrying. She rented a cottage, Clack's End, at Pangbourne in July, and took refuge there with Barbara whom she had taught 'to recite "Votes for Women" like a parrot.' From there she wrote to her mother:

> I still feel a real European war is incredible, but it looks as if it is actually happening.[66]

EVA HUBBACK (1886–1949)

One of Ray Strachey's contemporaries as a student at Cambridge was Eva Spielman. Eva came from a large and wealthy Jewish family. Like Helena Sickert and Evelyn Sharp, she had resented the greater attention given to her brothers and her parents' higher expectation of them. She was a precocious child; faced with inadequate governesses her parents sent her to St Felix School, on the Suffolk coast. She did not settle there, but the school stimulated her ambition to go to University. At Cambridge she put more energy into peripheral activities than into her academic study of economics. She was intensely happy. Although somewhat shy she would conquer her diffidence and talk in 'enthusiastic bursts'. A contemporary later told her daughter that Eva's most memorable characteristic was her 'intense enjoyment of everything . . . this joie de vivre she never lost.'[67] Life was at its most perfect for her on 'Reading Parties', when mixed groups of her contemporaries lived together; reading, walking, cycling, talking. This was the form of holiday she took through choice as a widow and a mother.

On leaving Cambridge Eva lived at home. There was no need for her to earn money, and her daily activities were the fruit of the social commitment which had drawn her into the Fabian Society at Cambridge. There was a family tradition of social concern, and Eva extended its boundaries beyond the Jewish community. She became the organiser for a Care Committee in Whitechapel and a Poor Law Guardian in Paddington. As a young woman she was impatient of this type of activity, feeling that committees evinced a 'tremendous gefuffle for the little that gets done.' After her first meeting in Paddington, she described her fellow Guardians as:

> composed of three elements: (a) white-haired conservative old gentlemen; (b) garrulous tradesmen; (c) competent women of fifty or more, who always dress in black and whom one doesn't often meet except on such occasions as C.O.S. committees or Church Missionary Societies.[68]

This letter was written to Bill Hubback whom she married in 1911, despite the disapproval of both their families. Bill was not a Jew, and his family was much poorer than Eva's. They had met in Cambridge, and he was lecturing in Manchester until the spring after they married when he started work at the Board of Education in London. Eva had joined the WSPU in 1910, but was never drawn into militant activity. Suffrage meetings were her only outside activity in 1912, the year her first child was born. She viewed her domestic role as an important one, taking cooking and dressmaking lessons before she married. The Hubbacks had a new house built for them near Hampstead Heath, employing a housemaid, a cook and a nurse. A month after war was declared, a second baby was born. It was the war rather than the suffrage movement which tore Eva Hubback's world apart.

MARY STOCKS (1891–1975)

In the summer of 1916, soon after the birth of her third child, Eva Hubback went back to Newnham College, Cambridge, as a temporary lecturer in Economics. There Eva met another young mother who was doing 'odd jobs of tutoring.'[69] Mary Stocks tutored Eva's students in economic history, and between tutorials she lunched with Eva. Mary Stocks was five years younger than Eva. She too had been born into a middle-class London family, and brought up among many cousins. 'Life was orderly, comfortable, and supremely secure.'[70] Mary was sent to St Paul's School, but she excelled neither at games nor at her studies, and left with relief, having failed to pass Higher Certificate, the university entrance qualification. Before she left she had been drawn into the suffrage movement by her Rendel cousins. At the age of sixteen she carried a banner in the 'Mud March' alongside her cousin Ellie Rendel, and Ellie's friend Ray Costelloe. She joined the NUWSS and acted as a steward at meetings, distributed literature, and went to annual conferences. She once addressed a street meeting in Hackney but her mother forbade her to do so again:

> I fear I did – though only once – at The World's End in the King's Road. The temptation to hear my own voice raised in public for so great a cause was, I fear, compulsive; and I suspect that I did it rather well.[71]

Mary's Rendel aunts and cousins were suffragists whose commitment to the cause stemmed from their social concern. Mary accompanied her Aunt Edith on visits to the St Pancras Workhouse. When she left school and was, like Margaret Thomas, a reluctant debutante, she became the honorary secretary of one of the care committees set up by the London County Council and attached to schools. The committee members visited homes to establish the need for medical treatment and free school meals. Mary's mother would not let her do any 'visiting', but she prepared and presented the case records. Education, if it could be relevant to social work of this sort, came to mean more to her. She retook her Higher Certificate in order to qualify for entry to the London School of Economics. Once there, she found academic study both stimulating and satisfying and graduated with a first-class degree in 1913.

At the end of her second year at LSE Mary had met John Stocks, a fellow of an Oxford College; 'a socialist, a Poor Law Guardian and a keen member of the Oxford Women's Suffrage Society'. They were married soon after she sat her final examinations. They lived in a house in the centre of Oxford which Mary's mother referred to as 'the little slum house'. Mary tutored students from the women's colleges and taught courses for the WEA in rural Oxfordshire. For Mary Stocks, as for Eva Hubback, the war disrupted this settled contentment.

It is difficult to make any judgement on the state of the suffrage movement on the eve of the war because of the shadow that cataclysm has cast. From what is discernible, there is no clear pattern. A woman's individual stage in life was one factor. Political factors included attitudes to the increasing militancy of the WSPU, and to the new alliance of the NUWSS with the Labour Party. The suffrage struggle had always been subject to changes in method and political context, but the events of the last two years before the war were particularly significant, and did lead to some realignment and to a reassessment of their position by individuals. Many of the women who had been deeply involved in the struggle for seven or eight years were exhausted. There was evidence of rethinking; of tiredness; of the distraction of motherhood; but also of a determination to persevere. There was no sign of despair. At the hub of suffragist activity were Catherine Marshall and Mary Sheepshanks. Both of them were exhausted after a heavy year of work, yet they hoped that women could bring pressure to bear on the government through the rally they organised in the Kingsway Hall on 4 August 1914.

3 Suffragists and the War

When war broke out it seemed to Helena Swanwick that England had woken 'from a deep dream of peace.' By the time the Women's Peace Meeting was held, it was clear to many people that Britain would not be able to remain neutral, and there was pressure to cancel it. But it was held, the hall 'crowded to overflowing by an excited and enthusiastic audience of women'. Two thousand women were crammed inside the hall and more had to be turned away.[1]

For the past ten years rallies such as this had given women a sense of their potential power: the outbreak of war fractured that conviction. The immediate reaction of very many suffragists was to deny responsibility for the war, and of many more to deny their own power. The calls for national unity in face of an outside enemy, combined with the almost unbearable sense of powerlessness, splintered the suffrage movement, although not irrevocably. Close cooperation between suffragists was eroded by the many different shades of attitude and commitment which the war revealed. The gradual dispersal of women who had worked together closely for a decade or more led to feelings of grief – and betrayal. It meant the end of the concerted drive to achieve votes for women, but active suffrage work did not simply stop: Evelyn Sharp and some of the United Suffragists continued to put the cause of suffrage first, and in the middle of the war, suffrage organisation was still sufficiently intact to take up the cause when there was hope of success.

Millicent Garrett Fawcett, president of the NUWSS, was the first speaker at the rally. She condemned the war and exonerated women from responsibility for it, and she declared that women must now put aside their 'precious national and international hopes'. Other speakers echoed her view that there was no way in which voteless women could influence foreign policy or the conduct of war. One woman stood out immediately against this view. Helena Swanwick declared in her speech that women who wanted the vote had 'a duty to think out what the war was about, how it ought to end, and what constructive policy to prepare to prevent its repetition.' For many women this stance would prove too difficult and the pressure to close ranks with men against a new enemy too strong. A resolution was passed in the Kingsway Hall which called on women's organisations to offer their services to their country.[2] The need to act proved paramount in the early months of the war. Garrett Fawcett, Marshall and Courtney, as members of the NUWSS executive, had already sent out a circular asking local societies what the Union should do if war was declared. On 5 August they read the responses: the overwhelming majority of those societies replying (200 out of 202; fewer than half had replied) were in favour of suspending suffrage work and devoting energy to war relief work.[3]

There was a general expectation that war must lead to immediate suffering on the part of the civilian population, and for some this expectation would be fulfilled. Eleanor Rathbone was instrumental in developing the Soldiers and Sailors Family Association in Liverpool to cope with the problem of the dependants of reservists who were called up when the war broke out.[4] It was difficult for women who were accustomed to organising to resist the urge to act immediately in some constructive way. At the executive meeting of the NUWSS on 6 August Kathleen Courtney reported that she and Catherine Marshall had offered the services of the office to the London Government Board for its work in dealing with offers of help. The Active Service League became the focus of relief work although many of its members, including its founder Mrs Harley, who was over sixty, soon found their way into more exciting tasks than relief work at home. A parallel organisation with roots in the WSPU was the Women's Emergency Corps, and Emmeline Pethick Lawrence joined this body of women. Writing much later of the outbreak of war, she declared that 'Divisions and conflicts were forgotten while the whole nation was united in the one purpose of serving our country in her hour of danger.'[5] Yet within months she was to become strongly associated with the wartime women's peace movement. Relief work moved very quickly beyond national boundaries. Mary Sheepshanks used the SIWA office as the centre for the organisation of the 800 or so German women whom the outbreak of war had stranded in an alien country. After the fall of Belgium, Sheepshanks, together with Chrystal Macmillan, who was a member of the NUWSS executive, responded to the plight of the refugees and sailed to Flushing with the first food convoy. They then put pressure on the British government to welcome the refugees, and many former suffragists became involved in refugee work.[6]

Mary Sheepshanks was beginning now to develop her ideas about how women could contribute beyond relief, asserting that women must use their brains and their voices to call for a non-punitive peace. These views were expressed in the IWSA journal, and they came into conflict with those of Millicent Garrett Fawcett. By June 1915 Sheepshanks was considering resignation from her position as editor because, in Kathleen Courtney's view, Fawcett had made her position intolerable. For Millicent Garrett Fawcett the war was the gravest national crisis that Britain had ever had to face and she believed that if Germany won it would mean the destruction of representative institutions.[7] For other suffragists the refusal of the men who ran those institutions to give women the vote was symptomatic of a much deeper malaise, and defence of those institutions could not be the first priority.

WOMEN AND WAR

In her autobiography Helena Swanwick recalled her disagreement with a delegate at the IWSA conference in Budapest in 1913 who had expressed surprise at the rumours of impending war. For Swanwick war was an all-too-likely outcome of the international system and situation. The views which she expressed at the Kingsway Hall meeting on 4 August were to be the basis of her political stance throughout the war. She thought that a 'stop-the-war' movement was pointless but that it might be possible to find means whereby the participating nations could extricate themselves. Later she wrote that she knew that she would have to speak out and that she would be accused of at best 'twittering', and at worst treachery, but she felt driven to take this stand as she had been driven to join the suffrage movement. She knew that this time there would not be that sense of 'unquenchable hope and buoyant comradeship'. In this new struggle she saw women as once again the sane, rational adults in a mad world. 'I felt that men had dropped their end of the burden of living, and left the women to carry on, while they played this silly, bloody game of massacring the sons of women.' In Swanwick's view, women had a greater understanding of war and violence because they were so often its victims, both individually and collectively. She agreed with Fawcett that militarism was associated with political structures which excluded women, but unlike Fawcett she saw the behaviour of the British government as militarist. Swanwick recognised that it would be difficult for many women to stand out against the pressure to support the war, and was prepared to act alone.[8] She had always been prepared to act independently, as her resignation from *Common Cause* demonstrated. She had, like Evelyn Sharp, learned to act alone in her loneliness within a large family.

Swanwick's first actions in the war were nevertheless concerned, like those of so many other suffragists, with relief – relief for other women specifically. She cooperated with the Richmond Suffrage Society in forming local committees to help women thrown out of work, and later to establish a nursery for the children of women who did find work. Then on 17 September, she read a letter in the press from several prominent Liberals which urged the necessity for 'democratic control' of foreign policy, advocated the establishment of an international organisation after the war and argued that the peace terms agreed at the end of the war should not be punitive. These ideas conformed with her own, so Swanwick joined the newly established group and was elected to its executive committee. She was to remain with the Union for Democratic Control until 1928, her only regret that she was unable to persuade her close friends in the NUWSS to come with her.[9]

In late 1914 some form of cooperation with the UDC was one of the possible choices for suffragists. On 6 October Catherine Marshall received a letter from Dr Ethel Williams, the chairman of the Newcastle Suffrage Society, who was contemplating joining the newly-formed branch of the UDC. Williams was anxious to avoid a schism in the NUWSS should there not be majority support for such openly-conducted links between the Union and the UDC. The attitude of the NUWSS to the war was discussed at an executive meeting on 15 October. Marshall was on holiday and was not present at that meeting when Helena Swanwick put forward a proposal to hold a general Council of the Union the following month 'to consider whether any policy should be adopted with regard to the European War'. Swanwick was in favour of the Union adopting the policy she had put forward at the Kingsway Hall Meeting on 4 August, and argued that it should press for a settlement of the war 'not by force, but by reason'. She recognised the possibility of a split in the Union over this question, but thought that whatever the outcome, it would not 'find itself in the same position as that in which it had entered upon the War.' Millicent Garrett Fawcett spoke strongly against the holding of a Council meeting and against inviting the Union to take any line on the war. She agreed that 'war was a gigantic crime' but was not prepared to support any peace initiatives such as those proposed by the UDC until the war was won, arguing that such moves would hamper the government 'in their conduct of the greatest crisis in history'.

Swanwick would not accept Fawcett's argument. She linked the work for peace with the suffrage movement: 'the question of peace and war, involving as it did the question of the relations of reason and physical force, was at the basis of the whole Franchise movement . . . ' Her emphasis was on the need to educate the public about war and the causes of war. Swanwick was warmly supported by Maude Royden, who argued that if the National Union 'confined itself to relief work and refused to consider the causes which made that work necessary their attitude would resemble that of the Anti-suffragists, who were content with dealing with effects.' She believed that if the union did not consider its attitude to the war, it might avoid splits but that the 'disintegration which would result would be far more harmful.'[10]

Maude Royden's analysis of the war was similar to that of Swanwick. She accepted that women's reaction to the outbreak of war had been as varied as that of men's, but argued that militarism and feminism:

> must be in eternal opposition . . . The Women's movement in all its aspects, but especially, of course, in its political one, is an assertion of moral force as the supreme governing force in the world . . . Women . . . are not equal to men in their capacity to use force or their willingness to believe in it. For them therefore to ask for equal rights with men in a world governed by such force is frivolous.[11]

Not all members of the National Union had as yet made up their minds where they stood on the question. Alice Clark, who would later resign along with Royden, suggested at the October executive meeting that it was perhaps too early to speak about possible peace terms. Yet she sensed the loss of identity and power involved in supporting the war effort. In a letter to Marshall in November she wrote that she could not see clearly 'what the National Union ought to be at', but felt that it could not expect to keep its members together by doing relief work, and that some policy guidance must be given to members, explaining to them the object of such work. She felt that she and Marshall and Courtney were standing in the middle ground between Garrett Fawcett on the one hand and Swanwick, Royden and Isabella Ford on the other. Courtney was also clearly groping for some solution at this time. At the committee meeting she was unhappy about the way the discussion was wandering shapelessly, and tried to bring the other members of the committee to come to some practical decisions. When the committee did vote on the question of whether or not to call a General Council, it was agreed that it was not desirable to do so, but that members of the executive were free as individuals to express their views on the war.[12]

A Provincial Council meeting was held in November and a resolution was passed which applauded a speech by Asquith made in Dublin in late September, in which he had rejected the use of force in the settlement of international disputes. Another successful resolution asserted that 'the enfranchisement of women would facilitate . . . the establishment of permanent peace.' The passing of these resolutions, which seemed to form a bridge between the views of Fawcett and Strachey on the one hand, and Swanwick and Royden on the other, encouraged Marshall and Courtney to believe that the Union would survive intact. Courtney wrote to Marshall at the end of November:

> I am glad to say that I have great hopes of finding a modus vivendi in the National Union . . . I think however that if we are to keep together we shall all have to sacrifice something.[13]

Eleanor Rathbone was also anxious that no split should occur in the Union. Although she had been a critic of the EFF she was still on good terms with Catherine Marshall, and wrote that she was 'aghast . . . at the idea of a possible exodus out of the Executive of yourself and the four others you mention'. She confessed that she did not know what side she was on, but was anxious about the effect of a possible division of the union on Millicent Garrett Fawcett. Mary Stocks's address to the Council when she stood for election to the executive in February called for the Union to stay intact, and to allow for individuals to support other organisations such as the UDC. At this time Fawcett was still hopeful of being able to continue to work with Marshall and Courtney. She wrote to Helena Auerbach, the treasurer of the NUWSS, after the provincial council:

> I was very much impressed by Catherine Marshall's speech. It showed a real grasp of the essentials of the situation.
>
> I want to talk over our future developments with the other officers or with the Exec. Com. I will try to see KDC first.[14]

Marshall was prepared for some sacrifice, as she made clear in a letter to Garrett Fawcett:

> I would refrain from doing a good many things which as an individual, I should like to do, if only the union will take some corporate action.[15]

It is not surprising that there should have been such a strong hope among suffragists that they could continue to work together. They had shared the difficulties and hopes of the struggle, and close relationships had been formed. Isabella Ford, an active suffragist from Leeds who joined the UDC, wrote an affectionate letter to Millicent Garrett Fawcett in November, assuring her that she would never do anything disloyal and that she did not feel any hostility towards Fawcett.[16] Helena Swanwick also wrote warmly to Fawcett at this time:

> The women's movement in England is what it is because you have lived an Englishwoman . . . Many things dear to us go under in war-time but the spirit of the women's movement will keep alive . . . And, dear Mrs Fawcett, if I do not always speak the same language as you, it is only language.[17]

Swanwick had a serious operation in January 1915 and went to Cornwall afterwards to recuperate. She was thus absent during the storms and stresses of the early months of that year. She kept in touch with Marshall during this time and offered her support and advice from a distance. She remained on good personal terms with Millicent Garrett Fawcett. But Swanwick felt that a split was unavoidable and had in essence already happened.

From the other side of the growing gulf Ray Strachey was also aware of the reality of the division in the union. At the beginning of December she reported to her mother that 'the suffrage world' was 'heaving and tossing', but at this stage her thoughts were most absorbed in her effort to conceive a second child. Then her doctor, Miss Turnbull, persuaded her that she was becoming unhealthily obsessed by the desire to become pregnant, and she returned to public activities. The language in which she described her view of the situation in the NUWSS makes the strength of her feelings apparent. She wrote of the need to 'defeat the intriguers of the peace party', and later of the hope that Oliver, who had been elected to the executive, would keep the opposition from 'extremes of folly'.[18]

Oliver Strachey was elected to the executive at the Annual

Council Meeting at the beginning of February. Both sides anticipated that this meeting would force some sort of decision, but those who were anxious for the union to concern itself with the issue of the war were not agreed on any policy of action. Ethel Williams of the Newcastle Society wrote to Catherine Marshall to suggest that those who anticipated that the union would adopt a policy they could not accept should meet before the Council meeting. Marshall wanted to avoid any 'conspiracy', but she did agree that there was a need for some sort of meeting with 'delegates from a distance who want to combine peace work with suffrage'. She told Ethel Williams that Kathleen Courtney was 'immovably opposed to taking any action immediately after the Council's decision', while Helena Swanwick was 'strongly in favour of immediate action'. As for herself, she admitted that she was 'still some way off making up my mind what I think the best course would be.'[19]

Catherine Marshall was to be in the eye of the coming storm. When the war broke out she was riding the wave of success of the alliance of suffrage with Labour. She was also deeply involved in extensive and persistent Parliamentary lobbying, which she believed would soon be successful in obtaining a commitment to Women's Suffrage from the Liberal Government. The war exploded into her activities and her hopes, destroying the alliances she had worked for, and bringing her great personal suffering. In the autumn of 1914 Catherine needed time to rest, to sort out her ideas about the war and to decide how best to use her energy and her hard-earned experience as an organiser and propagandist. Frank Marshall did not want her to go 'stomping the country on the preparation for peace, important as it is and well as I believe you would do it'. The pressure to do this came from three of Catherine's closest friends: Mary Sheepshanks, Helena Swanwick and Maude Royden. Marshall had not yet openly commited herself on the question of the war, and when she spoke in Newcastle in January, her speech was concerned about the need to continue suffrage work. She said that she could not accept that a moderation of the suffrage demand would be of any benefit to the 'men who are fighting for us. It is for the sake of the country, and for the sake of men as well as women, that we press it.' She accepted that there was a connection between suffrage and relief work, but argued that, 'It is a tragic necessity, not a matter for self-congratulation, that when we are engaged in conflict without we have to cease for the time being our conflict with evil within.' She was indignant when Mary Stocks suggested that she was trying to lead the Union away from 'the paths of Suffrage propaganda'. The war moved closer to Catherine Marshall personally when in that same month her brother volunteered for the army.[20]

Marshall had asserted in her speech in Newcastle that 'conflict was the very essence of life'. She may well have regretted those words as the crisis in the National Union moved towards a climax. Her efforts as the meeting of the NUWSS Council drew near were aimed at the avoidance of conflict. Ray Strachey had written to her stating that is was 'the one business of patriotic people' to support the war. In reply Marshall asked: 'surely you do not mean that patriotism is to end there? Are we not to work towards a right ending of the war?' The London Society of which Ray was a member had put a series of questions to candidates for election to the executive about future activities of the Union, which Marshall complained to Strachey were not amenable to a yes/no answer.[21] It seemed that Strachey's object at that time was to force those who composed what she called 'the peace party' to appear unpatriotic in their plans for the NU. Both Strachey and Fawcett had accepted the paramount demands of patriotism with its need to reject and condemn those who resisted.

PATRIOTISM

Helena Swanwick was fully aware of the force of patriotism. In *Women and War* she acknowledged that 'men fight for the love of their country, for the ashes of their fathers and the temples of their gods . . . ' The very language which Swanwick used was resonant of the education she had shared with men of influence whose 'horror of war', unlike her own, was swept away by a storm of emotion in 1914. Those images were partly responsible for the seduction of war which Swanwick understood, and rejected.

Two influential leaders of liberal, and formerly anti-war, opinion were Gilbert Murray and H.G. Wells. The two newspapers representing this strand of liberalism were the *Manchester Guardian* and the *Daily News*. Accustomed from pre-suffrage days to accept intellectual guidance from such sources, many women now turned to them again. Gilbert Murray spoke for the London Society at a meeting in December. Jane Harrison, who went with Ray and Alys Russell to this meeting, was a close friend of Murray and it cheered her to find that he 'seemed sure that the war was a righteous one that could not be avoided.'[22] Arguments put forward by influential people like Murray in the early days of the war were to lead to the concept of a 'Holy War', a concept which was both generated by patriotism and justified it. Many women accepted such arguments; some did not. Irene Cooper Willis was an active suffragist and a close friend of Mary Sheepshanks; later she worked with Helena Swanwick in the peace movement. Willis analysed the sudden *volte-face* in the Liberal Press when war broke out in a book entitled *Holy War*. She pointed out that letters to the *Daily News* and the *Manchester Guardian* in the days preceding the outbreak of war had urged the government to adopt a neutral stance. On 4 August a leader in the *Manchester Guardian* argued that the neutrality of Belgium could not be repaired by a violation of the neutrality of England. On the next day the *Daily News* admitted that it had been persuaded by Sir Edward Grey that British interests were vitally bound up with the neutrality of Belgium. The 'Holy War' had begun.[23]

Mary Stocks was staying with friends in Lancashire when war broke out: friends who were 'actively preparing to engage in a great peace campaign supported by the Manchester Guardian's influential editor, C.P. Scott.' They were, she asserted, 'unlikely to be responsive to a crude "King and Country needs you" appeal'. Looking back on the beginning of the war after fifty-five years Mary Stocks had no doubt:

> that the revulsion of feeling on learning of the Belgium invasion, which brought our Lancashire circle into wholehearted support of the war effort, reflected public opinion throughout Great Britain . . . It was seen as a monstrous, wicked, unprovoked act of aggression against a small neutral country which we were in honour bound to assist. The issue was as simple as that.[24]

The issue was not, of course, a simple one. The appeal to honour was powerfully persuasive – and ambiguous. Jane Harrison wrote to Gilbert Murray:

> One thing still troubles me – you have brought me up (a man may bring up, though he may not marry, his grandmother) to believe that it is never safe to trust emotion unless it is supported by reason – yet in a supreme case you turn on your own position and say honour is unanalysed, yet I trust my sense of it.

Helena Swanwick had an answer to Harrison's question: that those susceptible to the appeal of honour should ask themselves whether it was 'not a relic of the barbarous past, of the superstitious remnant of belief in ordeal by battle.'[25]

Later the press would submerge questions of honour and civilisation in the need to express hatred of the enemy. Many women, as well as men, needed to feel hatred in order to justify the horror of it. In her autobiography Margaret Mackworth wrote that she was far from accepting the *Daily Mail* view of the war, but that she 'knew very well, knew it quite consciously, that one could not carry on war without hating the enemy, and that one must just let oneself go to unreasonable hatred and think the worst of the enemy for the time being, even though a piece of one knew that one was believing many lies.'[26] She was unable to retain her identity as a feminist under the enormous centripetal force of patriotism. Yet that awareness that she was acting out of need, rather than conviction, meant that after the war she was able to rediscover her feminist self.

The rhetoric of patriotism also justified the war in terms of the need to defend women and children from the horrors of German militarism. It was particularly difficult for men of an age to volunteer and for the women who were their wives, sisters and mothers, to challenge this manipulation of their love for each other. Margery Corbett Ashby's letters to her mother at this time bear witness to the irresistible pressures which drove middle-class liberal men to volunteer:

> You won't tell Brian not to go will you dearest? . . . Brian was so miserable to be doing nothing but watch other men go about in khaki that I was in terror he would enlist for the front as an ordinary recruit.

Two days later she used her mother's own sense of commitment to social causes to justify her husband's willingness to serve in the war:

> You devote every instant of time and every oz. of energy on helping other people who can't help themselves. You treat with contempt the idle and prosperous who leave social duties to others . . . and then you round on a large young strong man with no business much to lose, with a wife provided for and happily looking forward to a wee companion and wonder why he should want to help in the only way he can![27]

Just before Brian Ashby left, Margery wrote again to her mother about how hard he found it to do so. The ambiguity of her feelings are clear as she wrote that she could not 'stand in a man's way when his conscience is involved', and at the same time that 'he hates soldiering, he loathes the idea of war and in fact shares your views precisely.'[28]

The terrifying immediacy of death for the men in the trenches resonated in the lives of the women at home. For the young, married suffragist the involvement of her husband in the fighting made it virtually impossible to reject the view that the war was being fought for some worthwhile cause. Margaret Hills, who joined the UDC with Swanwick, wrote to Catherine Marshall of her feelings about the war:

> I think it is just the sense that one's own man's conscience keeps him in hourly peril, agonisingly against the grain, that makes it impossible to feel tender to the man whose conscience keeps his body safe even in HM prisons . . . My man has just been home – his first leave & I still live in the afterglow.[29]

Mary Stock's husband 'endured eighteen months of trench warfare in France, including front-line fighting on the Somme'. For her, this period of 'acute and unrelieved personal anxiety' came to an end when she heard that John Stocks had been wounded.[30] Bill Hubback volunteered for the army, was at first turned down because of his poor sight, then given a commission. He was killed on 14 February 1917, leaving Eva with three young children.

Swanwick understood how the idealism and involvement of the younger generation made it impossible for many to speak out against the war. She was aware that it was easier for her to think clearly and act decisively than it was for many other women because she had no husband, son or son-in-law who would have to make the decision of whether to volunteer, or later on, to stand out against conscription. She was determined that she would keep control of her own thought and her own action when the ease with which women were sucked into the vortex of war was only too apparent. The war overwhelmed other commitments and made people anxious to be involved, to become part of some national effort. Jane Harrison felt for the first time in her life that public affairs were more important than her work, which seemed tasteless. When she went 'quite fatuously and uselessly' to pour coffee for the troops in a camp at dawn, 'the beauty of the tents in the mist almost undid me, it was so Old Testament-like'. This was the romantic, literary appeal of war which would appear in Rupert Brooke's poetry and, with a bitter twist, in Vera Brittain's

Testament of Youth. The bitterness would come with experience: in the early days of the war, people seemed to have been possessed by an overwhelming sense of excitement. As Jane Harrison expressed it: 'The war is so horribly exciting but I cannot live on it. It is like being drunk all day.' Observing the people around her at Cambridge she saw that the 'bugle call . . . whether it summoned to the hospital ward or the camp, has some quite compelling music'.[31]

A UNION DIVIDED

War raised the level of emotional intensity in political life so that the divisions in the suffrage movement were felt all the more acutely. The rhetoric of the war spilled over and differences were expressed in terms of loyalty and betrayal. Millicent Garrett Fawcett understood as desertion the actions of Marshall and Courtney, whom she had 'looked upon as friends and Miss Courtney in particular as a close and intimate friend'. To Courtney it seemed that after their resignations Fawcett became 'quite unbalanced. She is furiously angry with us I believe and for some reason, particularly so with me. She will not meet me if she can help it, and will not even write to me civilly.'[32]

The anxiously-anticipated National Council meeting of the NUWSS was held in February 1915. Fawcett, supported by Ray Strachey and Eleanor Rathbone, succeeded in achieving, as Ray put it, 'a mitigated triumph . . . not carrying what we wanted but thwarting what we most dreaded, and leaving an uneasy sort of compromise in which we shan't any of us actually split off nor actually feel satisfied'. Delegates supported a resolution calling for an IWSA conference in a neutral country, and another calling for the organisation of educational courses concerned with 'the study of the causes which lead to war . . . and the consideration of what means can be taken to prevent war in the future'. But a closure of the debate on another resolution concerned with Asquith's speech effectively stymied the possibility of action by the Union. The meeting also rejected resolutions which would have committed the Union to implement the proposals, and a resolution to 'sustain the vital forces of the nation' (a phrase which was used by all those standing for the executive who supported Fawcett's line), was passed. In Frank Marshall's view the opinion of the majority of the Council was behind those who wanted the Union to extend its efforts beyond informing the public about the importance of suffrage to an attempt to do the same about the importance of moral over physical force. This was not the impression of the Council that Catherine was left with. She and others now reluctantly faced the possibility of leaving the Union in order to be free to work as they wished.[33]

After the Council Meeting, Maude Royden gave in her notice as editor of *Common Cause*. Kathleen Courtney wrote a letter of resignation which was read out at the executive committee meeting on 4 Marsh. She had been very depressed about the situation in the NUWSS since before the Annual Council meeting and, according to Frank Marshall, was 'overworked and worried to death' and had 'helped to depress' Catherine's view of the situation. He believed that Catherine still had the confidence and strength to persist with the Union, but that Courtney had not. 'Her face as she sat on the platform haunts me. It is such an infinite pity if she breaks down.' He warned that Catherine would need physical vigour to avoid her tendency to 'become indecisive and capable of doing things at a rush and with an effort that robs them of their value'.[34]

Catherine was apparently so rushed and preoccupied that her letter of resignation as Parliamentary Secretary did not reach Millicent Garrett Fawcett before the executive meeting. Fawcett's angry response suggests that in fact Catherine's delay was the result of her inability to face the coming split. 'You tell me that you had definitely made up your mind to retire from the Parliamentary sec-retaryship on or immediately after February 18th. In that fortnight I think you might have found the time to write me an explanatory letter.' Marshall's resignation did not entail a total breakdown in her relations with Fawcett and they continued to correspond. But the unhappiness of that executive meeting confirmed the feeling among other members that it would not be fruitful to continue working within the NUWSS. Alice Clark had declared in her election address to the Council that she thought it was the duty of the women to educate themselves about the causes of war. When she heard the news of the resignations Clark wrote to Catherine Marshall to say that she thought it was 'worth putting up a fight and giving the societies a chance to decide which way they shall go.' She added that she wished 'to do what the rest of you do, and I am unable to do much to help in the fight if that is decided on. I am a poor fighter at any time, I hate it so much.' When she received a copy of the minutes of the executive meeting she wrote: 'What a horrible dark place full of emptiness, East Wind and bitterness we seem to have come to.'[35]

Helena Swanwick was back in London in March, and she offered Catherine the support of her cooler view of the situation. Fawcett called on Swanwick and after the visit Swanwick wrote to Marshall that she had 'told her that I intended to resign'. Swanwick had been persuaded to stay on the executive by Marshall and Courtney but she could see no point at all in doing so since she foresaw a 'period of stagnation' for the Union. In her view Fawcett was 'quite dreadfully embittered & unjust.' Two days later she wrote again:

> As I see things now, there is no use whatever in making a pro-longed misery of staying on the executive . . . Events (not only lately, dear Catherine, but for months past) have shown me that 'our lot' are not capable of making good on that committee. It is this feeling of the waste of you & KDC in particular that makes me beg you to get out of it. I can guess what you feel at the prospect of being once more an individual & not an officer speaking for thousands. But Catherine dear, do face the fact, that that has happened & then take courage at the confidence & affection & admiration that countless people have for the individual you.[36]

On 15 April Swanwick resigned from the executive of the NUWSS, at the same time as Alice Clark, Isabella Ford, Emily Leaf and Maude Royden.

Ray Strachey did not play a central part in the events of the spring. She had been in bed with a threatened miscarriage on 5 February, but by early March she was fit again, and considering filling one of the posts in the NUWSS which had been vacated. She left England later in the month and was still on holiday on the Italian coast towards the end of April. From there she wrote to her mother that Oliver had been one of those who had 'succeeded in driving the pacifists out . . . It is a marvellous triumph that it was they who had to go out and not us.' Ray saw the occasion of the split as the proposal to send a delegate to a Women's Congress at the Hague. Certainly it was this issue which led Millicent Garrett Fawcett to consider resigning in March. Fawcett had been shocked to discover that Emily Leaf, the Press Secretary of the NU and one of the 'peace party' had been using Union stationery in correspondence about the Congress, although it was made clear that it was not being organised by the Union.[37]

The Hague Congress brought the attitudes of many suffragists to the war into public view. The derisive terms in which the Press described the 'peacettes' helped to harden attitudes and widen the gap between the two sides. The Congress provided a focus for the efforts of women whose views of the war were similar to those of Swanwick, and it linked the prewar international suffrage movement with the postwar women's peace movement.

CONGRESS AT THE HAGUE, APRIL 1915

On 1 December 1914, Mary Sheepshanks had published a letter in *Jus Suffragii* from Dutch suffragists who suggested that, since it would clearly not be possible to hold the IWSA conference in Berlin in 1915 as had been planned, an 'international business meeting of the Alliance' should be held in a neutral country. They offered to be hosts to such a meeting. Chrystal Macmillan responded to this letter by circulating the twenty-six societies within the Alliance, declaring that it was the duty of women to take the initiative in discussing the possibility and terms of a negotiated peace. She stressed that she was not speaking for either the IWSA or the NUWSS committees, but she did propose that such a meeting should be organised by the IWSA. The national presidents of the IWSA did not support the proposal. Millicent Garrett Fawcett was strongly opposed to it and argued that it would be impossible to prevent 'national predispositions and susceptibilities' leading to 'violent outbursts of anger and mutual recriminations' which would harm the suffrage cause.[38] Her own identity as a suffragist had been submerged by her patriotism, and she expected that this would be the case with others; she was mistaken.

Macmillan had suggested that if the IWSA was not prepared to organise the meeting, a gathering could be summoned by individual women. In February a group of women met in Holland to plan for an international women's peace conference. The proposal to send delegates to such a conference was supported at the NUWSS council meeting in the same month, and Macmillan, together with Marshall, Courtney and Emily Leaf, met with German, Belgian and Dutch suffragists at the Hague. Then the incident occurred which angered Fawcett, when Emily Leaf used National Union notepaper for correspondence connected with the proposed Congress. At the March executive committee meeting, Fawcett argued that if official delegates were sent from the NUWSS it would damage 'the reputation of the National Union for common sense', and would indicate its 'total aloofness from national sentiment'. A compromise was reached whereby members were to attend the congress, but not as official delegates from the Union. [39]

A list of 180 women who wished to attend was drawn up, but the Home Secretary was reluctant to grant them the newly-introduced passports. After pressure he agreed to issue them to twenty-four women. Then, just a week before the women were due to leave, the Admiralty closed the North Sea to all shipping. The only women to reach the Hague from England were Macmillan and Courtney, who had already left. Emmeline Pethick Lawrence arrived with the American delegation: she had been invited to speak at a suffrage rally in New York in October, and had spent the winter in the States with leading American suffragists. The atmosphere at the Hague, contrary to Fawcett's fears, was one of harmony and concord. The twenty resolutions which were passed outlined the principles of a peace settlement: they bear a strong resemblance to Wilson's Fourteen Points of 1919.

Sensitive leadership was given to the Congress by Jane Addams who claimed that the delegates had come together to insist that in the truest sense, 'internationalism does not conflict with patriotism'. Some women heard of the death of son or husband during the congress, which lent bitter weight to Addams's reference to the fact that the women who were protesting there did so 'in the shadow of the intolerable knowledge of what war means'. Addams's message was that women must be prepared for a long struggle, for progress was always 'slow and halting'. [40]

Evelyn Sharp was one of the women who had hoped to attend the Hague Conference and she later recalled her brief involvement in the wartime peace movement with pride. One contribution she made was to write an assessment of the British press reports of the meeting which, in contrast to the proceedings themselves, were inaccurate and abusive. Sharp detected the note of fear in the reports; it reminded her of the press reports of suffrage activities. The fear, she judged, was that 'women might perhaps be right, might perhaps impress their belief on the women of other belligerent countries, might perhaps make their war really 'the last war.' On the return of the delegates to London a public meeting was held at the Kingsway Hall. There Jane Addams defiantly challenged the belief that war was inevitable because human nature was unchangeable, and Helena Swanwick asserted from the chair, 'We can change, if we will change.'[41]

THE WOMEN'S INTERNATIONAL LEAGUE

From the meeting at the Hague, and the participants' desire to change the conduct of international relations, was born the International Committee of Women for Permanent Peace. Its British section, the Women's International League, was officially established on 1 October, 1915. An unofficial committee was already in existence by then, and Helena Swanwick had been elected as Chairman; a post she filled until 1922. Maude Royden and Kathleen Courtney were two of the Vice-Chairmen; Emmeline Pethick Lawrence was treasurer and Catherine Marshall Honorary Secretary. When Marshall resigned because of her commitment to the No Conscription Fellowship, Irene Cooper Willis took over. Among the executive committee members were Isabella Ford, Mrs Barton of the Women's Co-operative Guild, Barbara Ayrton Gould and Helen Ward. Chrystal Macmillan worked in Amsterdam where the International body had its very small head-quarters. Macmillan thus kept the lines of communication open between the internationalists and the NUWSS on whose executive she remained throughout the war. Conferences were held, mainly in London, on a wide variety of subjects and for a period there were weekly discussion meetings. There was support for the WIL throughout the country and particularly in the North. By the end of its first year the WIL had 2458 members, organised into thirty-four branches throughout the country.[42]

Women other than those who joined the WIL and other organi-sations of women were prepared to make public their opposition to the war. Margaret Llewelyn Davies, the secretary of the Women's Co-operative Guild, was an active opponent of the war, as was Mrs Barton. WCG schools and conferences were held during the war to study international relations and 'the conditions necessary for an enduring Peace'. Resolutions 'embodying these conditions' were passed at the Guild Congresses of 1915, 1916 and 1917, but a resolution in favour of a 'negotiated peace with no annexations and universal disarmament' was defeated by 399 votes to 336 in 1918.[43]

Women who favoured a negotiated peace had to face fierce opposition, for the overwhelming assumption on the part of the vast majority of people was that to talk of peace was to undermine the efforts of the armed forces and to discredit those who were dying in the trenches. Ray Strachey wrote to her Quaker mother that 'Facts are facts, and if I were a man I should enlist. Quaker or not'. She felt that there was no point in 'passing resolutions at

congresses, and splitting hairs about words and interpretations . . . '
Helena Swanwick was to experience much harsher expressions of
patriotism than those expressed by her former associates in the
suffrage movement. In November 1915, her attempts to speak at
a UDC meeting were interrupted and the meeting broken up by
Australian and Canadian soldiers. In July 1917, Swanwick was again
on the receiving end of mob violence when a joint WIL/ILP meeting
was broken up by a crowd, mainly of women, who used benches to
attack the speakers. Undeterred, she continued to devote most of
her energy to the WIL, speaking 'almost every day' and collapsing
with exhaustion in the evening.[44]

THE EMPLOYMENT OF WOMEN

In the same way that the war intensified feminist commitment to
internationalism, the economic changes of the war stimulated the
search for economic equality. For many working-class women the
main focus of their lives in war and peace was the struggle to survive.
Very many of them earned a living in factories and workshops. One
of the first effects of the war on women had been a rapid increase in
unemployment because the industries hit by the war were precisely
those such as textiles, fishing and the luxury trades where women
were employed. The Central Committee on Women's Employment
was established on 20 August in recognition of this problem. Work
was provided for women at 'Queen Mary's Workrooms', but conditions there were poor, and the pay of 10s a week inadequate. The
potential for the exploitation of women industrial workers was to
increase as the early unemployment was replaced by an increasing
demand for women's labour with the development of the munitions
industry and the introduction of conscription for men. There was
theoretical negotiation of equal pay in industries where such 'dilution'
occurred but the negotiations with government and employers about
women's wages were complex, and women were often substituted for
male workers without receiving their rates of pay.[45]

One witness to the failure to secure decent conditions and equal
pay for women wrote that women munition workers were in rooms
without ventilation on twelve-hour shifts without a break. Such
women were placed in work by the efforts of former suffragists such
as Ray Strachey. The London Society established a Women's Service

Bureau in order to find women workers to replace men needed at the front, and from the summer of 1915 she was busy 'placing women in "war works" and trying to see that they are put in in such a way that they don't ruin the whole labour market by taking low wages'. Strachey was also involved at this time in negotiations with the Railway Unions about the wages of women clerks, and with the Civil Service about openings for women. She was delighted at this opening-up of opportunities for women, although frustrated by the load of work and lack of resources. She complained that the London Society was 'swamped with work – over 250 applicants a day, hundreds of posts, and no staff or the money to investigate the important new openings for women'. One of the most challenging and significant efforts, as Strachey saw it, was the attempt to get women welders classed as skilled workers. Such a classification would serve as 'a lever to all the thousands of semi-skilled women in engineering and a way of breaking down barriers to women's employment'. A small society of Women Welders was established under the auspices of the London Society, and it challenged the level of wages women were receiving, which was half that of male welders. The women sought the support of the Amalgamated Society of Engineers and they received an award which granted fully-skilled welders the same rate as men. However, it was not made clear what work was 'fully-skilled', and by the end of the war only twenty women had been so classified. Moreover, the ASE continued to refuse membership to women and only accepted equal pay awards for the duration of the war.[46]

Strachey's experience with the Women's Service Bureau was to extend her knowledge of economic and social conditions. She began to contribute articles on employment questions both to *Common Cause* and to other journals. The knowledge and skills as an organiser and negotiator which she gained during the war would provide a further impetus towards a political career after the war. She saw the value of unionisation for women, but she did not move closer to the Labour Movement. One reason for this was the absence of support for equal pay for women. Other suffragists moved closer to the Labour Party: Catherine Marshall in particular, but also Kathleen Courtney, Maude Royden and Alice Clark. Marshall had worked closely with women in the Independent Labour Party before the war and the committee of which she was secretary in the first months of the war was composed of women from the Labour Movement such as Mary Macarthur and Marion Phillips. In forging close links with

Labour she foreshadowed one choice which feminists made after the war, a choice which was to put pressure on their commitment to feminism.

THE STRETCHER-BEARERS

Ray Strachey rejected the widespread assumption that the best way women could contribute to the war was through relief. She was soon impatient with such work in the NUWSS. 'The tumult of voluntary workers is inconceivable', and in the following month she complained that 'Everyone is muddly, including myself, and the confusion and general rage is horrid. Fortunately there is practically no unusual distress as yet to be relieved.' Her involvement in finding employment for women gave her an alternative and absorbing occupation within the National Union. The women who left the organisation in the spring of 1915 sought for engagement elsewhere. In June 1915, Kathleen Courtney had confessed that she was 'suffering from an utter disgust with organisations of all kinds and feel extremely disinclined to put my hand to anything of the sort'. Courtney was essentially an active person and the slow, Sisyphus-like operations of the WIL did not suit her. As Helena Swanwick wrote, 'KDC is not a believer in the force of ideas as a constructive force in itself: she is not interested in theories except as they express themselves in something concrete and tangible.' In her old age Courtney recalled her conviction that 'it was essential for us to understand the causes of war, and to work in future to prevent it recurring,' but she then added that 'there was work to be done'.[47] Although she never accepted the necessity for war, she felt the need for an active, caring role when so many were suffering.

Ray Strachey observed that the London Society had been overwhelmed with volunteers, especially those who wished to nurse. Many thousands of women took on the traditional role of carers and healers. Elizabeth Robins was a librarian in a hospital during the war, and believed that women should become stretcher-bearers. May Sinclair, another novelist who was also a suffragist, tried to become a stretcher-bearer and has left a vivid description of the terrible seduction of danger which drew women close to what they inevitably saw as the heart of the war, the fighting front. Margaret Mackworth discovered her own physical courage on the *Lusitania* when the ship was sunk in mid-Atlantic. In the months afterwards she suffered from terrible nightmares and felt that she had shared some of the experience of the soldier in the trenches.[48]

In becoming stretcher-bearers – or doctors, or nurses – women sought an identity by sharing the danger which seemed to be the only reality in war. As individuals they were often successful: exposure to danger and horrific conditions revealed to them their own physical courage and increased their self-respect and sense of solidarity with other women. But the respect that women in general thus gained from men was less durable.

For those whose job it was to heal wounds the desire to do so on the front was compelling. The suffrage cause had been supported by many women doctors, among them Ray Strachey's friend Elinor Rendel. Rendel went to Serbia with one of the Scottish Women's Hospital Units; these were medical teams staffed entirely by women and equipped by the NUWSS. The first unit had been established in France, and Ray Strachey visited it in August 1918. There she found that the four women surgeons on the staff had done 2000 operations in two months. One surgeon was ill so that another had been operating for 36 hours at a stretch after four hours' sleep. 'And yet she seemed to find a refreshment in walking round with us! An odd taste.' Raising of money for this and other units became one of the main focuses of NUWSS activity during the war. Five units had been established by the end of 1915, operating in Corsica, Salonika, France and Serbia. The French government also accepted an offer from Louisa Garrett Anderson and Flora Murray who established a hospital at Wimereux, near Boulogne. Evelyn Sharp visited this hospital soon after it was set up, and commented on 'the bitter irony of our civilisation' which compelled men to tear each other to pieces and women to heal the wounds thus inflicted.[49]

Kathleen Courtney satisfied her desire for practical activity in a less dramatic way. Towards the end of 1915 she applied to work as a volunteer with the Serbian Relief Fund. She landed in Salonika in January 1916, and worked for a while in a transit camp for Serbian refugees. 'My job is to look after half the tents and see that the right people have beds and give them tickets for clothes and try to make them get ready with passports for Corsica.' Courtney herself moved to Corsica at the end of January when the SRF and the SWH set up a hospital at Ajaccio for the refugees. In March she wrote to her sister: 'I certainly never thought when I left London for Salonika that I should find myself the Directrice of a hospital in Corsica.' In May she went to Baxtia, on the northern coast of Corsica, where

she was in charge of the reception of refugees who were then sent
on to Ajaccio. Courtney and the administrator at Ajaccio, another
suffragist, crossed swords with the officials on the island whom they
found inefficient. She wrote to her family:

> By the way you say you don't think my temperament is suited to
> dealing with alien races, but I must tell you that I am considered
> a great success with the authorities here, tho personally I don't
> see where the success comes in except in not quarrelling with
> them which I was determined not to do.[50]

When Courtney returned to England her abilities as a coordinator
were much in demand as she played a formative role in the renewal
of suffrage activity.

VOTES FOR WOMEN

In the NUWSS efforts had been made to keep political activity at
a deliberately low level since the resignation of those who wanted
to make peace an issue for the Union. It was Ray Strachey's view
when she returned to England from France in May 1915, that the
'effort to beat the pacifists out of the suffrage society', was not,
as she had hoped, yet over. In June she was elected to the post
of Parliamentary Secretary of the Union, 'just filling in the breach
and keeping out some poisonous pacifists'. She was irritated by the
'great deal of trouble with the people whom we turned out of office',
and felt burdened by the 'legacy of the policy we used to pursue, of
supporting Labour because Labour supported us. I hold that things
are so changed that we must all start with a clean slate.'[51]

In October the underlying differences of opinion about the
relationship between the Labour Party and the NUWSS emerged
when a no-conscription candidate was selected in Bristol. When the
NUWSS decided to suspend work on his behalf the local suffrage
society reacted angrily. Their officers pointed out that the society had
been built up on the basis of support for the Labour Party, and they
considered withdrawal from the NU. A compromise was achieved at
the Annual Council Meeting which followed in February, 1916. The
resolutions of the Council stated that the 'Union is free to abstain
from definite Party action in preparation for the next election,' but
confirmed the undertaking not to oppose candidates of the Labour
Party whose attitude to women's suffrage was 'satisfactory', and

agreed to support 'those candidates to whom it has been definitely promised in certain specified constituencies.'[52]

The relationship between the Labour Party and the National Union temporarily ceased to be a contentious issue as the possibility of a Suffrage Bill became a reality, but the link between feminism and socialism would again become controversial after the war.

One suffrage society, the United Suffragists, had not suspended suffrage activity during the war, although many of the members were too busy to do very much. A small group continued to 'keep the question alive', among them Evelyn Sharp and Barbara Ayrton Gould. Sharp had made the conscious decision not to become heavily involved in any branch of the peace movement, despite the fact that she was a pacifist by conviction and that her commitment to pacifism grew stronger as the war progressed. As a result she felt isolated from those who thought as she did. She confessed in her autobiography that she would have liked to be in the position to say, in response to a question about her wartime activities, 'I tried to stop the bloody thing.' The only 'war work' she did was on the land, picking gooseberries and currants during the few holidays she took during the war. She felt that the provision of food for the civilian population was not an impossible task for a pacifist.[53]

Evelyn Sharp's enthusiasm for keeping the suffrage issue alive was stimulated, paradoxically, by the official reaction to her continued refusal to pay taxes. Unlike other tax resisters she did not begin to contribute at the outbreak of war; ' a war fought to save democracy did not seem to me to provide the best reason for supporting the principle of taxation without representation'. When she received the usual tax demand she ignored it once again. By this time the amount due had reached the sum of £50, at which level the Treasury were able to hand her over to the bankcruptcy court. Having rejected the Court's offer to come to some arrangement, Sharp arrived home one day to find a bailiff sitting in her flat. After six weeks of sharing the flat with a friendly bailiff, her possessions were constrained, and she found that she missed the unobtrusive presence of the bailiff in her best armchair. She missed the armchair more literally, for she was left only with her clothes and a bed, having failed in her plea that she should be allowed to retain 'my typewriter, without which I could not earn my living, to say nothing of my need as a writer of a table, chair, and books'. Friends loaned her furniture, and gave a guarantee which made it possible for her to be supplied with gas and electricity. A fund was set up to which many suffragists contributed. She was only finally discharged when she began to pay her tax bills after she had been allowed a vote. She especially resented the official decision to force the tax issue at a time when she did not feel justified, because of the war, in appealing to public opinion. In 1916 Sharp received a gift from 'A Few Suffragists' with the following message:

> We feel that without your true courage and devotion, especially during these terrible times, when the attention of so many is directed to other interests, the cause of Woman Suffrage could hardly have been maintained as a living question.[54]

Suffrage became a 'living question' in 1916 when it seemed likely that the government would enfranchise the fighting men before the war was finished. In December 1915, Sylvia Pankhurst called 'an informal conference' of suffrage societies. A proposal that two delegates be sent from the NUWSS was put by Alys Russell, and seconded by Ida O'Malley, but it was rejected. The suffragists who attended Pankhurst's meeting in December organised a conference in the Essex Hall on 21 January, and delegates from the NUWSS did attend this time. Pankhurst was determined to press for full adult suffrage; the United Suffragists were also committed to it, as was the Women's Freedom League, and there was support for the idea from within the NUWSS and the WIL. She moved a resolution demanding 'a vote for every woman and man of full age', and was supported by 'Miss Royden, Miss Marshall, Mrs. Swanwick and Mrs. Pethick Lawrence, and others'. Evelyn Sharp moved an amendment which was couched in less importunate terms, urging 'all Suffrage Societies to insist that if the Parliamentary register is so revised as to extend the franchise to every adult man, the vote shall be granted to every adult woman.' In the end an amended resolution from the WIL was passed, urging the Societies 'to demand a Government measure of Women's Suffrage now'. Ray Strachey spoke against this resolution on the grounds that the present Parliament might come to an end before the war ended, and in those circumstances it would be 'unwise to press the question of Women's Suffrage at such an election'.[55]

The NUWSS was cautious in its approach, but there was a willingness to initiate activities directed towards the suffrage. Delegates from the Union attended a Joint Conference of Suffrage Societies in February and requested the Parliamentary Secretary to 'see a member or members of the Cabinet to find out whether there is any proposal at present for extension or alteration of the basis of the

Franchise'. Having received a positive result to these enquiries the NUWSS initiated a recruitment drive in the spring: there had been a steady decline in membership of about a quarter since the outbreak of war. Meanwhile members of the executive were negotiating behind the scenes. Ray Strachey was still cynical about the question as late as 12 August, reckoning that 'we are and always have been, perfectly powerless, and that its no good buzzing'. Three days later she was at last hopeful, believing that it was the Union's pressure which was forcing the Government's hand.[56]

A consultative committee of twenty-three suffrage societies was set up in March 1916, with Eleanor Rathbone as Chairman: within it the arguments over adult suffrage continued. At a meeting of adult suffragists in August, Henry Nevinson suggested that a Speaker's conference be convened for the purpose of framing agreed proposals to form the basis of a Franchise Bill. In the Autumn the government announced that it would hold such a conference. The adult suffragists then formed a National Council, with Nevinson in the chair, and Courtney, Llewelyn Davies, Marshall, Royden, Swanwick and Sharp on the executive. They were dismayed when the recommendations of the Speaker's Conference were that there would be full adult suffrage for men based on a residential qualification, but that women's suffrage should be limited by age and by property qualification, thus excluding many of the munition workers among whom the NUWSS was agitating. The suffragists who had come so close in this final effort to achieve their goal were once again divided by these proposals. Catherine Marshall and Sylvia Pankhurst joined forces to pressurise the ILP to support a widening of the franchise for women. On the NUWSS executive Fawcett and Strachey proposed that there should be no criticism of the recommendations. Kathleen Courtney could not agree with this, although she did modify her views later at an adult suffragist meeting. Margaret Llewelyn Davies told the NUWSS executive that she would continue to work for adult suffrage until she was convinced that there was no hope left. As the Bill passed easily through its parliamentary stages, most suffragists who were actively involved moved towards reluctant acceptance of a limited measure for the present, hoping that as soon as the war was over, full franchise for women would be achieved. They were cheered by successes such as that, in which Eleanor Rathbone played a leading role, when the government put on the whips to oppose an amendment which extended the existing women's franchise on local government registers. The NUWSS organised such a deluge of telegrams, letters and deputations that the government backed down and allowed a free vote, and the amendment received a majority.[57]

The limitations of the Representation of the People Bill which received the royal assent on 11 February, 1918, marred the sense of achievement for some suffragists; for others there was guarded satisfaction and the beginnings of a new confidence. Ray Strachey was moved by the sense of shared effort: 'And such a great handshaking took place – after all we've had a good stiff year of it together.' This good stiff year had done much to bring together the divided halves of the National Union. In November Catherine wrote to Millicent Garrett Fawcett:

> I do hope, as all Suffragists must – that the crowning of all the year of hard work and hope and patience of the N.U. will come whilst you are still its President.[58]

Fawcett found it difficult to forget the events of 1915 and regretted Courtney's decision to stand for the NUWSS executive in March 1918, but once Courtney was elected they worked well together.[59] Such renewed working relationships were to form the basis for cooperation after the war.

THE NO-CONSCRIPTION FELLOWSHIP

Catherine Marshall was absent from the NUWSS in 1918. She resisted the call of patriotism, but she moved away from solidarity with other feminists to work with conscientious objectors. The isolation she suffered as a result contributed to her collapse towards the end of 1917. She resigned as secretary of the WIL after many months of attempting to combine that post with her growing involvement in the No-Conscription Fellowship. Opposition to conscription was one of the ideals of the WIL and Marshall went as a delegate to the first National Convention of the NCF in November, 1915. She was especially impressed with the personality and ideals of Clifford Allen, the chairman. It soon became apparent to Catherine Marshall that her talents as an organiser were much needed in the NCF. Responding to this need was not an easy choice to make, for to do so meant that she had to neglect other work with long standing friends from the suffrage movement. At first she tried to do both, but Swanwick urged Catherine to make a choice between the NCF and the WIL. She felt that the work of the NCF was not 'wide enough,' but added, 'if you do, it's right that you should do it'.[60]

Marshall undertook an enormous amount of work for the NCF. A record was kept of every CO who came before a tribunal with the aim not just of accuracy of recording, but so that each objector would know they were not being swallowed up in the military machine. She corresponded personally with many relatives of those in prison. What she came to mean to those who where imprisoned is apparent from a letter written when she had collapsed through overwork in the autumn of 1917:

> The news of your illness reached us in Maidstone. I think if you could have seen its effect upon us and heard the expression of affection for you and deep concern, you would have felt rewarded to some extent for the labours of the last three years.
>
> There is little opportunity these days for us to express our gratitude to you, but the day will come – for our hearts are full.[61]

This letter must have meant a great deal to Catherine Marshall, for her work with the NCF was problematical as well as arduous. Apart from keeping in touch with the situation of COs, she undertook the bulk of the word connected with the organisation's efforts to apply political pressure against conscription. There was a daunting propaganda task facing the NCF in trying to give the objectors a sympathetic hearing in the press and thus before the public. Marshall worked with Bertrand Russell in the political efforts of the NCF and developed a close, although turbulent relationship with him. For the first year they worked well together, supporting each other when exhaustion and frustration depleted their strength and optimism. In the autumn of 1916 Russell prescribed for Catherine's 'fatigue & bad attack of missing' Allen, 'sunshine, moonlight, woodfires; walks, talks, reading aloud (I hemmed three prs of curtains!) poetry, philosophy, fun'.[62]

By the end of 1916 the best period of their partnership was over. Russell was elected Acting-Chairman of the NCF during the imprisonment of Clifford Allen, but his distaste for administrative work exacerbated the growing tensions in his working relationship with Marshall. Catherine had worked well with other women in the NUWSS; she found it difficult to adjust to working with some of the men in the NCF – although not all of them. In the spring and early summer of 1917 she was under increasing pressure. In

March Swanwick tried to persuade her to come to Cornwall for a
holiday in May. 'You are very white and look as if you must have
a holiday soon.' Catherine replied that she wanted 'desperately to
go to Kynance Cove with you. I long for it so much that I hardly dare
let myself think of it'. But May was the month of Clifford Allen's
next court-martial, 'and I must be with him then if possible . . . '
To her anxiety about Allen was added criticism from the Quaker
wing of the organisation of Marshall's political efforts on behalf
of the NCF. Her method of working in the NUWSS had been to
develop contacts and good communications with those in authority,
and she had followed the same practice in the NCF, forming a liaison
with General Childs, director of personal service at the War Office
and the man responsible for ensuring good treatment of COs. The
Quaker view was that no effort should be made to alleviate the conditions of prisoners. When Russell added his influence to the other
critics, Marshall resigned from her political responsibilities in July
1917. Her workload was still large, since she was responsible for
servicing NCF committees, keeping in touch with prisoners, and
visiting branches. Moreover, it seems that the lightening of her load
came too late.[63]

Another source of continual tension for Marshall was the knowledge that the work she had undertaken was not understood or
appreciated by others. A cousin wrote to her that he thought
the COs were 'plainly . . . cowards, or suffering from some brain
lesion which has unhinged their minds'. Worse was the knowledge
that those close to her did not believe that her work was of value.
Her mother wrote in September 1916, that she could 'see no sign
of the least support of COs among our sort.' A month earlier
Maude Royden had written to try to persuade Catherine to leave
the NCF, equating their approach with that of the militants in the
suffrage movement. Marshall justified her determination to continue,
despite everything, to work for the NCF by her belief that there was
a close connection between the women's movement and the pacifist
movement as interpreted by the NCF. But above all she felt bound
by a promise she had given Clifford Allen that she would not leave
while he remained in prison. She missed his presence acutely: one
comfort was that she acted as his official correspondent and visitor.
However, this placed an added anxiety and burden on her, for Allen
suffered acutely both psychologically and physically when in prison.
Marshall tried to reassure him, telling him that her experience of

visiting him in prison enabled her to be more effective in helping others when they came out of prison.[64]

On 9 September, 1917, Catherine Marshall was returning from a visit to Chester when she was 'overcome . . . with such an immense fatigue that I could hardly last out the two and a half hour journey home and literally could not carry my bag across the platform'. She took refuge in the country where she slept for 'about 16 hours out of the 24! – on a balcony at night, and on a hillside by day – the best kind of cure there is'. As she rested, she thought about the war and her feelings indicate the stress placed on anyone who was prepared to speak out against the war:

> I can't not see, and understand the point of view of the average person who thinks war is – not good, as some of our own people keep assuming – but just as horrible as we think it, only inevitable under certain conditions. I can't not feel with the thousands of young men to whom participation in the war has meant agony of mind and soul as well as of body, and the sacrifice of all they value in life; I want our gospel to bring comfort and hope to these people and not only a challenge and a rebuke. I want to be tender with them, just as I want to be tender with the CO who has given in.[65]

She hoped that she would soon be back at work, and she was back in harness for some time in October, but she was not fully recovered. She had reached the breaking-point which her family and friends had forecast. Helena Swanwick wrote in distress:

> I never in my life have felt so desirous of influencing the will of another . . . I think you know how I dislike the idea of influencing people under normal conditions – Still more, my great regard for your mind and character and my respect for your free will would ordinarily make me refrain from volunteering advice . . .
>
> *Resign definitely from the NCF. They will do better without you now.*[66]

She persuaded Marshall to see Dr Elizabeth Bolton, who advised total rest in order to save herself for the work of reconstruction, for which Marshall's talents would be needed. Catherine was able to take this advice because Allen had been released from prison that month. She was not released from the strain of worry because Allen was

physically in a state of collapse, and was plagued by insomnia and
nightmares. His health recovered slowly, but Catherine's depression
deepened. She now felt that she had been out of place in the NCF
and confessed that it had been:

> unutterably hard . . . to give up the work I loved and probably
> all prospect of the future work I had hoped for to fill my life, and
> to incur the reproaches and opposition of all the friends I value
> most in order to carry on the NCF work for men in prison.[67]

While Allen was recovering she was unable to sleep or eat; she
was losing weight and feeling 'profoundly unhappy.' In February
Allen came to stay with the Marshall family at Hawse End and he
and Catherine then spent time together. Helena Swanwick wrote to
Allen that she hoped that his presence and a complete rest would
lead to Catherine 'regaining all that she was'. In this letter Swanwick
wrote that she had seen friends 'drop around me, either by a definite
breakdown of health or else by the wearing-out of motive power or
thinking power.' Some of her former colleagues had become 'inert
in mind (or, what is worse, were rabbits scurrying about) and quite
useless for constructive thought.'[68]

Catherine Marshall did not return to active life before the end
of the war, and she was much missed by her friends. Kathleen
Courtney wrote:

> I miss you badly all the time and wish we could work together
> again; there is no-one else with whom to talk things over with the
> same sense of understanding and satisfaction. I constantly feel like
> a lower [*illegible*] one of whose legs has strayed away.[69]

Helena Swanwick found herself wondering 'What would Catherine
have thought?' whenever she was faced with a dilemma or a problem.
Although it had been a long time since Swanwick had been able
to 'consult quietly with her, yet I never miss her less.' Eva Kyle,
who had worked as Marshall's secretary, wrote to ask if she had
'disappeared off the face of the earth altogether? I've been reporting so many meetings lately where Miss Royden, Miss Courtney and
Mrs. Swanwick were floating around, and it always seemed to me
that you were missing – a kind of "vacant chair" business.' Helen
Ward wrote a long letter to Catherine in September, telling her of
all the political stirrings in London, and punctuating her letter with
the question, 'What do you think?' The future of the NUWSS was

under discussion and the questions of 'equal pay for equal work' and the 'State Endowment of Motherhood' were at the front of her mind.[70]

MOVING BEYOND SUFFRAGE

The issues beyond suffrage which had engaged feminists before the war were now discernible as potential postwar campaigns. Like suffrage itself many of these questions had not been totally submerged by the war, and women had been active in preparing the way for the presentation of these issues to the public once the war was over. But the war altered irrevocably the pattern of the lives we are tracing, and the emotions of war drove a wedge between some of them, drawing others closer together. Women who had been involved in the suffrage struggle were accustomed to discord and tension; the experience of a country at war brought them an even deeper understanding of how destructive fear can be of political convictions and structures.

Seven of the fourteen suffragists had opposed the conduct of the war: they suffered a second ordeal as members of a persecuted minority. Swanwick, Pethick Lawrence and Sharp seem to have survived without bitterness, although the direction of their lives after the war suggests that they may have felt the need to seek less stony paths. To Catherine Marshall the war had brought suffering from which she never fully recovered, although she continued to work in the peace movement in the twenties, as did Mary Sheepshanks. Maude Royden was committed to the peace movement, but her life was centred on the church which gave her a structure, purpose and sense of continuity, linking her work before, during and after the war. She resisted Kathleen Courtney's attempts to persuade her to remain active in the feminist movement, but it was she who exhorted Courtney not to despair of feminist organisations.[71] It was indeed Kathleen Courtney who was able after the war to hold together three strands of feminism: peace; the search for equality, and the compulsion to heal the wounds of war.

The three young married women whose husbands fought in the war knew the terror of fear for one they loved and the burden of caring for children whose fathers might soon be dead. Ray Strachey briefly shared the experience of her contemporaries when Oliver was in a ship which was torpedoed. He had been sent to Egypt by the War Office in November 1916, at the time of the birth of their son. Only Eva Hubback suffered the full horror and challenge of young widowhood. She had already set out on the path of solitary independence when she accepted the teaching post at Newnham which she continued to hold until the end of the war. None of these four women could sympathise with those who opposed the war. Ray Strachey was fiercest in her condemnation of the 'lunatics' who went to the Hague, and those who talked about peace in the safety of drawing-rooms. But even Ray defended the 'anti-conscription people', because she knew that her sister and brother-in-law's opposition to the war was 'founded on genuine belief.'[72]

Eleanor Rathbone, Elizabeth Robins and Margaret Mackworth did not oppose the war, neither did they condemn those who did. They did not fully share Catherine Marshall's need to 'be tender with' both the soldier and the conscientious objector, but their patriotism was neither blind nor exclusive. Mackworth had discovered her own physical courage in the war; in others a different sort of fortitude was revealed. The rewards for the faith and perseverance of all women suffragists seemed to be coming to fruition as political life stirred in the last year of the war.

4 Time of Hope, 1918–1920

Catherine Marshall hoped that after the war women would respond to poverty, disease and exploitation with the same passion and concern with which they had responded to the sufferings caused by the war. In a letter to Helena Swanwick she commented on how delighted she was that Asquith had attributed his conversion to suffrage to his recognition of the need for women to contribute to the 'reconstruction' legislation it was anticipated would follow the ending of the war.[1] Did Marshall notice the warning to optimistic feminists which Asquith delivered when he said that women would have a special claim to be heard on the questions which would affect their interests? One of these, he suggested, would be large displacements of labour. The question of women's employment after the war would be one of the most intractable of the inequalities which feminists challenged in the 1920s. The dimensions of the problem became evident in the first year of peace, although the full weight of the difficulties which needed to be overcome was not felt by feminists, who were elated by the apparent change in the political atmosphere.

Catherine Marshall was physically and mentally exhausted in the last year of the war, nevertheless she was one of those who gave time and energy to forming plans for the future of the suffrage movement when a limited degree of suffrage had been obtained. For others who had shared her views on the war, the need to press for peace still took precedence. A temporary surge of hope for peace occurred at the end of 1917 and gave impetus to the WIL and to another women's peace initiative. The Women's Peace Crusade had been initiated in 1916 by two suffragists in Glasgow. In July 1917 a demonstration was organised in Glasgow which attracted at least 12 000 people. The Peace Crusade had established thirty-three groups by the autumn, and in September a meeting was organised by the WIL for speakers to report on the progress of the Crusade. During the winter, propaganda work continued. By the end of the war there were about a hundred branches of the Crusade in existence, with perhaps 50 members each. In 1918 Helena Swanwick was 'stomping the country', speaking for the UDC, the ILP, the WIL, the WPC. '(Do you know your alphabet?)' she asked Catherine Marshall.[2]

In the spring of 1918 a 'Women's Demonstration for peace by

Negotiation' was planned by the WIL, with the support of the ILP and the Women's Co-operative Guild. Evelyn Sharp and Barbara Ayrton Gould from the United Suffragists were asked to take part, marking the strengthening of links between different branches of the suffrage movement. Ayrton Gould became a member of the WIL executive in June, and was to be very active during the rest of the year. Another member of the WIL executive, Margaret Llewleyn Davies, was 'bound from headquarters not to engineer Peace by Negotiation', although she encouraged the WIL to seek support from individual branches of the WCG. The speakers at the rally were to include Barbara Ayrton Gould, Emmeline Pethick Lawrence, Evelyn Sharp and Helena Swanwick. The last-minute prohibition of the meeting was a backhanded compliment to the women's peace movement, and also a reflection of the grim stalemate in the fighting of the war right up to its final months.[3]

WOMEN'S INTERESTS

The WIL was concerned not only with issues of peace and war, but also with the 'emancipation of women and the protection of their interests'. The impulse to extend the scope of women's influence, already demonstrated by the efforts towards peace during the war, was to be a characteristic of the women's movement after the war. There was nothing new in this – Victorian feminism had ben wide in its range of interests and activities – but the focus on the suffrage struggle during the Edwardian period had tended to disguise this fact. Suffragists in 1918 began to make the choices which would lead to new alliances, to separations between old colleagues, and to reunions between those who had been divided by their attitude to the war. A hint of the sort of issue which would lead to this regrouping is given by Catherine Marshall's reaction to a series of 'six Wednesday Conferences' held by the WIL in 1918 on 'Problems of Population'. The titles included 'Problems of Population: How Can Peoples be made free, healthy and pacific?'; 'Is there a Connection between Militarism and the Birthrate?'; and 'Should the Birthrate be Restricted?' The speakers and chairpersons at these conferences included Helena Swanwick and her close friend Dr Elizabeth Bolton, Irene Cooper Willis, Maude Royden and Emmeline Pethick Lawrence. Birth control was not at this time widely discussed. Even for radical women it was not necessarily accepted as a subject for open discussion. Catherine Marshall wrote on the back of her programme for the conferences:

> I'm doubtful about the wisdom of having public discussion of things which are largely so intimate and personal as some of these subjects – at any rate until we are ready to put forward a definite policy as to the part the State should play with regard to them.
>
> People who lack personal experience will be very ready to expand all sorts of academic theories. People who have personal experience will probably be very reluctant to speak of it in public.[4]

Birth control did become a public issue in the 1920s, and we shall look at the way it was regarded by feminists in the next chapter. Marshall's doubts about the political wisdom of the open discussion of birth control were shared by many women in the Labour Movement, and did not reflect any lack of interest in issues which concerned women as wives and mothers. Marshall was not an advocate of equality with men without any reference to the difference between gender experiences. Indeed, she was concerned to emphasise the difference between men's and women's perspectives. Her thinking at this time is apparent in notes she made for proposals put before the Keswick Suffrage Society in May 1918. Marshall began her notes with a defence of the need for the continuation of separate women's organisations. She argued that women were inevitably less politically mature than men and they needed time to develop politically. Women, she believed, had a different political perspective: 'things which have been dealt with from exclusively masculine points of view, must be looked at in future from a woman's point of view in order to achieve a "balanced vision".' She accepted that women did not all think alike, and that they would join different political parties, but the effect would be to spread women's influence into each party. The focus of women's interests in the political sphere would be different from that of men; women would be more concerned with 'all the things that make or mar the happiness of homes, or concern the conditions of young lives'. For Marshall, politics was concerned with the relations between human beings, including those between husband and wife, between parent and child.[5] In these notes Catherine Marshall touched on what would be contentious issues for political feminists in the years after the war: separatism; women's role in the political parties, and whether that role made links between women in other political parties possible;

and the question of what feminists should be concerned with and could achieve in the political sphere.

The problem facing former suffragists was how to make room for the many issues which demanded attention and would be subject to debate and some disagreement. In February 1918, an article appeared in *Common Cause* on 'The Future of the NUWSS', written by Eleanor Rathbone. In it she asserted that to 'many of us for many years "The Suffrage" – i.e. the Parliamentary vote – has been merely the keystone of the edifice the National Union exists to build.' But, as she pointed out, 'Until the keystone was firmly implanted, we could not begin on the rest of the building, because its basis would not be secure.' The NU now needed to look at the complicated question of what the building should look like. Rathbone suggested that the sphere of interest which belonged to the union was the sphere of feminism. But she recognised in the very next sentence that such an assertion would not be acceptable to some women who found the word feminism repugnant. So she suggested that the motto of the union should be: 'I am a woman, and nothing that concerns the status of women is indifferent to me.' As a rhetorical statement, this was powerful. As a definition of the interests of women, it was open to more than one interpretation. She went on to recognise that there were problems inherent in the existence of other organisations which represented the interests of women, but Rathbone believed that there would not be an overlap, and that there was no need for fusion between women's organisations.[6] In these early, sanguine months, it seemed to feminists that there was room for diversity of organisation.

Rathbone's article was published after the future of the NU had been discussed at length at an executive meeting, and just before the subject was to be on the agenda of the Council meeting. The executive proposal to the Council was that the National Union should work for equal franchise, and 'all other such reforms, economic, legislative and social, as are necessary to secure a real equality of liberties, status and opportunities between men and women.' At the Council meeting Ray Strachey, Ida O'Malley, Chrystal Macmillan and Alys Russell all spoke in support of the proposal. There were others who wanted to broaden the scope of the resolution so that it would include domestic reforms such as 'are necessary to secure not only real equality of Liberties and status between men and women, but also freedom of opportunity for women to make their full contribution to the affairs of the Nation'. This amendment, which was defeated, was supported by Maude Royden, Kathleen Courtney and Isabella Ford. Courtney believed that if the National Union:

> adopts the Equality Formula, I think it will be condemning itself to death . . . The societies especially those in the country simply cannot keep together on a doctrinal basis like 'equality', especially when the members are all burning to do practical things.

She thought that the broader proposal would lead to the resignation of Ray Strachey and that there would then 'be a change of building up a vigorous feminist society which would eventually I should hope unite with the WIL.' Courtney's prognosis that societies would be unlikely to remain active on the basis of the 'equality formula' was to be echoed the following year by Rathbone, who had favoured the narrower definition of the union's programme in 1918. Mary Stocks was also loyal to the executive proposal, although she would later press for issues to be included in the union programme which arguably went beyond 'equality'. The divisions in opinion were intricate, and shifting. Helen Ward, who was an active member of the WIL, did not agree with Courtney and Royden, believing that 'the implications and ramifications of every sort bound up with the "equality formula" provide more than enough work . . . ' She confessed to Marshall that she was unable fully to understand either 'school of thought'.[7] For the present there was a general willingness to continue to work together on the basis of the executive resolution.

The debate was further complicated by the development of the Women's Citizens Associations. Such associations were not new in 1918, but they were given a fresh impetus by the partial achievement of franchise for women. In June Rathbone complained that the suffrage societies were being 'bled white' by the WCAs. The following week came a response to this complaint by Ray Strachey who agreed with Rathbone's concern about the closeness of the links between the societies and the citizens associations, but disagreed with her conclusion.

> Miss Rathbone fears that they will bleed our societies white, that our members will be interested in citizenship and not in our own objects, and, therefore, that unless we allow them to camouflage their loss of interest we shall expire.[8]

Strachey argued that the NU must retain its independence: 'Let us keep our money, our strength, our organisations, and our enthusiasm for our own objects.' Her opposition to close links with the Women's

Citizens Associations was rooted in her belief that they would not limit themselves to educational work; she foresaw that efforts would be made towards their 'banding together and gradually developing a Woman's Party programme.' She had expressed these fears earlier in the year and had opposed proposals by Rathbone which, in her view, 'would clearly necessitate the addition to the objects of the NUWSS . . . of some such thing as "to encourage women to make collective use of their votes."' Strachey did not believe that women shared a particular political viewpoint. She did believe that the NUWSS should continue to work politically for equality: 'In the equality programme we have before us lies the most vital of all the reconstruction problems, namely, women in agriculture and industry. To arrive at a solution to that problem is not easy, but it is *our* problem . . . '. She was optimistic about the situation in the spring and summer of 1918 when the newly enfranchised women were suddenly a political and electoral factor. She was determined to make the most of this power before an election, after which, she predicted 'we shall be a pricked bubble.'[9] For the present the interests of women appeared to be a political priority, and this meant the interests of women in the home as well.

One of the main focuses of feminist activity in the 1920s was the welfare of women, especially working-class women. Many suffragists had been involved in 'Settlement Work.' Their experiences in working with working-class women had often fed directly into their support for suffrage. Eleanor Rathbone was one such, and her war-time experience had given her practical experience of the operation of a scheme where wives were given an income by the state. In articles published in 1917 Rathbone argued for 'direct provision' to women through allowances for their children.[10] She then brought together a small committee for the purpose of writing a pamphlet to advertise the idea more widely. The Committee included four suffragists who had been concerned with the welfare of working-class women before the war: Rathbone herself, Mary Stocks, Kathleen Courtney and Maude Royden. Their attitude to war had divided these women; their hopes for the future now brought them together again. The pamphlet contained an outline of a scheme for the payment of 'family endowment' to all mothers at the level then paid out to the wives of servicemen.

The arguments put forward in support of family endowment linked it firmly with the question of equal pay. To those who argued that men needed more pay to support their families, it was pointed out that at any given time most men had no children dependent on them, either because the children were as yet unborn, or because they were grown up. A blanket level of pay to cope with the period when there were dependent children in a family was uneconomic; direct provision for the children through family endowment would be an appropriate way of dealing with the problem. Family endowment and equal pay were at the forefront of feminist thinking as the war drew to an end. Barbara Ayrton Gould drafted a resolution for the WIL executive in support of both 'state payment of motherhood' and equal pay in September 1918, and a similar resolution was put to the WIL Council in October. Maude Royden wrote a pamphlet for the WIL on the subject, and Helen Ward asked Catherine Marshall: 'Are you interested in State Endowment of Motherhood? I am. I think it wants a tremendous lot of ventilating as "Equal pay for equal work" is surely fundamental and yet under the present wage system almost unobtainable.'[11] The issue was indeed 'ventilated' in the years that followed, as we shall see.

Commitment to the welfare of women was a new departure for the WIL; to other women's organisations it was a continuation of their work. The suffrage movement had not distracted the Women's Co-operative Guilds from their prior commitment to improve the conditions of life for working-class women. The Guilds were active during the war, both in their support for peace and in their concern for the conditions and pay of working women. As the largest organisation representing married women, a priority for the Guilds was the care of mothers and young children. In 1915 a collection of letters from Guild members describing their experience of childbirth had been published. Mary Stocks later wrote:

the impact of these published letters was shattering. Of course I knew that childbirth was a very different matter for those who could not command the skill and comfort available to me. But the letters were so vivid, so personal, so immediate and so horrifying.[12]

Mary Stocks would look to family endowment and birth control as solutions: the Women's Co-operative Guilds for the present continued to press for the establishment of Maternity Centres. They believed that 'infant mortality and disease were largely due to the serious neglect of maternity problems by the medical profession and the public and the impossibility of working women getting the medical aid which is needed in pregnancy.' Apart from Maternity

Centres which were run by volunteers, some Local Authorities had established centres, and the NUWSS had cooperated with the WCG in pressing them to do so. Indeed, the exigencies of war made women's health a popular issue. One of the resolutions passed at the Annual Council Meeting of the NUWSS in 1916 called for individual societies to 'do all in their power to further the welfare of infants and mothers in this country.'[13] A combination of pressures thus led to the passing of the Maternity and Child Welfare Act in 1918. This Act required local authorities to set up Maternity Committees, and empowered them – although it did not make it mandatory upon them – to provide child welfare and ante-natal clinics.

The victory won for the consideration of childbirth in the political arena, as indeed for women's welfare in general, was partly the result of a growth in 'concern for motherhood. The ideology of motherhood was then, as it is now, a weapon which could be turned against women, as Eleanor Rathbone was well aware. The appeal to and of woman as mother was compelling. Labour women who represented the interests of industrial women workers were subject to it. Marion Phillips and Mary Macarthur wrote and spoke during the war of the importance of protecting the health of women who were or would be the mothers of future generations. The adoption by women in the Labour Movement of the cause of motherhood was not new, but the war and the hopes of suffrage intensified and sharpened the commitment. A collection of essays entitled *Women in the Labour Party* was published in 1918 and addressed the issues of what newly-enfranchised women could hope for and offer to the Labour Movement. Margaret Llewelyn Davies drew together the demand for maternity services and 'National Endowment' of mothers and children in one of the essays. The question of equality in the factory was taken up by Mary Macarthur in another essay in this volume. She did not put in any strong plea for women to remain in the factory after the war. Her aim was 'to secure as wide a sphere as is possible, consistent with the maintenance of health and the welfare of the race'. Like Davies, she was hopeful that 'politicians would take more interest in the questions that specially interest women', but for her these issues were not concerned with equal pay or employment opportunities. 'Women', she claimed, 'desire above all else to conserve the race. Big questions of domestic policy will appeal most to women in so far as they affect the welfare of children.' When discussing the pledges given by the Government to the Trade Unions when 'dilution' occurred. Macarthur assumed that 'no individual woman would desire to retain the job of any soldier or sailor who may return to claim it.'[14]

This assumption that women in industry would quickly be replaced by demobilised men was an accurate forecast of the situation which occurred when the war ended. Few women expected a transformation in the structure of women's employment in industry after the war, yet the climate of hope in 1918 was such that radical change did seem possible. Ray Strachey was determined to make the most of a situation in which the new women voters were being courted. She had been made aware of the difficulty of persuading unions to allow women a foothold in well-paid work through her wartime attempt to negotiate membership in the engineering union for women, yet she was for a short time hopeful that change was possible in the political climate towards the end of 1918. She was in a buoyant mood in the autumn, revelling in political activity, despite her distaste for what were assumed by most to be 'women's interests'. In September she wrote a confident and optimistic article for *Common Cause* in which she asserted that 'the belief in equal pay for equal work has taken root in this country, and can never be dislodged again.' As evidence she offered the outcome of the bus conductors' strike, and of the long struggle between May and August of the National Federation of Women Teachers. She linked these successes to the emergence of women as voters, and her article was titled: 'Does Having the vote Raise Wages?'[15]

Strachey attended the Labour Party Conference in October and wrote to her mother while supposedly listening to a speaker:

> As I write Miss Llewelyn Davies is holding forth on the new ministry of health. I can't think how often I have said that 'health was the sort of question women voters were interested in' – but oh! this woman voter is not![16]

By October 1918, the prospects were looming of an end to the war, and of a new parliament which not only would be elected by women voters, but could contain women members.

THE FIRST ELECTION

A government bill enabling women to stand as candidates for Parliament became law just in time for the election in December. Ironically, the age of eligibility was the same as that for men, so that women between the ages of 21 and 30 could stand for election although they could not vote. Suffragists were greatly encouraged by the rapidity with which this radical change was put through Parliament, and they had already begun to consider the question of who might be chosen to stand before the Bill was passed. The NUWSS was aware that there was insufficient time to be ambitious, but they hoped and planned to run six candidates, two from each party. Ray Strachey wrote to Selina Cooper, an NU organiser and Labour Party member from Nelson in Lancashire, to tell her of this plan, asking if she would be willing to stand for the Labour Party and if so, whether her local constituency party would adopt her. But Nelson, like many other constituencies, had already chosen its male candidate and Cooper's efforts in two other North Western constituencies were fruitless.[17]

Four women were chosen by the Labour Party. Two of them were very well-known suffragists, Pethick Lawrence and Charlotte Despard. They were also well-known as pacifists, however, and Pethick Lawrence felt that her campaign in Rusholme, Manchester, showed that war-fever was still raging there. She also made clear her position as a feminist and issued a 'Letter to Women from the Woman Candidate'. In Battersea, where Despard stood, it seemed to one feminist that the only canvassers were 'WIL women' and that there was 'no organisation apparently – a mass of poor streets where hardly anyone knows or apparently cares about politics – 9000 absent voters and the result will be the "Will of the People". It is a huge farce.' The fourth Labour candidate was another former suffragist, Mrs Mackenzie. *Common Cause* reported that there was practically no organisation in existence in her constituency either, and that all the work had fallen on to the inexperienced candidate.[18] Because of these political and organisational barriers, only Mary Macarthur of the Labour women candidates stood any chance of winning.

Four women also stood as Liberal candidates, and one of these was Margery Corbett Ashby, who stood for the Ladywood division of Birmingham. During the war she had given shelter to homeless girls when the NU was involved in relief work, and she had helped at the baby clinic her mother organised in the family home, but she had been mainly occupied in looking after her own son who was born in 1915. In April 1918, she agreed, somewhat reluctantly, to speak at a National Union meeting in Northampton in place of Alys Russell, who was ill. Corbett Ashby agreed to speak partly because of the topic which was 'the responsibility of the vote', about which she felt strongly. Then, in October, she was approached by the Liberal party in Birmingham to stand. She did not at first take the offer very seriously, but when she mentioned it at an NUWSS committee meeting she was told that 'it was one of the best offers made to any woman and I was pressed to take it on'. The offer by the local party to pay her expenses was crucial; the cost of an election deterred women as it did working-class men. Margery Corbett Ashby did not expect to get elected, a factor which encouraged rather than discouraged her from standing. Indeed her main reason for standing was not a desire to be elected, but a sense of duty to the suffrage cause. 'Besides when I am very old it will really be fun to think I fought at the very first election possible.' She also felt the pressure of her mother's long commitment to suffrage, and she saw that 'so many women have refused who would have made good candidates.' Her reluctance to stand was shared by others. Ray Strachey was asked by the Liberal Party as early as July 'to suggest 20 women for them to run – but they must be Liberals and these are hard to find.'[19]

The press tipped Christabel Pankhurst, Macarthur and Violet Markham, a former anti-suffragist, to win, and suggested that Ray Strachey stood an outside chance. Strachey was acting again as Parlimentary Secretary of the NU in the spring and summer of 1918. In July she told her mother that she was:

> trying to worm my way into the inside of the Conservative Party, to see whether I can bear to join them or not. Up to date I fear I can't, but I haven't given up hope. But I can't swallow 'the war after the war' and the economic weapon and all that, nor can I swallow Lloyd George and all his dishonesty. However, its great fun worming in.[20]

Strachey got nowhere with the Conservative Party, which refused to see her. The party's central office, she found, was 'violently opposed to women MPs'. She refused the offer of a Liberal candidature in South Kensington because it was a safe Conservative seat, and because she still did not consider herself a Liberal. Then, in November, when she was still busy trying to find good women candidates who were 'refusing to stand for one reason or another', the possibility opened up of being selected as a Coalition candidate for Brentford and Chiswick. She was shortlisted, and before appearing at the selection committee collected 'testimonials' from three Liberals and three Conservatives, of whom only two were women; Lady

Strachey (her mother-in-law and a staunch suffragist) and Millicent Garrett Fawcett. She was not selected at the first meeting, and only became the candidate when the man chosen withdrew the following day. She was 'alarmed and overjoyed' at this reversal of fortune, and turned immediately to the pressing problem of finding the necessary money for her campaign. She threw herself into electioneering with vigour and enthusiasm and conducted the most lively campaign of all the women candidates, according to *Common Cause*. She stood as an Independent Coalitionist because she could not agree to support Lloyd George's government on every single issue. Strachey, like Markham, was decisively beaten. It was the independent line taken by many women candidates that *Common Cause* believed was one of their handicaps. Apart from Pankhurst and Strachey, four women candidates stood as independents, including two members of the Women's Freedom League. One of these was Edith How Martyn, who argued that women should remain independent of party until all inequalities had been removed.[21]

Two women candidates stood for the Sinn Fein whose policy was not to recognise the Westminster Parliament. They therefore had no intention of taking their seats if elected, yet one of them was the only woman to be elected: Constance Gore-Booth, Countess Markievitz, who was in Holloway Jail for her part in a 'German Plot.' From jail she wrote to her sister Eva, a committed suffragist herself:

> By the way, shall you 'stand' for Parliament? I wouldn't mind doing it – as a 'Shinner', as an election sport, and one does not have to go to Parliament if one wins, but oh! to have to sit there and listen to all that blither![22]

This was the paradoxical conclusion of the first election in Britain in which women had played an active part. There was confidence at the time about the impact made by women on that first election campaign. Ray Strachey was astonished at the difference in the attitude towards women once the Franchise Bill had been passed. 'I come into the office in the morning to hear that the Liberal Whip's office is on the telephone, the Labour Party want me to ring them up, the Ministry of Reconstruction will see me at 11 and a dozen representatives of this and that are asking for appointments.' Catherine Marshall corresponded with her local coalition candidate during the campaign and he wrote: 'I have been told that so far I have neglected women and I intend to say something about that subject on Tuesday at my meeting here.'[23] In the light of such encouragement, the results of the election were a grave disappointment.

The women who stood in 1918 were all politically committed and active, and the WIL and the NUWSS had supported women candidates with money and effort. But women had not been eager to become candidates, as Strachey had found. Much of the suffrage struggle had been conducted on non-party lines, and many women would have preferred to remain independent of party. Of the suffragists whose lives I have focused on, Eleanor Rathbone and Ray Strachey were intensely interested in Parliament as an arena of activity, but were uncommitted to any political party. Strachey stood in 1918 and would stand again, her enjoyment of politics and her inherent optimism overcoming the memory of past defeats. Rathbone also stood more than once as an independent, and was eventually elected – a rare phenomenon in twentieth-century British politics. Five of the others were Labour Party members, but of these only Pethick Lawrence stood for election, and then only once. From the years of the war until her death Helena Swanwick concentrated her energies on international rather than national affairs, and the same is true of Catherine Marshall, although she did once consider standing as a Labour candidate. Maude Royden was invited to be a Labour Party candidate in 1922; she refused. Evelyn Sharp was asked 'once or twice to let my name be put forward as a suggested candidate for Parliament', but she never agreed to this, believing that involvement in parliamentary politics would have meant acceptance of compromise, which would have 'troubled me to the point of rendering me either obstructive or ineffective'. Margery Corbett Ashby had felt able to give the necessary time to her election campaign only because her doctor, Louisa Martindale, had told her that it would be good for her young son and for herself to be away from each other for a while.[24] In fact, Corbett Ashby did stand again; she was, as we have seen, firmly committed to the Liberal Party.

The results of the election were an overwhelming victory for the coalition government and a defeat for all candidates connected with pacifism in any form. As Strachey commented, 'the sting of being beaten is quite taken out by the company in which I find myself. If two ex-cabinet ministers forfeited their deposit, and dozens more were rejected, why should I grumble? I don't.' None of our suffragists celebrated the results of the election and the victory of Lloyd

George's coalition. The experience of the NUWSS before the war had led to a deep distrust of the man whom Swanwick referred to as 'the little scoundrel'. Writing much later, Swanwick recalled that the war cast such a pall over the political scene that 'though, of course, I used my vote, it was with no hope and no rejoicing'. As for the effect of women voters on the results of the election, Evelyn Sharp contributed a humorous footnote to this controversy in a dialogue between party politicians, all of whom blamed women for aspects of the election which they disliked.[25]

RELIEF

The election was held in the month after the war ended. On Armistice Day Catherine Marshall was undergoing treatment in Edinburgh, and she celebrated by going into the empty cathedral and singing Schubert's *Litanei*, with the refrain 'All souls may now rest in peace.' Helena Swanwick was on a speaking tour in Scotland: 'I seemed to be crying all the time inside and I had to hold myself tight'. The end of the war had brought a sense of relief to all, but it was a relief muted by the knowledge of so many deaths, so much intolerable and irreparable damage. Ray Strachey wrote:

> You would be astonished, Mother, and probably incredulous, to find how little excited anyone is about peace . . . things happening so fast, and we had all settled down to war as a permanent condition and so don't believe it. And perhaps we are a little afraid of peace.[26]

When she heard the news of the armistice, Margery Corbett Ashby got on her bicycle, and 'jumped off in the woods half stumbling and then something broke and I shook and cried and cried because the awful terror of these years was over.'[27]

Mary Stocks's chief memory of the end of war was of a sense of relief and a certainty that such a war could not happen again. The determination to take this certainty into international politics had been and was to continue to be the driving force behind the Women's International League. One of the WIL's first activities during peacetime was concerned with the relief of suffering. In April and May special meetings of the WIL executive were called to discuss the pending prosecution of Barbara Ayrton Gould for posting bills dealing with the food situation in Europe on hoardings in London. Rumours were abroad that the prosecution was for 'obscene literature'; in fact she was summonsed for contravention of a regulation under the Defence of the Realm Act (still in operation) because the posters accused the allied blockade of causing the famine conditions. Helena Swanwick pointed out that the prosecution could only argue she was guilty if the blockade was considered to be an 'act of war', and if that was the case, the allies were breaking the armistice. Nevertheless, Barbara Ayrton Gould was found guilty and was not given the option of going to prison as she wished. Her fines were paid by Irene Cooper Willis and the WIL, and the fine on her printer by Miss Marian Ellis, the Quaker, and Eglantyne Jebb.[28]

The WIL began to work with Marian Ellis, Eglantyne Jebb and her sister, Dorothy Buxton, in the Fight the Famine Council at the very end of 1918. The Council had emerged from immediate postwar efforts by Quakers to give aid to occupied Germany, and was launched in January at a public meeting at which Maude Royden spoke. The link between the Fight the Famine Council and the WIL was forged, according to Emmeline Pethick Lawrence, at a protest meeting in April. After the meeting she and Barbara Ayrton Gould marched to Downing Street under a banner demanding 'Lift the Hunger Blockade'. The links were strengthened when Mary Sheepshanks became secretary to the Fight the Famine Council in August. In the following month, Dorothy Buxton read a report on the famine conditions in Russia to the WIL executive, which then agreed that a resolution condemning the blockade should be conveyed to Winston Churchill. For some members of the WIL such efforts were not enough. In March 1920, Ethel Williams reduced her donation to the WIL on the grounds that it should have been involved in bringing to England the starving children of Vienna. The executive committee's response was to say that the WIL was a political and not a philanthropic organisation.[29] Other women offered their own skills. Dr Hilda Clark, Mary Sheepshanks' friend and Alice Clark's sister, established and ran a Quaker Relief mission to Vienna. She worked together with her friend Edith Pye, with whom she had collaborated in establishing maternity hospitals in France during the war. Kathleen Courtney offered advice and help regularly to Hilda Clark's relief mission between 1920 and 1922.

Evelyn Sharp joined those suffragists who felt that they must contribute in some way to the relief of suffering. In 1919 she was writing regularly for the Labour newspaper, the *Daily Herald*. A recurring theme of her articles was the destitute state of the German people, especially the children, and the refusal of the British public to recognise or relieve this distress. In a cutting little dialogue – one of her favourite forms of journalism – she had the father of a middle-class English family recommend that the starving babies of Germany drink cocoa, while his wife insists to their own demanding and well-fed child that cocoa is bad for babies. By the end of the year Sharp decided that her efforts to stir up public opinion would be strengthened were she to see what the conditions were in Germany at first hand. She decided to go where she believed the situation was at its worst, confessing that: 'the worst of having been a suffragette is that, ever afterwards, you think public work cannot be worth doing unless it is the most unpleasant task you can find to put your hand to'.[30] The relief work that Sharp did under Quaker supervision over the next four years was second only to her suffrage work in its influence on her life.

PEACEMAKERS: THE WOMEN'S INTERNATIONAL LEAGUE FOR PEACE AND FREEDOM, ZURICH, 1919

Before she went to Germany Evelyn Sharp had attended the second Congress of the International Committee of Women for Permanent Peace, of which the WIL was the British branch. The committee had been set up because its founders believed that women should never again have to be the providers of relief during and after a war. From its inception it had been the intention of the organisation to hold a Women's Congress to coincide with any official peace conference at the end of the war. The decision to hold the peace conference in Paris meant that the ICWPP could not meet alongside the treaty-makers, because women from the defeated powers would not receive permission to travel to France, and the ICWPP had no intention of excluding them. In May, 1919, the Women's Congress met in Switzerland, in Zurich. Among those from Britain who attended were Helena Swanwick, Catherine Marshall, Kathleen Courtney, Emmeline Pethick Lawrence, Mary Sheepshanks, Chrystal Macmillan, Margaret Ashton and Isabella Ford. Barbara Ayrton Gould, newly active in the WIL, could not come because her court case was pending.

The meeting was an emotional occasion, as women whose countries had been at war met in peace. The climax of feeling came towards the end. One of the French delegates arrived late because of difficulties in obtaining a passport. She had spent the war years in the

Ardennes, where she had watched terrible destruction take place. As she arrived, a German delegate, Lida Gustava Heymann, who had just finished speaking, clasped her by the hand. The delegates rose to their feet and repeated the words of an American woman who cried out, 'I dedicate my life to the cause of Peace.' Helena Swanwick thought that she had 'never witnessed or imagined so remarkable an affirmation. Such schemes can, of course, be staged, but only intense feeling can cause them to occur spontaneously, as this did.'[31] This testimony to the solidarity of feeling among the delegates came at the end of a conference where difference of opinion had arisen but had not destroyed the consensus of the delegates. At the Hague in 1915 there had been an embargo on discussion of where responsibility for the war lay. In Zurich, news of the effects of the blockade was given by 'a representative of the victor states' and the invasion of Belgium was denounced by a German delegate.

While responding to the immediate crisis, the Congress also considered the long-term position of women in Europe. The ICWPP was renamed the Women's International League for Peace and Freedom, and the headquarters were moved to Geneva. A special Feminist Committee was set up to deal 'with proposals concerning a radical change in the position of women'. The committee drew up a Woman's Charter which they proposed should be included in the Peace Treaty so that it would be accepted by all signators. The charter began boldly with the declaration that 'the status of women – social, political and economic – is of supreme international importance.' Subsequent clauses asserted the mutual interdependence of men and women, and thus the injury done to a community when women were kept in a position of dependence, and recognised the service of women not only as wage-earners but as 'mothers and homemakers'. A list of principles was drawn up specifying the policies which were necessary to achieve a just status for women, including suffrage; property rights; maternity and guardianship rights; equal educational opportunities; equal pay, and 'adequate economic provision for the service of motherhood'.

The main items of immediate concern at the conference were the Treaty of Versailles; the possibility of continued violence as revolutionary movements in Eastern Europe attempted to wrest control from autocratic governments; and the famine conditions in much of Europe. The Congress called for the raising of the blockade and immediate international action to supply relief. Attitudes to revolutionary violence were ambivalent. The result of the debate was a narrow victory for a resolution whereby the congress accepted 'special responsibility to counsel against violence' but 'declared its belief that there was a fundamentally just demand underlying most of the revolutionary movements who were everywhere seeking to make an end of exploitation and to claim their world'.

The news of the terms of the Treaty of Versailles were made public after the conference had assembled, and delegates spent a whole day and night studying them before they were discussed. In Swanwick's view the terms were 'worse than anything we had anticipated'. The Congress adopted a resolution in response to the treaty which expressed 'deep regret' that its terms 'should so seriously violate the principles upon which alone a just and lasting peace can be secured.' The imposition of reparations and the disarmament of the defeated were condemned. Great hopes had been pinned on the establishment of a League of Nations, but the terms of the Covenant of the League laid down at Versailles were a bitter disappointment and led to differing reactions from delegates. Some wanted to condemn the covenant outright, but the view prevailed that 'the child was born, the important thing is not to kill it'. This was the response of a group which considered the question of the League in detail, basing their analysis on a pamphlet by Helena Swanwick. The final text of the resolution accepted by the Congress called for amendments to the Covenant, the most important of which would allow for open membership of the League and 'immediate reduction of armaments on the same terms for all member states'.[32]

Members of the WILPF were not the first women to attempt to have some impact on the Peace Conference. Ray Strachey had been in Paris with the first group of suffragists to attend the Peace Conference. When the war ended the French section of the International Woman Suffrage Alliance had advocated that a Conference of Women Delegates take place in parallel to the Versailles Conference: Ray Strachey and Millicent Garrett Fawcett were the British delegates. They were not optimistic about the results of their efforts, although they did succeed in establishing the eligibility of women to offices in the League. In her diary Millicent Garret Fawcett wrote that the conference was 'rather desultory.' Ray Strachey's comment on her experience in a letter to her sister-in-law was that 'there has been so much that is purely ridiculous.'[33] After Strachey and Fawcett had returned to England, the NUWSS sent Margery Corbett Ashby and Margery Fry as delegates to the Paris Conference in an attempt to ensure that women would be represented on the various international bodies which were being established. They were not successful. From Paris Margery Fry wrote wry letters to Eva Hubback, who was soon to become secretary to the NUWSS; in the last one she concluded:

> I will say that of *all* muddles, undemocratic, unpractical bodies this conference simply takes the bisc [uit] We practically never met, we have noted the resolutions and we couldn't get them altered. The preambles are a simple disgrace to the human intelligence, I consider.[34]

Corbett Ashby's letters to Fawcett reveal the enormous frustrations which faced them in their position of total powerlessness. 'I would write more often but alas there is really no news. We are waiting from day to day in increasing despair . . . the whole situation here seems very depressing.' She opposed the suggestion of sending yet another delegation from the IWSA to continue to press for their demands. She said that the proposal to do so 'seems to me to show a lack of sense of proportion. The men in Paris are under the impression that we have been wonderfully well treated by them and have acquitted ourselves very well'.[35]

Although international feminists were unable to make any impact on the structure or philosophy of the League of Nations, the efforts of the two groups of women, which ran parallel in 1919, did converge to some extent in the following year. In June, 1920, the IWSA held a congress in Geneva which saw the gathering together of feminists who had been divided by the war. Ray Strachey went reluctantly, writing to her mother that she had to go, since it was important, but referring to it as that 'filthy' congress; 'I can't tell you how much I hate it.' In the end Strachey found Geneva 'really very entertaining'. Although she found the Congress dull, she enjoyed the company of Lady Astor, and met many 'really interesting people from whom I got a lot of fascinating information.'[36] For Strachey the interest of the congress lay in discussions on women's employment. One of the questions discussed at Geneva concerned the question of legal restrictions on women's right to work. The differences of opinion that emerged in the debate on this issue were the herald of a division in feminist thinking which would later become crucial.

Margery Corbett Ashby was also there, finding 'The German women so quiet and subdued, they are making it very easy for everyone.' From the WIL came Helena Swanwick, financing herself by using a present given to her of £50, and Emmeline Pethick Lawrence. Kathleen Courtney represented the NUSEC, and Eleanor Rathbone was also there. On Sunday 6 June Maude Royden was invited by the Cathedral consistory to be the first woman to preach from Calvin's pulpit. Royden saw this as a recognition 'that, at such a time in the world's history as this, if women felt that they had something to say, they should be heard'. In her sermon Royden declared that women had come to Geneva with 'a sense of the world's need' and 'a hope – a faith – that we women have some answer to that need'. Corbett Ashby commented that Royden preached 'quite well'; adding that she was 'a little disappointed but the Swiss lady next to me murmured "magnifique" and shook me warmly by the hand to express her emotion'.[37]

Geneva marked the reunion of feminists divided by the war. A symbol of that reunion was the Charter that was there proclaimed. With the addition of a clause on the question of labour legislation, the charter was identical to one which Chrystal Macmillan had drawn up in the previous September, which was in turn based on the Charter of the WILPF conference in Zurich.

LABOUR, FEMINISM AND PACIFISM: THE WIL, THE NUSEC AND THE LABOUR PARTY, 1919–1920

During the war relations between the WIL and the NUWSS had been strained, but the links had been there. The ideals of the women in the two organisations were the same; the arena in which they chose to work was different. One former suffragist believed that these two groups of 'equally able women' were 'now happily friends again'; and that 'in their ultimate hopes and desires for permanent peace the two organizations do not differ by so much as a hair's breadth'.[38] In Geneva the two groups were reconciled. Would they also come together in the national context?

The executive committee minutes of the two organisations reveal their common concerns, including support for equal pay and family endowment. To some extent they shared a common membership. In 1919 women from the two organisations considered their futures, and among the options which faced them was whether they should make the existing links between them more formal. Delegates from the WIL had attended NU meetings about Widows Pensions and the extension of suffrage. In September the possibility of formal affiliation between the two organisations was discussed at a WIL executive meeting: it was shelved.[39] By that time decisions about the future activities of the NU had been made; the WIL was more uncertain, at least about its national role.

The future of the NUWSS was decided in March 1919. Proposals put forward by Ray Strachey, Eleanor Rathbone and Oliver Strachey came before the Annual Meeting of the Council. Ray Strachey's scheme would have abandoned the national federation of societies, and would have limited the work of a renamed 'Fawcett Trust' to the provision of information. Eleanor Rathbone's amendments to this proposal would also have concentrated the work of the Union in one Society, but with a wider vision of its objects. Oliver Strachey's scheme was the most ambitious and it was adopted with some modification. The object of the Union was to be retained; 'to work for a real equality of status, liberties and opportunities between men and women'. Affiliation to the Union was to be opened to any society which had equality between the sexes as one of its objects. This scheme was seen as an attempt to reunite 'the scattered elements that are seeking, in different ways and under different names, for solutions of the sex equality problem'. In some ways it was also a recognition of what was happening in reality, and an attempt to retain a relationship with some societies which had already moved away from the NU. The 1918 Annual General Report referred to 'a year of some difficulty'. It was proving difficult to recruit young women who had careers, and other women were giving their energies to the Women's Citizens Associations or Women's Institutes. The report stoutly maintained that these women would 'soon discover that the political education of women tends to the production of feminist principles'. Articles in *Common Cause* in the summer of 1918 exhorted societies not to disband, and urged women who joined other groups and parties to 'hold the union forces together as well'.[40]

The extension of the work of the Union was reflected in a new name: the National Union of Societies for Equal Citizenship. Millicent Garrett Fawcett resigned as President and was replaced by Eleanor Rathbone. Fawcett had been wanting to resign from the presidency since the autumn of 1917, so this was not a precipitate or resentful move. In March 1918 she had pressed the London Society to enlarge its aims to include the newly-adopted objects of the NU, which does not suggest that she was opposed to them. The London Society made its own decision about the future a few weeks before the National Union Council Meeting in March, 1919, and that decision was to narrow, not widen its objectives. It resolved to continue to 'stand for equal suffrage and equal opportunities for women' but 'to concentrate its efforts for the present on obtaining economic equality for women'. Ray Strachey had been one of those who had advocated this evolution by the London Society: she was unhappy about the decision made by the National Union to loosen its structure. She wrote to her mother after the council meeting:

> Oliver and I have been stirring against each other to the universal interest of the delegates . . . Oliver won all the time, and is left in my judgment with an unworkable and paper scheme.[41]

Despite the loosening of the structure of the NU, the WIL did not move any closer to it, in organisational terms at least. The decision as to whether or not to affiliate to the NUSEC was postponed on 3 September, and again on 18 September. On that occasion Emmeline Pethick Lawrence argued against affiliation on the grounds that it was not appropriate for an international organisation to affiliate to a national one. She did express sympathy with the objects of the NUSEC and a willingness to cooperate with them. On 16 October the decision was reached not to affiliate on the grounds put forward by Pethick Lawrence. Perhaps this constitutional argument was the one that prevailed in the minds of women like Swanwick, Marshall and Courtney who had worked in the NUWSS, unlike Pethick Lawrence and Barbara Ayrton Gould. However, it does seem likely that there were political considerations acting to hinder the possibility of a reunion. There was much in common in the feminism of the two groups, but they differed in their attitudes to the existing political parties. The fact that women had to – or felt they had to – cooperate with the political and patriarchal system prevented the evolution of a strong and united feminist political organisation or viewpoint. The question of what the relationship of the WIL should be to the Labour party occupied the minds of the executive of that organisation as much, if not more than, their relationship with the NUSEC.

At an executive meeting in January 1919, letters from Mary Sheepshanks and Isabella Ford had 'opened up the question of our relationship to the Socialist International and the Labour Party'. Swanwick said that she thought the question an urgent one, given the results of the election. In the discussion that followed 'it was emphasised' – by whom is not clear – that 'to join the Labour Party would limit our scope outside it'. It seems that the accepted view was that the women in the WIL could best use their energies – 'even for Labour' – in efforts to 'convert the middle classes'. There was a need for a 'progressive feminist movement'; the NUSEC was clearly not seen as sufficiently 'progressive'. Pethick Lawrence was enthusiastic about the political side of the WIL work and pressed hard for the setting up of a 'political department'. Other members were doubtful about what purpose this department would fulfill; more pressing problems were lack of money and of women willing and able to take on the work. In September Barbara Ayrton Gould gave up the job of secretary because of her heavy involvement with the *Daily Herald*, and Swanwick had unwillingly to carry that burden as well as the post of Chairman. She found it difficult to persuade anyone to take on the work entailed in either of these roles. In February, Catherine Marshall said that she could not be an active member of the executive because she was not always in London; she was persuaded not to resign. At the same meeting, Swanwick warned that the income of the League was falling, and the financial situation continued to deteriorate until October.[42] The WIL was suffering the same difficulty that faced the NUSEC; women were being attracted into other organisations, or were simply too busy to give time to political activity. For Helena Swanwick and Catherine Marshall, who had been so active during the war years, there was also the question of their health, as is apparent in a letter written by Swanwick to Marshall at this time:

Please don't leave us yet.

I am glad you are staying at home for a bit and living a good deal out of doors. I hope you may gradually get stronger . . .

I have been rather under the weather for some months and have found it very difficult to keep going. Mere weariness, when it is extreme, is a tiresome complaint. I have been very lame for a long time and the mere fag of dragging one's aching leg about is a source of great fatigue.[43]

Swanwick's weariness does not seem to have curtailed her activities to any great extent, but she was clearly troubled by the difficult choices facing feminists. Her publicly-expressed belief was that 'the great task before the WIL was to re-twist the three strands of the League – labour, feminism and pacifism. After the peace, pacifists must support labour and feminism as inter-dependent.' But in private she was all too aware of the problems of the relationship between these three strands when faced by immediate political decisions. Writing to Catherine Marshall about the use of the strike method, she confessed that she could not welcome it and added:

I am more and more struck with two facts (1) that scarcely anyone ever sees or tries to see beyond his nose (2) that nearly everyone is entirely blinded as to methods, if he desires the result.[44]

The link between suffragists and the Labour Party was a long-standing one, and the pull towards socialism was felt by a very large number of feminists. Mary Stocks believed:

Women's suffrage alone is a palliative. The economic basis of feminism rests upon these points: Women's Suffrage, the Endowment of Motherhood, and Socialism. And yet the writer has met Suffragists who are not Socialists.[45]

Not all Stock's colleagues within the NUWSS accepted this assertion. Rathbone made it clear in a discussion about the continued employment of NUWSS organisers that Mrs Annot Robinson would not be kept on because she was 'heart and soul for the Labour Party and it was impossible to expect her to work on non-party lines.'[46]

That there were hurdles facing middle-class feminists in their commitment to socialism is implicit in the subject of a talk Stocks herself gave in 1920: 'Women Opposed to Class War'. For middle-class feminists, the question of class would continue to be a problem. Helena Swanwick, Mary Stocks and Helen Ward hoped that Guild Socialism would offer a less divisive socialism, but here they came across a different obstacle: the lack of recognition of 'motherhood as an occupation'.[47]

The relationship between socialism and feminism has never been a comfortable one, and the postwar years would prove no exception. The dilemma which faced feminists from the Labour Movement was apparent in a letter which appeared in the renamed *The Woman's Leader and Common Cause* in April 1920, from Ada Nield Chew, another Northern working-class suffragist. It was entitled 'Should the Special Interest of Women come before Party Considerations with Women Voters?' Chew reported that her local WCA had provided a list of questions on women's issues to be put to political candidates. The Labour Party man had provided the least satisfactory answer to the questions; his worst response being a 'bold "No"' to the question of whether the council should employ married women. 'I object to his representing me to this effect in a public capacity', wrote Chew, but added that she found her dilemma 'very unpleasant, and the decision I came to equally so'.[48]

Evelyn Sharp did not admit to any doubts about the choice she made. She joined the Labour Party in 1918, and at the same time moved away from the influence of other feminists. In October 1920, she wrote to the WIL criticising their continued existence as 'a purely women's league'. She did retain personal links with other suffragists who were in the Labour Party. In August of that year Sharp, together with Henry Nevinson, had been invited by Catherine Marshall to speak in Cumberland. In his reply Nevinson wrote that 'Miss Evelyn Sharp says she has a conscience which will not allow her to come unless she can speak three times for the Labour Party!'[49] This did not cause any problem, for Marshall was herself very active in the Labour Party at this time. However, like Swanwick, Marshall did not find her commitment to socialism trouble-free.

In January 1920, Catherine Marshall wrote to Arthur Henderson, General Secretary of the Labour Party, to explain that illness had prevented her from being active. In the following month she was the only woman at the conference at which a Divisional Labour Party was established. In April she attended the National Conference of Labour Women together with Helena Swanwick and Mrs Annot Robinson. When she returned to Hawes End she wrote a long letter to Jim Middleton, deputy secretary to the Labour Party, in response to his expressed regrets about the 'dearth of active women in the Labour Movement'. Marshall wrote that middle-class women 'get a very strong impression that they are not welcomed . . . from the head-quarters of the Women's Sections, and the platform of Labour Women's meetings'. She mentioned Marion Phillips, who had been appointed as the first Woman's Officer for the party, as especially responsible for this attitude, but exonerated Margaret Bondfield. She also pointed out that the Labour Party did not offer any training to younger women or give them the opportunity to 'develop and practice their powers of initiative and leadership. . . . There are so far as the outside public is concerned only 5 women who can be produced whenever the representation of Labour women is required on any Committees, delegation etc.' As a result, Marshall maintained, her attempts to urge women to 'to throw their energies into the Labour Movement' had failed.[50]

Middleton had suggested that Kathleen Courtney might become an 'organizer of propaganda' in the Party, and Marshall herself 'secretary to the advisory committees'. In reply Catherine agreed that Courtney would be 'quite excellent', but for the fact that she was not 'whole-heartedly in sympathy with Labour propaganda'. For herself, she believed that her illness had destroyed her 'executive capacity', adding, 'some spring seems to have broken, and I have no longer any confidence in myself – which is fatal'. She agreed to do her best 'to persuade KDC to come and work for the Party', for she would 'love to help her' and thus restore a 'fruitful partnership'. Kathleen Courtney had hoped that a union between the NUSEC and the WIL might occur, and she wanted very much to work closely with Marshall again. 'I miss you badly all the time and wish we could work together again; there is no-one else with whom to talk things over with the same sense of understanding.' Nevertheless she refused, partly because of her involvement in relief work in Vienna, but also because she felt incapable of 'initiative propaganda'. She suggested that a younger woman should do it, but thought Swanwick should be asked first. Swanwick in turn said that she was 'tired of initiating and organising' and was looking for half-time, paid, intellectual work.[51] These three women who had worked closely in the NUWSS might have done so again in the Labour Party: they might thus have formed a bridge between the NUSEC, the WIL and the Labour Movement.

Just before the war Courtney and Marshall had been at the centre of the suffragist effort to influence the House of Commons. One effect of the war on their lives – especially on Marshall's – was to remove them from that arena in the postwar years. However, there is a hint that one of them might have become adviser to the first woman member of Parliament were it not for the fact that this woman, contrary to all expectation, was a conservative.

WOMEN IN THE HOUSE OF COMMONS

On 1 December, 1919, Nancy Astor took her seat in the House of Commons. She was the American born wife of Lord Astor who had been a Member of Parliament for Plymouth until his elevation to the House of Lords. She won this same seat at a by-election by an overall majority of 1000 over the Labour and Liberal candidates. She was greeted on her arrival at Paddington by a small group of suffragists. Their welcome was muted. Nancy Astor was no suffragist, and had shown no personal interest in politics. Suffragists had assumed that the first woman MP would be 'one of ourselves . . . a woman of tried political experience, knowledge and wisdom.' Now they would be represented 'by someone entirely outside our own world'. Her election was not the result of any organised effort, but 'of a complex of accidental happenings'.[52]

Common Cause at the time of Astor's election gave her a warm welcome, despite her lack of feminist credentials, denying the relevance of her party and pointing out that she had proved her faith in equal opportunities for women 'practically, and in a way which will make it easier for other women to prove theirs'. Astor's response was equally gracious: 'I feel that it is a great responsibility to be the first woman to sit in Parliament, and I know that I shall need all the help that other women can give me.' An article in *The Woman's Leader* in 1923 claimed that within a year of her election came 'the realization that Lady Astor was doing all the work which we had dreamed that our first woman in parliament could do'.[53]

Ray Strachey's immediate reaction to the prospect of Nancy Astor's election was as ambivalent as that of any other suffragist. She did not think she was 'a good specimen for the first woman MP;' but added: 'However, she's quite sound really, and Christabel would be far worse!' After speaking to Astor, Ray offered:

> to run her Parliamentary work for her. It is so very important that the first woman MP should act sensibly and she, though full of good sense of a kind, is Parliamentarily ignorant of everything she ought to know. I am not offering to be her paid secretary (though that too was among the alternatives we considered) but simply to run her work for a time and write her memoranda and speeches, watch events for her, prepare her Parliamentary questions, see her despatches, select what invitations she must accept and so on . . . .
>
> I have two objects in doing this. First of all to make sure that the first woman MP doesn't break down somewhere, and that she is the maximum use to all the things we want to get done. Ly A being what she is, and I being what I am, I think we'd make a good combination for that purpose . . . .
>
> My second object is purely selfish. I want to get further into political things . . .

Ray concluded that she was the only person who could do the job; 'the only other person I can think of to take on the job is too violently labour to be willing to try'.[54] It seems likely that Ray Strachey was thinking of Courtney, Marshall or possibly Mary Stocks.

Thus a firm link was made between the largest suffrage organisation and the first woman MP. At first all went well; Ray dined with Lady Astor on her first night in the Commons, and was established in the Lady Member's Room in the House of Commons every afternoon. 'I think it is all going to be not only useful but *great* fun.'

In February she was 'frantically busy' coaching Astor for meetings
and for her maiden speech: 'she is a hopeless speaker'.[55] But Nancy
Astor did not need coaching for long. In the summer Strachey left
her to concentrate on her writing.

When Ray Strachey offered her assistance to Nancy Astor, the
early hopes of feminists about what could be achieved in the first
postwar Parliament had already fallen from a peak reached in the
spring. In April, Strachey had listened to the debate on the 'Women's
Emancipation Bill' and her impression was that 'There was not a rag
of the old prejudice left, not an echo or a squeak, and the only fault
anyone could find with the bill was that it did not go far enough.'
In June she heard MPs making speeches on the Bill which she 'had
just put in their mouths'.[56] But the original, sweeping bill, which,
among other things, would have equalised the franchise and admitted
Peeresses to the House of Lords, was defeated in that House. The
Disqualification Removal Act which was secured granted general
legislative freedom from disqualification by gender. Under the Act
women entered the legal profession and joined professional bodies
such as the Society of Chartered Accountants. The Royal Society
opened its doors reluctantly after a test case involving Mrs Hertha
Ayrton, Barbara Ayrton Gould's mother. Women were now also
able to serve as magistrates and on juries. The appointment of
the first women magistrates was another symbol of success for the
women's movement, and one which gave status and some power
to a few women. Included among the first JPs to be appointed
were Millicent Garrett Fawcett, Eleanor Rathbone, Margery Fry,
Margaret Rhondda, Jane Harrison, Mary Macarthur and Margaret
Bondfield.

In her presidential address to the NUSEC in March, 1920,
Eleanor Rathbone had admitted that she was one of the 'happy
innocents' and 'dreamers' who had been give 'a rude awakening'
by 'the first fruits of the first Parliament elected partly by women's
votes'. Rathbone was complaining about an Act which 'has the
effect of legally excluding women, for the first time in British
history, from nearly every department of skilled industry except a
few trades traditionally their own'.[57] The Act to which she referred
was the Restoration of Pre-War Practices Act. By this Act powers
were given to trade unions, according to pledges previously given,
whereby they could compel employers to restore any customs and
practices which had lapsed during the war. The Act covered any
new industries or new branches of industry that had grown up.

DEMOBILISATION

Ray Strachey had become deeply interested in the question of women's employment during the war and she was to retain this interest for the rest of her life. When the National Union had accepted Oliver's scheme, she confessed to her mother that she was 'secretly glad, because I am myself quite clear from it all . . . I feel as if a ton weight had been removed from my back, and I can now buckle down to the work I like.' After the war the London Suffrage Society transformed itself into the London Society for Women's Service whose object was that of 'obtaining economic equality for women . . . by means of propaganda, political work, the collection and distribution of information.' The letter which announced the change to members of the society declared that 'the forces which threaten the economic position of women today are of a most serious and threatening nature and that action is immediately needed for the protection of women workers'. The letter also averred that the society 'united in principle and experienced in practice will be able to give immediate support to the demobilised women'. Women came to the London Society 'in a rage with their employment exchanges'. They had been deprived of their unemployment benefit for refusing to go into domestic service.[58]

By the spring of 1919 thousands of women had left their wartime occupations, willingly or unwillingly. Within a year of the armistice, there were three-quarters of a million fewer women employed. The demobilisation of women took place in an entirely disorganised and unplanned way. Despite warnings by a committee of the Ministry of Reconstruction that at the end of the war women workers would pose a greater problem than demobilised men, no new machinery was set up by the Government. The unemployment donation scheme did not cover all women laid off, and those who were eligible faced being cut off if they refused any kind of work, even if it paid less than the inadequate level of benefit. Despite protest there was no woman representative on the committee which administered the donation scheme. Almost the only jobs available for women were in domestic service, and women showed a determined resistance to returning to the long hours and poor conditions which accompanied such work. The government reaction to this resistance was to reduce the donation. At the end of the year, when the Government suddenly withdrew unemployment benefit, the number of unemployed women was estimated by the National Federation of Women Workers as

100 000. Yet Mary Macarthur was certain that no women would wish to keep the jobs of men returning from the war and the NFWW supported the Restoration of Pre-War Practices Bill. The NUSEC did not: in the pages of *Common Cause* Ray Strachey wrote angrily about the situation. Early on she identified the position of women as a weakness of the trade union movement. While she also attacked the Government's attitude over the question in the summer of 1919, it was the attitude of the trade unions which she described as 'barbarian', although she added that some unionists were 'enlightened', and she did hope that things would change. Eleanor Rathbone suggested in a letter to Strachey that the question of women's employment be added to the immediate programme of the NUSEC. Strachey felt that this was indeed 'our one big job', and pointed out in her reply that it was Rathbone who had been chiefly instrumental in the decision of the union to 'plunge into the Women Citizens business' and pay 'little attention to the big industrial problem'. Strachey herself had been the only person at the 1919 council to bring up the subject, although demobilisation was 'thick upon us'. In her view, it was 'too late to change the general drift now.'[59]

In their last minute efforts to turn the tide the NUSEC were joined by the Women's Industrial League. The League was headed by Margaret Mackworth, now Lady Rhondda, and its aims included equal employment opportunities and equal pay and working conditions for women. Strachey and the London Society for Women's Service had been actively lobbying against aspects of the bill, especially the clauses which extended the exclusion of women to new industries and branches of industry for longer. None of these efforts were successful. Moreover, relations between women active in the Labour Movement and suffragists were not improved by the division in attitude about the Act. The Women's Industrial League was distrusted by the Labour Movement, and *Woman Worker* warned women not to join it.[60]

Catherine Marshall had built up strong links with the Labour Party, and she retained an interest in and concern with the conditions of employment of women during the early years of the war, keeping in touch with Ray Strachey about the issue after she left the NUWSS. In August 1915, a meeting took place with Anderson, an influential member of the Independent Labour Party, at which Ray Strachey and Catherine Marshall were present. They discussed the 'industrial problems which would arise after the war'. Anderson expressed the opinion that to concern themselves in such questions would take the NUWSS out of its depth. He agreed that it was a good idea to encourage women to join trade unions, but 'this would not come about easily. It must be done from the inside and from the workers themselves. If middle-class women were to start an agitation on these lines it would be regarded by the workers with great suspicion.' Anderson also asserted that the aid given to the ILP by the NU before the war had 'embarrassed them'.[61] Distrust of feminism in the Labour Movement ran deep and disrupted cooperation on the question of women's employment throughout this period.

A WIDE DIVERSITY

Parliament was proving to be a frustrating arena for feminists. The disappointing end to early hopes suggested a need to establish agreed priorities. The resolution of the London Society to the NUSEC Council in 1919 stated that its members were 'convinced that the experience of the last 8 months has shown that the attempt to work for the whole field of equality of men and women at the same time leads to the dissipation of energies and not to effective organisation'.[62] However, the confidence inspired by partial enfranchisement had not been entirely dispelled and there was still very widespread agreement about the injustices that remained. In Chapter 5 we shall look at the goals of women like Eva Hubback and Margaret Rhondda, who devote their energies in the first half of the decade to 'lobbying for equality.'

Behind the widespread agreement about feminist aims lay the beginnings of divisions which the frustration – and the challenges – of the postwar years would carve into the women's movement. One of those challenges was the international peace movement which, as we shall see in Chapter 8 was taken up to varying extents by Helena Swanwick, Evelyn Sharp, Mary Sheepshanks, Kathleen Courtney, Catherine Marshall, Maude Royden, Ray Strachey and Margery Corbett Ashby. The devastation wrought by the First World War was a forceful stimulus to women's involvement in the peace movement. The war ironically also added resonance to the ideology of motherhood. The writings of Marie Stopes did much to popularise the idealisation of woman as mother: she also gave widespread publicity to changes in attitude towards women's sexuality. Eleanor Rathbone, Maude Royden and Mary

Stocks understood women's interests as extending to their domestic and maternal roles and they were beginning to argue that it was in these areas that progress could best be made. In the next chapter I want to consider whether the women in this study were influenced by new ideas on sexuality or by the ideology of motherhood.

5 A New Morality?

In the spring of 1918 *Married Love* by Marie Stopes was published. Maude Royden reviewed it for *Common Cause*, giving it a warm welcome: 'Marie Stopes has made a beginning. We shall look for future enlightenment from her with great expectation.' Royden specifically welcomed Stopes's challenge to 'the old assumption that desire is all on the side of the man'; an assumption which she believed had 'led to a complete ignoring of the needs and nature of women'.[1] Caroline Marshall wrote to Catherine about the book later in the year:

The lack of understanding the nervous and emotional nature of a woman is a very real one. I know she is right in much that she says on this point. Also that ignorance of that fact that a corresponding orgasm in woman is necessary is probably v. true.

But Victorian women – the nice ones – were and are so absolutely reticent and the others so gross that I personally have only my own observation, knowledge to go on. Mainly I hated the actual act – but certainly was capable of passion. I never knew the possibility of orgasm in the act. I do know one woman to whom it the act was never anything but great pain. v. nervous sensitive passionately loving one.

I cannot see how people get or the man gets through the long time of pregnancy chaste if all this is so calculated an enjoyment and industry. Nor can I see how the woman stands it. Life is *so* tiring and family ties so compelling that sexual fatigue must be very wearing.

Also I do know that in times of sorrow and difficulty and trouble, when the sympathy and close personal contact is most precious and comforting the idea of sexual enjoyment or satisfaction or need for it is entirely absent *would be unthinkable*. That seems to me to place sex – in its rightful proportion. And I still think the happiest state is most free from it. But I have not probed the heights and the depths of it. I find myself often wondering how much or how little I know about it all – v. little I believe. What Stopes says of the unconscious effects of sex disturbance seems also true and explains a good deal of the vague longings and pantings for greater freedom. It *is* bad to be forced to renounce legitimate longing for variety and experience and an eager woman become a drudge is so common a sight that no one sees the tragedy of it or the bitter sense of injustice it brings. And the fact that it is perhaps, finally, accepted as *the* sacrifice demanded of her, does not make it just or creditable on the part of the blind who do not perceive its nature or value its cost. All the same I do not think women can sit in Parliament and do their duty to babies. From Stopes account life would seem a long uninterrupted honeymoon if only sex conditions were duly observed. But that is not so.

At the same time – the immediate sex problem is so hideous and so acute that anything that tends to rise above vice and profligacy must be welcomed by those who are in the slough of sex turmoil and suffering. For suffering it is.[2]

Caroline Marshall reveals here both her own attitudes, formed as they were by her Victorian upbringing, and the new expectations which would mould the thinking of her daughter's generation. Her definition of passion challenges the new emphasis on sexual intercourse as the exclusive focus of sexual enjoyment. Tenderness and the comfort of close personal contact seem to her to be in danger of being replaced by pleasure achieved by calculated moves. Nor does she accept the supposition that every woman needed or would benefit from a satisfying heterosexual relationship. Marshall has doubts about her own knowledge of the whole subject, hinting at how the new ideology could undermine a woman's faith in the validity of her own experience. Nevertheless, she accepts that the subject is an important one, and in what might seem a sudden leap to the prospect of women MPs neglecting their babies, she shows how sexuality and motherhood were seen as politically important and connected issues.

The glimpse Caroline Marshall gives us of sexual attitudes and experience was multiplied a hundred times as letters poured in to Marie Stopes. Stopes was not the first to claim that women were and should be able to enjoy sexual intercourse as much as men, but her book had a very wide circulation. Its publication coincided with and helped to foster a change in women's attitude towards sexuality. This change did not affect all women – far from it – but the wider acceptance of women's sexuality was seen by some feminists to be an essential part of their emancipation. A 'new morality' had been expressed in the pages of *The New Feminist* just before the war, based to some extent on the writings of Havelock Ellis. Some of the contributors believed that increased physical enjoyment of heterosexual relationships was potentially liberating for women.

The feminists whose lives feature prominently in this book left little evidence of their views on the question of sexual relations: they were not accustomed to discuss such questions even among their friends. Judging from the letters written to Stopes and Caroline Marshall's reflections, the silence covered pain and ignorance. The breaking of that silence and the wider acceptance of women's sexuality can be looked upon as the severing of a link in the chain of their bondage – or as forging another link in a chain of sexual slavery.[3] In this chapter I am going to look at the attitudes and feelings towards sexuality of the women whose lives are central to this book. I want to try to find out what part the new ideas on the importance of sexual enjoyment played in their understanding of feminism. Were feminists distracted from their fight for equality and their challenge to male sexual domination by the celebration of sexuality? Feminists who celebrated sexuality tended also to support the birth control movement, and the position of that movement in feminist thinking is another contentious issue which I shall look at through the eyes of some of these suffragists. The birth control movement is in turn closely linked to the campaign for the endowment of motherhood, and I will consider what lay behind their support for this concept.

SEXUALITY: LIBERATION OR ANTAGONISM?

In Mary Stocks's view the strong association of Marie Stopes with the birth control issue tended to make people forget that *Married Love* was 'primarily a moving plea for recognition of the emotional and spiritual significance of mutually satisfying and reverently conducted sex relations.' Stocks implied that this aspect of the book accorded with her own thinking, but she did not say whether her own reading of it affected her married life. Naomi Mitchison was less reticent in her autobiographical volume about the postwar period. Mitchison was born in 1896 and was just too young to be an active suffragist. She was not too young to be cramped by an Edwardian upbringing. Her sexual ignorance, which was shared by her husband, was responsible for 'some damage' to their sexual relationship. They were both virgins on marriage and Mitchison 'got little or no pleasure . . . the final act left me on edge and uncomfortable . . . I began to run a temperature'. They were rescued when Naomi 'heard about and bought Marie Stopes's *Married Love*, rushed out, bought a second copy and sent if off to Dick.' Writing in the late 1970s, it seemed 'incredible' to her that 'this book was such an eye-opener. Why had none of these elementary techniques occurred to either of us before? Well, they hadn't. It was not the kind of thing young people talked about or, in spite of the poets, thought about.'[4]

The ignorance in which girls like Naomi Mitchison faced marriage was condemned by Maude Royden. In *Sex and Commonsense*, published in 1921, Royden wrote that she had 'known marriage after marriage wrecked by the almost unbelievable ignorance that has been present on all sides.' In this book Royden accepted the idea that many women suffered from sexual repression, although she also noticed a contemporary tendency to exaggerate the importance of sex. She found the root of repression lay in ignorance and a condemnation of sexuality:

> One need not go all the way with Freud – one may, indeed, suspect him of suffering from a severe 'repression' himself – while admitting, nevertheless, that much of the folly that surrounds our treatment of sex-questions is due to the pathetic determination of highly respectable people to have no sex nature or impulses at all.[5]

Maude Royden did accept the new ideology in so far as she accepted the idea that repression could be harmful to body and mind. She saw sexuality as a creative force, and argued that 'the man or woman who works hard at some congenial and absorbing task – especially if it be creative work – finds the virtue of continence well within his grasp . . . '. She is describing here her own experience. In writing on sexuality she admitted that she had to 'generalize very rashly from a very narrow experience', and it may well have been Royden, among others, whom Catherine Marshall feared would speak on sexual matters without sufficient experience.[6] Royden did eventually marry Hudson Shaw, the man she had loved for forty years, when his wife and her friend, Effie, died. Royden was then in her late sixties and he was in his eighties. He died two months later.

Royden wrote a description of her relationship with Effie and Hudson Shaw in *The Threefold Cord*. She had loved both of them, as they loved her and each other. But 'Effie was repelled by passion' and had 'forced upon Hudson a completely celibate life.' In Royden's view Effie was not 'normal' in her fear of passion, and could not 'understand what normal people feel about it.' The theme of the suffering of the man who considers 'passion's fulfilment' to be 'most literally a sacrament', while his wife sees it as 'a concession to his lower nature', appears more than once in Royden's writing. She did not appear to believe that sex education could help such women, but rather that it was a matter of 'temperament', and she condemned those women who 'elevate' such a 'defect into a quality'. In a letter to Emmeline Pethick Lawrence who had written to say how much she had enjoyed the book, Royden explained that 'I wrote the book to relieve my heart . . . But the woman – a stranger – who typed it out, said it would have helped her to fight for her (failed) marriage and said she thought it would help others.' Although Royden accepted that passion was associated with the fulfilment of heterosexuality, she believed that the lack of such fulfilment in her own or Hudson's life 'neither crippled nor repressed' them, so that they 'lived their lives to the full'. And the three-sided relationship was kept together by love of a different kind. 'Without Hudson [Effie] would have had no life in the real sense at all. That sweet and lovely nature could not have known what happiness was. She would have withered.'[7]

While accepting the importance of sexual passion for a woman, Royden does not adopt the idea contained in the writing of Ellis, that women's sexuality was receptive and responsive, while men were 'open and aggressive'. 'The old idea that women like to be mastered will die . . . the abandonment of self-control in the intoxicating sense of being mastered belong alike to the pathological side of sex.' She argued that the association in women of virtue with the passive qualities was designed to keep them in a servile state.[8]

In *Sex and Commonsense* Maude Royden condemned the 'bland assumption that a man has a perfect right to play on a woman's sex-instincts till they are beyond control, and then call her the guilty one because they are beyond control'. Elizabeth Robins also wrote about women's 'burden' of preventing the 'sex impulse' from carrying both the man and the woman 'over the brink'. H.G. Wells's comment was that 'Miss Robins thinks that she is at war with men; she is really at war with sex.' Such a comment resounded with male determination to scorn women who did not celebrate sexual relations with men. One of the themes which run through Robins's novels is that it is possible for women to live full and happy lives without men. Robins believed that 'sex antagonism', including its sexual manifestation, was rooted in the contempt with which men's view of women was deeply imbued. She did not believe that this view was much altered by the war and the legislative changes which came at its end. In *Ancilla's Share* she traced the 'origin and effect of sex antagonism' through history in the contemporary statements of 'man', and she examined 'the fact that he has lost no occasion to substantiate, namely that, broadly speaking, his concern with woman has begun with her sex function and culminated in her use as a cheap and docile servant'. She observed that women have learned well the lesson of shame: 'that livelihood, security, ease, honour could come to her only through her sex-relationship to man'. In her view women have shared 'the Kaffir woman's pride in the fetters on her ankles', and the heavier the fetters the greater has been her sense of worth.[9]

The central concern of *Ancilla's Share* is with the public, not the private emancipation of women, but Robins clearly believed that private confidence entailed public value. In this book her condemnation of men's sexual abuse of women is less strong than in her earlier novels. It is therefore possible that her open attack on male sexuality had been blunted by the dominance of the new ideology. We will return to the feminist campaigns against sexual abuse later in the chapter, and try to judge whether they were deflected or indeed broken by a wider acceptance of woman's sexuality. For Robins it is apparent from a later book that she continued to believe that male sexuality was central to 'the woman question, and I mean her Question: not man's view of it'.[10]

Elizabeth Robins's closest friend in the postwar years was Octavia Wilberforce. In her autobiography Wilberforce included letters written to her by Margaret Rhondda about the writings of Freud, and these letters offer another glimpse of the views on the sexuality of feminists of the period. It is implicit in Rhondda's replies that Wilberforce rejected Freud's ideas about the central importance of sex, but that she was herself more open to them:

> But to try and suppress Freud because you detest him – that is indeed 'allowing hugely for sex' its admitting you're afraid of it . . . you'll never get sex into its right proportion if you put a veil round it and say 'Please don't look.'

In a later letter Rhondda was anxious to convince Wilberforce that she 'never did believe Freud's theories', and that 'of course I don't think its impossible for men to be chaste – I think . . . (it would take too long to set down)'.[11] Since it was such a lengthy subject we shall be left in ignorance of Rhondda's view in detail, but what is apparent is that she shared to some extent Wilberforce's rejection of the power of sex. It is not surprising, therefore, to find that she challenged some of Robins's ideas in *Ancilla's Share*. In a review of the book in *Time & Tide* Rhondda denied that 'men's attitude towards women's work . . . is founded on sex antagonism'.[12] The phrase which Rhondda could not accept was the one quoted above in which Robins asserted that men's concern with women 'has begun with her sex function and culminated in her use as a cheap and docile servant.' There was nothing in Rhondda's experience which could help her to accept Robins's trenchant analysis.

Rhondda's description of her own education and ideas about sexuality are probably typical of the educated suffragist of her generation. Her mother's attitude towards the relations of the sexes was 'exceedingly strict. Indeed she went so far as to believe that no nice girl ought to enjoy talking to men as such.' Rhondda did not accept her mother's views, even at twelve when she 'ferreted out the main facts concerning child-birth and procreation . . . and now believed that I knew all there was to know about sex'. But she suspected that her mother's view had a 'considerable effect' on her. After her marriage, and as a direct result of her involvement in the suffrage movement, Rhondda read Havelock Ellis's *Psychology of Sex*. She found it in the Cavandish Bentinck Library which supplied 'all the young women in the suffrage movement with the books they could not procure in the ordinary way'. At that time Rhondda recalled, 'one had to produce some kind of signed certificate from a doctor or lawyer to the effect that one was a suitable person to read it'. She recommended it to her father, who was amused and indignant that he was at first refused a book which his daughter had already read. The book 'opened up a whole new world of thought' to Rhondda, although she 'was far from accepting it all'.[13]

Helena Swanwick was closer to Robins in age but was much closer to Rhondda in her attitude to sexuality. Her mother refused to talk about sex, so Swanwick, like Rhondda, 'found out what I could by such means as were available, and I was distinctly conscious that, by my own standard, this was right, although I was well aware that by hers it was wrong'. Knowledge did not shake her belief that 'sex-experience seemed properly reserved for adults.' At university she again came up against 'prudery on the part of authority', when she had to have a chaperone to lectures. In her view the result of these precautions was to retard 'the growth of respect and comradeship in the male undergraduates' towards the women. Swanwick later understood this prudery as a survival of the idea of 'Woman' as 'the legendary snare and lure of the devil', and as a refusal to treat students as 'real individual women, with qualities and capacities and ambitions and difficulties quite unconnected with sex'. Even as a young woman she was in 'revolt against the indignities to which women were submitted merely on account of their sex'. Her discovery that the reason why she was not allowed out after dark was that she might be 'insulted by men', had made her 'incoherent with rage at a society which, as a consequence, shut up the girls instead of the men'.[14]

Swanwick came to believe that 'sexual intercourse is as necessary for woman as for man.' But she retained the fear of venereal disease common among feminists of the time, and was determined that women should no longer feel that it was 'their part to endure all and never to refuse'. Her advocacy of sex education did not aim to increase sexual pleasure. There is no sign in her writings that Swanwick was especially concerned with the power of sexuality at the level of personal relations, although she was anxious to guard against the effects of excess. She makes a brief reference to Freud in her autobiography in which she, like Rhonnda, suggests that, properly understood, his ideas should lead to a reduction in the over-emphasis on sex.[15] For Swanwick the essential questions involved in sexuality were those key concerns of feminism in general; women's independence and self-respect.

Of the women in this book who have left some record of their ideas on sexuality, Emmeline Pethick Lawrence may have come closest to acceptance of the 'new morality.' Emmeline's childhood had been as protected as any other woman of her generation and class. Indeed, she suggests in her autobiography that reticence even extended to conversation among women friends. Mary Neal told her on the evening of their first meeting with Fred Lawrence that Emmeline would one day marry him. Emmeline was surprised, not just at the prophecy, but that Mary should break a taboo in speaking of such a subject. Although we cannot know about the sexual dimension of the marriage that Mary so accurately foresaw, it was certainly a close one. Many of their letters to each other have survived, and the early ones are passionate love-letters. They reveal the way in which Fred saw Emmeline as a woman complementary to himself as a man, an idea which is present in the writings of Havelock Ellis. Her femininity for him is interwoven with her maternal role. Emmeline had read and admired Ellis's work and asserted that there was link between his work and the 'Movement for Women's Freedom'. She believed that he helped women to find their own standards of 'morality in the realms of sex, love and motherhood'.[16]

To read and admire Ellis's work was not necessarily to adopt his view on the central importance of sexuality: this seems at least to have been Rhondda's stance. Evelyn Sharp read Ellis's *Impressions and Comments* when on holiday in the summer of 1921. She found the book 'soothing and charming, for he seems to have solved the problem of realising the pain of the world without letting it obsess him'.[17] In her novels Sharp presents women who are searching for independence, while feeling the need for loving, heterosexual partnership where equality is the keynote. In the utopia she invented in *Somewhere in Christendom*, there is total equality between the sexes. In her earlier novels the younger women are endangered and constrained by their own ignorance of sexuality, but the ideal Sharp presented is one of the meeting of two minds. She placed little emphasis on sexuality in her writings and a great deal on spirituality. In the 1920s she felt and wrote increasingly and with passion about political rather than personal questions. In a short piece written in 1919 she put these words into the mouth of a woman's 'lover':

> Though famine and pestilence stalk through the land, you will find passionate men and women who have learned to put things of the spirit first; who care for freedom before comfort, and fraternity before prosperity.

The man who speaks these words came to the woman 'at her bidding as he always did with his humorous eyes, and his brilliant intellect, with his heart that loved the just and the unjust, and his spirit that was too fine for despair.'[18] It seems likely that Evelyn Sharp is here describing Henry Nevinson. Their long and loving pre-marital relationship was almost certainly asexual. As a young woman Sharp had lived and loved in a circle which was accused of unconventionality bordering on indecency. For Sharp the freedom she enjoyed there was the freedom to think and to act as she wished and not according to convention, but she was not so unconventional as to break the code of sexual morality.[19]

Feminists of the period could appreciate the freedom other women might feel in sexual liberation without necessarily needing or wishing for this sort of freedom for themselves. Harriet Weaver, the editor of *The New Feminist*, was conventional in her behaviour. May Sinclair welcomed in her novels the freedom to rebel which she did not exploit in her own life. Before she had read *The Well of Loneliness*, for which Radclyffe Hall was convicted of obscenity, Mary Stocks felt 'rather on the side of Miss Hall . . . whatever she may have written my sympathies go automatically against censorship, Judges, Police, Bishops and governments in all such disputes. All the same she does sound rather an obscene woman.'[20]

As far as we can judge, there was a wide variety in attitudes towards sexuality and its relationship to feminism among the women whose ideas and experiences are central to this book. Robins and Royden saw sexuality as a strong force and understood how it could be used to make women servile. For Royden a woman's passion was a positive force; Robins was more ambivalent. Others are reticent, or silent. The glimpses we have of the reception of the 'new morality' suggest that liberal feminists – Swanwick, Sharp, Rhondda, Stocks – welcomed freedom from censorship and control, but retained a distrust of promiscuity or 'excess'. For all of them sexuality was defined in relationship to men. They have left no sign that they saw the deep love they felt for their women friends as in any way sexual, yet for most of them women were more important in their lives than men. This is true even of those who were married, or who had close relationships with men. With the possible exception of Emmeline Pethick Lawrence and Maude Royden they did not consider that a greater recognition of her sexuality was a necessary part of a woman's emancipation.

THE LOVE OF WOMEN

For most of the women central to this study marriage and relationships to men were incidental rather than crucial to their feminism. The exception is perhaps Emmeline Pethick Lawrence. She and Helena Swanwick had long-lasting marriages to men who supported their public lives; openly in Pethick's case, tacitly in Swanwick's. Maude Royden and Evelyn Sharp had long and almost certainly platonic relationships with men whom they married in late middle age. Of the younger women Mary Stocks and Margery Corbett Ashby were happy in their marriages, as was Ray Strachey, despite, if not because of, the very independence of hers and Oliver's lives. Robins and Hubback were both widowed early and remained unmarried. Margaret Rhondda was the only woman in our study who was divorced, but there is no sign that the failure of her marriage was relevant to her feminism, except in so far as it consolidated her independence. It is possible that Catherine Marshall's relationship with Clifford Allen affected her choice of direction during the war, and the subsequent breakdown in her health. She, Mary Sheepshanks, and perhaps Elizabeth Robins, may have suffered as a result of their relationships with men. Kathleen Courtney and Eleanor Rathbone, neither of whom seems to have had a close relationship with a man, were happy and confident spinsters.

All these women loved other women. The intensity of the relationship varied, but there is a common element of feminism rooted in a deep appreciation of and interdependence with other women. This is less true of the younger women, if only because four of them were both married and mothers. Ray Strachey had a very close relationship with Elinor Rendel: Ellie was devastated when Ray married, coping in the end with their separation by training as a doctor.[21] Margery Corbett Ashby, like Ray, belonged to a close-knit family and did not feel the need to break away from it. They both lived in a community of women at Cambridge and worked closely with women in the suffrage movement, and in the 1920s they lived and worked closely with women related to them. Ray had an especially close friendship with Pippa Strachey, with whom she worked closely before and after the war, and it was said that Ray had married Oliver in order to be able to work with his sister.[22]

Eva Hubback and Mary Stocks lived in family units, but they took holidays together, joined sometimes by Eleanor Rathbone and Elizabeth Macadam. Rathbone and Macadam enjoyed 'numerous and varied' holidays together. Rathbone found that 'she could think and work much better away from her own study with its incessant preoccupations'. Macadam did the housekeeping in the cottages they rented, and was, as she put it 'privileged to be her only companion' because she left Eleanor 'uninterruptedly absorbed in her subject'.[23]

The experience of being restored by holidays taken with friends was one that Helena Swanwick valued. Her companion on such holidays towards the end of the war was Elizabeth Bolton, known to her friends as 'the celestial surgeon.' She was indeed a surgeon, and operated on Swanwick in 1915 and again in 1921. Swanwick's 'paradise on earth' was Kynance Cove in Cornwall whence she escaped from the 'turmoil' of wartime 'with a loved friend' in May 1917. This must surely have been Elizabeth Bolton, of whom Swanwick wrote to Catherine Marshall soon afterwards: 'I love her more than words can say.' In the same letter Swanwick described her 'dream of a cottage somewhere & a group of good playfellows, – Evelyn Sharp, Irene Cooper Willis, Elizabeth Bolton, you??? That may not come off till after the war; but the combination would be

quite a happy one I think, with the gentle Wolf added.' The 'gentle
Wolf' was Eva Mcnaghten. It was Eva who wrote often to Catherine
Marshall during 1918 when Catherine was ill, keeping her in touch
with events in the Labour Party and the WIL. In February Catherine
sent four bowls of flowers from Hawse End to her friends in London,
and Eva watched Swanwick arrange them:

> I love seeing Nellie's hands touch flowers, or indeed anything,
> they are in fact more suggestive of spirit than matter, and so
> characteristic.[24]

Elizabeth Robins's awareness of women's need for rest in com-
panionship with other women led her to establish her own home,
Backsettown, as such a refuge. Robins herself went to Backsettown
to rest, living mainly with Octavia Wilberforce in Brighton. To
Octavia she offered:

> a sheltering protection while leaving me the liberty of choice in
> all my actions. As a result I never felt the urge to escape. On the
> contrary I welcomed and sought more and more the harbour of her
> affection which proved both stimulating and comforting . . . [25]

Margaret Rhondda remains as elusive and reserved as she seems
to have been in life, but she gives a glimpse of what the friendship
of other women meant to her in her autobiography, where she wrote
that the chief attraction of feminist activity for her was such friendship. Like Ray Strachey and Margery Corbett Ashby, she was sustained by the love and support of women within her own family, and
after the war she was close to Theodora Bosanquet who was literary
editor of *Time & Tide*.[26]

We have seen how Catherine Marshall suffered when her involvement with the NCF moved her away from her suffrage friends, and
how she longed to work again with Kathleen Courtney after the
war. Although she would never work so closely with them again,
she did return to her network of friends, a network which had
become international. Courtney had lived close to Maude Royden
and Ida O'Malley before the war. Later her work with Hilda Clark
and Edith Pye in Vienna led to friendship with them, and a shared
household when they returned from Austria. Mary Sheepshanks lived
with other suffragists at her house in Barton Street, and among these
friends there was one whom she loved deeply – Irene Cooper Willis.
Mary gave up her work with the WIL when she felt that she had lost
Irene's love to another woman. Her reticence made it hard for her to

share her feelings; to other women she appeared lonely in the years that followed the war, but she had one close friend in the 1920s, Margaret Bryant, to whom she owed 'more than I can say.'[27]

Evelyn Sharp never became as withdrawn as Mary Sheepshanks, but she too moved away from the intimacy of the suffrage years, and lived alone in the 1920s. She had suffered the same experience of feeling that she had been replaced in the affections of a close friend by another woman. Just before the war she became intimate with Louisa Garrett Anderson, whose deep affection is reflected in her letters to Sharp. During and after the war Louisa worked and lived with Flora Murray. Meanwhile Sharp moved away from women's organisations and concentrated on her writing, although she kept in touch with Emmeline Pethick Lawrence, Elizabeth Robins, Kathleen Courtney and Maude Royden. After the death of Henry Nevinson in 1942, she began to keep a diary again and in it she recorded receiving:

> a tragic letter from Louisa Garrett Anderson telling me she has cancer and they say she may live 6 months – It has been a great shock to me, for although F.M. came between us all those years ago, just before the last war, and our friendship seemed broken, I have always felt a great love for her, and much pity, after F.M. died (also of cancer) and she has often been lonely since, I am afraid . . . It was a lovely letter, about her love for me, and her admiration for my courage in starting my life afresh – courage! – Me!

Two days later she is thinking of Louisa again, and wonders whether she is welcoming death:

> thinking it is her way back to the friend whom she loved more than me – yet, did she, ultimately? A line in her letter seems to suggest a wish to tell me that she never faltered in her love for me; I can only hope that does not worry her now. I tried to tell her in my letter that all was well between us.[28]

In her autobiography, Evelyn Sharp is silent about her love for Louisa. There she wrote that when she was at school, her admiration and love for others girls had been firmly controlled by the 'sensible' attitude of teachers and pupils, and had never become, in her own words, 'unwholesome'.[29] The survival of Evelyn Sharp's papers makes it possible for us to know something of her love for Louisa Garrett Anderson. For others who did not keep diaries and whose letters have not survived there is only silence, a continued reticence. It is impossible for us to know the depth and power of the love these women felt for each other. The reserve of the older generation has combined with the later fear of love between women being in some way 'unwholesome', to veil the intensity of these friendships between women. If they are mentioned, it is usually in the background of a tapestry of relationships. The acceptable view was expressed by Vera Brittain in the introduction to her life of Winifred Holtby, a book which she hoped would 'show its readers that loyalty and affection between women is a noble relationship which, far from impoverishing, actually enhances the love of a girl for her lover, of a wife for her husband, a mother for her children'.[30] The new ideology may have restricted the free expression, both on paper and perhaps in life, of women's love for each other. The contrast between what Swanwick and Sharp wrote in their autobiographies with what we find in their surviving letters does suggest that they were unwilling to expose the depth of their feeling about their women friends, although this may well have been reticence, not suppression. These women did not challenge heterosexuality explicitly but implicitly in the strength and significance of their friendships.

AN EQUAL MORAL STANDARD

Sexuality may not have been central to the thinking of the feminists in this study, but the search for an equal moral standard in sexual mores was – at least for some of them. As young girls Margaret Rhondda and Helena Swanwick had rebelled against the categorisation of some women as prostitutes. For Rhondda the treatment of prostitutes was central to her feminists beliefs. At the age of thirteen or fourteen, she had:

> discovered the existence of prostitutes as a class set apart. The discovery made a deep impression on me, and I took a vow to myself that all my life I would do what I could to see that the terrible injustice of scorning them and treating them as untouchables simply because they performed the sexual act for money should be done away with. It was one of the only two vows that I took to myself through my whole childhood.[31]

In *The Future of the Women's Movement* Helena Swanwick condemned both the treatment of a prostitute as 'a pariah', and the expectation that she should 'lead a life of penitential expiation for ever and ever'. Swanwick's attitude is different from Rhondda's: she condemns the seducer and does not suggest that some women might have a right to be paid for performing the sexual act for money. Yet another shade of opinion on the question of prostitution is found in Maude Royden's writings. She was concerned that women should not be condemned for choosing to express their sexuality.[32] Swanwick's ideas are close to those of the nineteenth-century 'social purity' campaigners; in Royden's we see the link with the welcome given by some feminists to greater heterosexual freedom. The efforts of feminists to remove the injustice to prostitutes in the 1920s had complex motives and inevitably gave rise to ambivalent feelings. They were a continuation of the campaign against the double standard which had its roots in the nineteenth century, but the challenge to the double standard now contained the idea that women had sexual needs and desires.

The earlier feminist campaigns against the double standard had their genesis in the fight against the Contagious Diseases Acts, and aimed to 'transform the sexual behaviour of men', or, as a campaigner put it, 'to demand purity and righteousness in men'.[33] The women who took part in these campaigns believed, like Elizabeth Robins, that sexual intercourse lay at the root of women's oppression, and marked men's contempt for them. One of the practical aims of these campaigners was to reduce the sexual abuse of girls by raising the age of consent. A bill to raise the age of consent was introduced in 1914, and reintroduced in 1917. This second bill was greeted with mixed feelings by feminists because of the inclusion of a clause which made it possible for convicted vagrants and common prostitutes to be detained. The pressure which led to this clause was fear of VD, a fear which was shared by many feminists. Feminists such as Christabel Pankhurst and Cicely Hamilton declared the solution to be voluntary avoidance of marriage and sexual intercourse, and total independence for a woman. Some of the 'social purity' campaigners welcomed the clause of the new bill, seeing it as a form of protection for women, while others protested that it was directed against women only, and objected to the use of the phrase 'common prostitute'. The complexity of the arguments, and the diversity of feminist response to the Act, is illustrated in the pages of *Common Cause*. Maude Royden, who had been active in 'social purity' campaigns before the war, confessed that she was becoming doubtful about the efficacy of legislating on the question. Helena Swanwick replied that legislation would be effective, provided that it was not introduced in a panic.[34]

The Act did become law in 1922, after a concerted campaign by

feminist organisations. The campaign was coordinated by the Association for Moral and Social Hygiene, which had been founded in 1913.
Alison Neilans, a committed feminist and in the 1920s a member of
the executive of the NUSEC, was secretary of the AMSH. In October
1921, thirty-four societies supported a resolution demanding that
a bill be introduced. In the debate in the House of Commons it
was asserted that 'men could not defend themselves against a young
girl who uses all the artifices of her sex to achieve her object. She
gradually sees him being lashed into the elemental and aggressive
male . . . '[35] The image of woman as the eternal temptress continued
to haunt twentieth-century debates on sexuality.

After the successful adoption of this Act into law there was no
further major legislation on sexual offences in the 1920s. There is
apparent some lack of faith in legislative changes on the moral issue.
The demand for an equal standard was included in the Women's
Charter drawn up at Geneva in 1920, but even in that buoyant year
an article in *The Woman's Leader* maintained that 'in the direction
of the equal moral standard the position seems to be stationary, if
indeed it has not actually changed for the worse'. Just over three
years later, *The Woman's Leader* concluded that 'The Equal Moral
Standard is something intangible. It cannot be brought about by one
or a dozen Parliamentary Bills, only by a change of heart, of mental
outlook, on the part of society and its members.' Yet feminists did
not give up and the NUSEC questions to Parliamentary candidates
included one on the support of legislation raising the age of consent
to 18. Both Nancy Astor and Margaret Wintringham, who had
been elected to Parliament in a by-election in October 1921, were
staunch supporters of 'moral hygiene.' The AMSH campaigned for
the adoption by the government of the recommendations of a report
in 1925 which would have removed the anomalies of the 1922 Act,
whereby the 'reasonable cause to believe' clause was retained for
sexual intercourse, but not for indecent assault. *The Woman's Leader*
and *Time & Tide* continued to support this campaign.[36]

The 1922 Act had met the main aims of the campaigners. Writing
in the 1930s, and taking a long-term view, Alison Neilans believed
that 'Many of those who fought the battle for an equal standard of
moral responsibility . . . would hardly recognise the world of today,
so great has been the improvement.' She had no doubt that the improvements were 'made possible by the women's movement . . . The
results have not come only from having the vote, but also from the
long agitation for the vote and the repercussions of that agitation

on the development of a more awakened conscience.' The successes she described are increased protection from seduction and indecent assault, improvements in the position of the unmarried mother and the ending of the double standard of morals in the marriage law by the Divorce Acts of 1923 and 1925. She admitted that efforts to eliminate legal discrimination against any woman described in the law as a 'common prostitute' had failed. Women arrested and charged with solicitation for purposes of prostitution to the annoyance or obstruction of inhabitants or passengers were fined or sent to prison without any corroborating evidence. Efforts to alter the solicitation laws continued throughout the 1920s, and Neilans used the pages of *The Woman's Leader* and *Time & Tide* and the NUSEC summer schools to keep the issue on the feminist agenda. In 1925 Lady Astor introduced a bill drawn up in consultation with Neilans: it would have repealed all sections of Acts of Parliament which created 'for police court purposes, a special class of persons called "common prostitutes."' The bill was warmly welcomed by an article in *Time & Tide*, which must surely have been written by Rhondda:

> How many of those who stand in the feminist movement today can remember that their first impulse towards taking their place in its ranks came when they realised that there was a class of women set part and branded as common prostitutes, an outcast class, almost a slave class . . . ? Lady Astor is one of the few whose horror of injustice does not get blunted by familiarity.[37]

Neilans undoubtedly continued the tradition of feminist campaigns which challenged what had been identified as the 'dominant sexual ideology' propounded by sexologists, yet she cited Havelock Ellis in support of her views on prostitution, and referred to him as 'the greatest authority of our times on aspects of sex problems'. However, she did not welcome the changes in moral standards and practice which she associated with the advent of birth control:

> Women were united to abolish the double standard; an irresponsible one for the men and one heavily weighted with responsibility and punishment for women . . . the advent of birth control has placed the woman, if she chooses, in almost the same position of irresponsibility as the man . . . Thus the end of the double standard is definitely in sight, but it is not ending in the way anticipated by the pioneers who fought for it.[38]

Neilans understood that this change had brought 'the women's movement to a parting of ways'. She recognised 'that women, as such, have not necessarily a common objective in regard to sex matters'. This may be a sign of a loss of confidence in her own judgement as a feminist, although she then clearly defined her own understanding of the feminist aim:

> that law, custom and public opinion should accord to women as a natural and inalienable right the same liberty of action and the same standard of responsibility, neither more or less, that are accorded to men.

Men were, in her view, equally responsible for children. Neilans also recognised that for women in poverty birth control had 'undoubtedly been a palliative for many of her worst anxieties.' She knew that poverty was 'the greatest problem that men and women have to solve'.[39] For many birth-control campaigners the issue was not individual liberty, but increased economic freedom and improved health for women.

BIRTH CONTROL

A week after the war ended Marie Stopes's *Wise Parenthood* was published. *Married Love* had contained one chapter on birth control, and the second book was 'an attempt to answer innumerable enquirers' asking for 'wholesome information' on the subject. In her introduction Stopes referred to the pamphlet advocating 'control of conception' which had been published by the Malthusian League and which advocated *coitus interruptus* and douching.[40]

Rejecting these methods as ineffective and harmful, Stopes recommended the use of a rubber cap known as the 'check pessary' and she gave detailed instructions as to how to insert it. The book sold well immediately, a second edition coming out two months later, and two more in the following four months. Stopes and her husband established the first birth control clinic in Holloway, North London, in March 1921, and at the end of May a meeting was held in the Queens Hall. One of those who attended was Emmeline Pethick Lawrence, who temporarily provided a link between Stopes and the WIL. Her feeling was that Stopes's 'message' brought 'a light into the darkness'. She promised: 'In my own way I shall do all I can to spread this light that you have thrown.' Later that year she was more hesitant and refused to speak in public on the subject. Although she still felt that it was 'a tragedy and a wrong to bring unwanted children into the world', she wanted to 'stand aside until I have made up my mind fully with regard to the whole question.' One wonders how much her husband's position in the Labour Party – which, as we shall see was divided on the issue – was responsible for Emmeline's caution. Some years later Fred wrote to Stopes to decline an invitation to both of them:

> I think it only fair to add that while I go a long way with you in your campaign particularly in the matter of breaking down existing taboos, I feel that the acceptance of your invitation would imply an identification with your views to a greater extent than I am prepared to go.[41]

Another early feminist supporter of Stopes's work was Eva Hubback. In 1914 Hubback worked as a volunteer at one of the maternity centres whose development was stimulated by the war. The Maternity and Child Welfare Clinics established by local authorities after the war seemed to supporters of birth control to be an ideal source for the dissemination of information. But in 1922 Miss E. S. Daniels, a health visitor in North London, was suspended for giving the address of Stopes's clinic to a patient. In the following year Rose Witcop and Guy Aldred were prosecuted for publishing *Family Limitation* by Margaret Sanger, an American campaigner for birth control. Birth control was now a public issue, and organisations and individuals began to declare their views. The Women's Co-operative Guild, whose members had long wanted information on the subject, came out in favour. The Guild saw birth control as part of the campaign for maternal and child welfare, as did Maude Royden, Eleanor Rathbone and Mary Stocks.

Mary Stocks watched in admiration as another young feminist took birth control into the party-political arena: she referred to the efforts of Dora Russell to convert the Labour Party as a 'sex-war.' Russell was concerned that 'the working wife and mother' should 'get the advice she might desperately need.' Her aim was to make it legal for birth-control advice to be given in organisations under the control of the government. The advent of a Labour Government at the end of 1923 gave cause for hope, and Russell organised a deputation of doctors to go to the House of Commons. She claimed that she 'stirred up the Labour Party no end, to speak vulgarly, and I think it will do good'. Russell had drawn up a petition which was distributed widely, and was chiefly designed to put pressure on the Minister of Health from within the Labour Party. She succeeded in getting overwhelming support from the Labour Women's Conference, despite the opposition of Marion Phillips who protested that 'Sex should not be brought into politics.' In 1925 the Labour Women's Conference reiterated its support for birth control, and in the following year Dora Russell spoke in Durham, Scotland and Wales before proposing a resolution at the Labour Party Conference in October. She was opposed by Ramsay MacDonald, Prime Minister of the Labour Government of 1924. Russell's motion in favour of a commitment to the right of maternity centres to give advice on birth control was successful. Stocks wrote of the debate at the Conference:

> It was a fine stroke on the part of Dora Russell, wasn't it? I like to think of that young creature standing up to Ramsey MacDonald and beating him![42]

But the victory was an empty one, since the party executive did nothing to implement it and the following year a resolution in favour was lost. In 1928 the Labour Women's Conference also voted against birth control, and in subsequent years the issue was subsumed in resolutions on maternal mortality. Stocks herself placed great value on the question of birth control:

> I regard this particular question as one which is bound up not merely with the freedom of women but with the actual survival of civilisation.[43]

Stocks wrote a series of articles in *The Woman's Leader* which prompted Marie Stopes to write to her. They began a correspondence which was to continue through the 1920s. Stocks was joint editor of *The Woman's Leader* and her first letter to Stopes was concerned with the refusal of the directors of the paper to accept advertisements for Stopes's clinic or society 'in response to a number of protests from subscribers'. The paper had at first printed articles on the subject, including one by Stopes. In May 1921 advertisements for Stopes's books appeared, and in October information about the Society for Constructive Birth Control. The topic was dealt with in a series entitled 'Burning Issue' in the spring of 1922. The paper then fell silent. Stocks was determined to break that silence, especially since the NUSEC had decided to promote study of the issue. In June 1923, she succeeded in persuading the directors to allow an advertisement from Stopes and an article by herself to be published in the following issue.[44]

In 1924 the Stocks family moved to Manchester and Mary gave her first talk on the subject of birth control in the North of Liverpool in February. The meeting had been assembled 'after much heart-searching and controversy' by the National Council of Women (formerly the National Union of Women Workers). Stocks saw the willingness of this cautious and conservative organisation to hold such a meeting as 'a flaming sign of the times'. She then decided to become actively involved in the offering of birth-control advice. Whereas Russell was committed to the political struggle, Stocks shared that characteristic of many feminists, the urge to do as well as say what she believed. She welcomed the birth-control movement because 'Here, at any rate, was something that could be done.' With a group of friends, and the support of the local Labour Party and Women's Co-operative Guild, she 'acquired two rooms in a working-class area, found a woman doctor bold enough to officiate, and two nurse-midwives bold enough to assist her', and in 1925 opened what seems to have been the first provincial birth-control clinic. Together they 'staffed the weekly clinics, undertook preliminary interrogations, and kept the records'. Stocks also spoke at many meetings, 'because the subject was in great demand at women's meetings all over the north-western area and outside it.'[45] She continued to press for the NUSEC to advocate the availability of birth-control information, and in 1925, the Annual Council passed a resolution to that effect.

Mary Stocks thought of what she was doing as a continuation of the 'social work' she had done before the war. The women who came to the clinic were 'for the most part, mothers with over-large families or sad stories of miscarriages, and deplorable health records'. There is an element of the Victorian 'visiting' approach in the attitudes of middle-class women in the birth-control campaign. *Time & Tide* assured its readers that in the birth-control campaign what was in dispute was not 'whether the people with incomes of more than £400 per annum shall practise birth control – they do so now. What we are discussing today is whether the information which has spread amongst the well-to-do behind doors shall be made publicly available to working-class parents.' There was also a strong moral undertone in feminist writings on the subject. In a series of articles in *Time & Tide* which appeared in 1924, the author accepted that the question was a feminist one but was anxious to avoid the association of birth control with sexual promiscuity. She advocated the spread of information so that individual men and women could make their **own** decisions, but added that 'knowledge of the facts must include knowledge that . . . it is never possible to evade the consequences of prolonged self-indulgence'. The NUSEC secretary was anxious to make clear that the resolution which was adopted in 1925 did not advocate 'artificial methods of birth control for all women', but did demand 'that married women should have the right to decide for themselves whether they require this information which affects them so intimately'.[46]

There were undertones of anti-working-class feeling, yet the birth-control movement was also still seen as a radical movement. Mary Stocks pointed out that the subject was 'still not discussed in polite society and by many people not discussed at all.' *Time & Tide* admitted that 'We of this generation pride ourselves on our frankness but we none of us find it easy to discuss birth control without lapsing into vagueness just where, if we are to reach the root of the matter, we must face facts and not shirk detailed discussion.'[47] Dora Russell's frustrating battles in the Labour Party, Pethick Lawrence's caution, and the circumspect policy of the NUSEC offer evidence that it was no simple matter to declare publicly and actively in favour of birth control.

Active supporters of birth control tended to become ardent advocates, and this in turn hardened the divisions within the women's movement which we shall look at in Chapter 7. Naomi Mitchison was concerned about the violence with which the 'fiercely blind' attackers and defenders of birth control conducted their arguments. She, like Emmeline Pethick Lawrence, gave a cautious welcome to birth control. Although she believed that birth control was at least partly responsible for the changes in the 'accepted ideas and practice of marriage and of extra-marital relationships', she also wrote that to contemporaries, the birth-control movement of the 1920s was 'mainly thought of as family spacing and helping in the emancipation of women'. Mitchison believed that for most women the use of contraception at that time was dictated by economics. For the women she met in the clinic where she worked as a volunteer, it meant that 'life becomes possible again'. For women of her own class the use of contraception was part of the compromise that women had to make between their desire 'to have masses of children by the men they love', and their wish 'to do their own work, whatever it may be'. She did not suggest that men had to make the same compromise, although she did believe that one day women would have 'sufficient control of their external environment to ensure that their work will be compatible with having babies, or when the whole business of having babies becomes a real job in itself, carrying with it social respect and economic independence'.[48]

For Naomi Mitchison, as for Russell and Stocks and many other feminists in the 1920s, 'liberating the mothers' was a legitimate economic aim for feminism. The two strands of their liberation came together in 1925 when the Annual Council of the NUSEC passed a resolution demanding the availability to married women of birth-control advice, and another which placed family endowment on the programme of the union. Mary Stocks felt that the union's programme now embodied 'a complete charter of the rights of the married woman to have children under decent conditions when she wants to, and to have no more than she wants'.[49]

LIBERATING THE MOTHERS

As Russell listened to the working-class women she met at the Labour Women's Conference in 1924, and as she went out on speaking engagements, she 'began to wonder if the feminists had not been running away from the central issue of women's emancipation? Would women ever be truly free and equal with men until we had liberated the mothers?' She was 'astounded at the fury against child-bearing' expressed by the delegates. Here were women fiercely repudiating what had been preached at us as the noblest fulfilment of our womanhood.' The letters from Guild members included in the collection *Maternity* revealed both the ignorance of birth control of the authors, and the bitterness they felt about their frequent, painful and exhausting childbearing. They also pressed for payments to the mother for each child, or for wages for women at home.[50]

On the face of it some financial support for families with children may appear less contentious than the demand for birth control, and likely to receive wider support in a society where the ideology of motherhood was often propounded. Yet an incident described by Mary Stocks suggests that women were more interested in curtailing their families than in being rewarded for having children – or perhaps they saw birth control as the more attainable goal:

> Eleanor Rathbone, with whom I stayed last weekend, said that recently she went to Poplar to address a meeting on Family Endowment. The audience was violent [*sic*] pro-Birth

Control, and wouldn't listen to F.E. until she had declared herself
in favour of it.

According to Stocks, Rathbone welcomed the birth-control movement because it 'offered some chance of bringing the burdens of
parent-hood into relation with the physical and economic capacity
of those called upon to bear them.' Rathbone also contributed
money to the establishment of voluntary clinics. However, she did
not play an active part in the campaign, concentrating her energies
on the struggle to obtain acceptance for her idea of offering financial
assistance to mothers. She met with opposition from the start, and
she welcomed the open discussion on the subject among feminists.
The debate on this issue in the NUSEC Annual Council Meetings
reflected the division of opinion among feminists. When the union
eventually came out in support in 1925, Stocks commented that the
carrying of the resolution on family endowment followed a 'much
stiffer fight' than the one conducted for birth control.[51]

Early in 1921 an article in *The Woman's Leader* claimed that a
slow conversion to 'Family Endowment' was taking place, but argued
that this was not a 'feminist reform', nor a 'tribute to the dignity of
motherhood', but that it was a part of the reform of the economic
structure along with wage awards, unemployment benefit and separation allowances. From the start family endowment was put forward
as part of the struggle to achieve equal pay for women. In February
1921, Rathbone wrote an article on equal pay for *The Woman's
Leader* which dealt with the difficulties feminists were encountering
from the reluctance of women within the trade union movement
to challenge their male colleagues on the issue. To Rathbone it
was equal pay which was beginning to look intractable; others
disagreed. A resolution before the Annual Council of the NUSEC
in February 1921, declared that it was 'unnecessary to couple with
the urgent demand for "Equal Pay" any scheme for National Family
Endowment, which, if accepted as desirable in itself, may take many
years to accomplish.'[52]

The election addresses of the candidates for the executive committee of the NUSEC in 1921 indicate that the issue of family endowment was a question on which each of them was expected to declare
their views. Eleanor Rathbone and Mary Stocks declared in favour,
and they were joined by Margery Corbett Ashby who saw it 'as the
only way of assuring real security to a mother for the adequate discharge of her duties to her young children'. In her election address

Ray Strachey firmly declared that the 'economic position of women is by far the most important of the problems before the NUSEC', but did not state whether she felt that family endowment was one way of dealing with that problem. For her the equal pay question was the most crucial. 'I care hardly at all for the other points of the programme.' Interestingly, Rathbone's close friend Elizabeth Macadam, while declaring in favour of endowment, added that she did not think it was appropriate that it should be introduced yet.[53]

The attitude of the NUSEC towards family endowment was cautious. After 'a brilliant exposition of the tactical case for some form of family allowances' by Mary Stocks in 1922, the Council reiterated its support for the investigation of the question by local societies, but rejected by eight votes a 'resolution to the effect that it would welcome experiments in family allowances'.[54] The concept received a strongly feminist attack from Ada Nield Chew in September 1922. She asked:

> In what way would endowment lessen the real subjection of women? . . . the money would still be earned largely by men, more so, even, than at present, because the result of endowment would inevitably be that fewer women than ever would work outside their homes . . . Men are dead against married women working now. By endowment we should be handing them the means to forbid it . . . Why seek to shackle poor women to domestic work for ever?

Mary Stocks's reply was that proponents of endowment 'propose to add the occupation of motherhood to the number of occupations in which women can achieve economic independence under decent and dignified conditions of work'.[55] Thus feminists on both sides of the argument defended their stance in reference to women as workers.

Some space in *Time & Tide* was also devoted to airing arguments for and against family endowment, although the debate was usually limited to the correspondence columns. In December 1925, a report in the paper found 'unanswerable' the case put forward by the Family Endowment Council for a scheme for the mining industry. By that time the NUSEC had committed itself to 'support of the principle of Family Allowances.' The debate at the Council in 1925 had been 'one of the finest that has ever taken place on a National Union platform'. The atmosphere of the debate was tense, and the audience interrupted the speakers with 'frequent ejaculations and questions'.

Despite strong feelings on both sides, good humour prevailed. Margery Corbett Ashby was in the chair, keeping 'a delightfully light touch on the reins', and Millicent Garrett Fawcett introduced 'many characteristic touches of humour and racy and apposite anecdotes'. Fawcett opened the case for the opponents of family allowances; she had already put her case in the pages of *The Woman's Leader* in January of that year. Elizabeth Macadam – and the fact that it was Macadam, Rathbone's closest friend, shows how willing feminists were to have the question debated openly and without personal rancour – asked Millicent Garrett Fawcett to write 'a statement of the reasons which cause me to differ fundamentally from Miss Rathbone in regard to the tremendous step she is advocating . . . '. Fawcett did not argue on feminist grounds against the proposals. She disliked the scheme because she thought it would allow men and women to avoid 'the financial responsibility for the upbringing of their children'. She was also opposed to the burden it would place on the taxpayer. She confessed that she had at first regarded the proposal to add to the burden on the Exchequer 'three or four hundred millions a year as fantastic, simply from it own inherent disadvantages, but it seems to me now that I was mistaken and that it may become a real danger'.[56]

In her response Rathbone stated clearly that a universal scheme paid for out of taxation was 'not at present, nor probably will be for many years within the sphere of practical politics.' A much more practical possibility was a contributory scheme with the State stepping in when a man was unemployed. Her main defence of her proposal was that it was the only practical way of helping families whose incomes were below subsistence level. Rathbone had provided a much more detailed and more widely distributed defence of the principle of family allowances in her book *The Disinherited Family*, which was published in 1924. She is less restrained there in replying to the accusation made by Fawcett, and by others, that the payment of such allowances would weaken parental responsibility. She pointed out that the prediction of 'moral injury to the family' was only 'applied by well-to-do people to working-class people, never by well-to-do people to members of their own class . . . Most well-to-do parents indeed would be aghast at the idea of a cherished daughter running such a risk as is undertaken by nearly every working-class woman who marries within her own class.' This strongly feminist statement is typical of the tenor of her thinking in *The Disinherited Family*, although she did make an appeal for the plight of the child in the family and her final recommendation was that the provision should be 'a sum on account of each child'.[57] In making this proposal and diluting the feminism of her original proposals, Rathbone was demonstrating her characteristic willingness to compromise. She was, as always, out to persuade, and willing to negotiate.

Rathbone's early arguments for family endowment had been linked to women's claims for equal pay. Just before the NUSEC Council of 1921 Rathbone had reiterated her view that equal pay was impracticable without the introduction of family endowment. For Rathbone the attainable goal was the financial independence of mothers, not equal pay for working women. As equal pay became less and less a realisable aim, so Rathbone emphasised other aspects of her case for family endowment. By the time she wrote *The Disinherited Family* Rathbone was arguing that in the context of the 1920s, it was not possible for equal pay to 'make much headway, so long as the forces which had led in the past to unequal pay remain unchanged.' In *The Disinherited Family* Rathbone continued to argue that the introduction of a system of family allowances would mean that employers would lose 'their one valid excuse for paying women less than men, when their work was really equal.' She added that 'This would not by itself secure equal pay or equal opportunity for women', but that it would make it at least achievable, given good organisation and possibly legislation.[58]

The main thrust of the argument in the book is a feminist attack on the concept of the 'living wage' adequate for the needs of 'our wives and families' demanded by working men. In Rathbone's view women were 'either consciously or subconsciously in revolt' against a system which made them dependent on their husband's wages. Women's grievances were finding 'their most articulate expression through the membership of such bodies as the Women's Co-operative Guild, the Women Citizens associations, the Women's Institutes and Village Councils.' Those who felt the grievance, she argued, were not limited to the membership of these bodies, for 'the habit of joining societies and attending meetings is comparatively new among women and is limited by the circumstances of their lives'. She predicted that 'the development of this sense of sex grievance into a sense of sex solidarity and an articulate demand for the economic independence of women is I believe only a question of time'. What was hindering this development was family and class loyalty. Women who were unmarried or 'fortunate in their own marriage', lacked the sense of 'sex antagonism', and 'the vertical cleavage of class seems to them more important than the horizontal cleavage of sex'. Rathbone believed that women were being 'marshalled behind party banners'.[59]

THE IDEOLOGY OF MOTHERHOOD

Eleanor Rathbone's argument for family allowances is thus staunchly feminist and based on economic arguments. She makes no claim for motherhood as a morally uplifting occupation: she described it as a craft with children as the mother's product. Certainly, she still saw the raising of children as the woman's task, although not exclusively so. The feminists in this study who were also mothers saw motherhood as an important role, but not one which could or should absorb all their energy. Eva Hubback worked long hours at a variety of jobs, including her work for the NUSEC. Later it was said of her that she had 'watched the perilous journeys of her political children with that same unceasing care that a mother shows for its offspring'. One of her human daughters:

> actively resented the pressure of work on her, when it meant she arrived home late and tired. And frequently she was so obviously preoccupied that I felt her attention to my conversation was perfunctory. I remember being depressed at coming home from school and seldom finding her there to talk to about the day's happenings.[60]

Margery Corbett Ashby's election literature emphasised her role as the devoted mother, and during the war she did experience the sense of being trapped with a young and demanding baby.[61] Later she was dependent for support and help from her mother who looked after Michael when she was abroad. Ray Strachey enjoyed her children but she had no hesitation in leaving them with other women while she pursed her own interests. She depended on help from her aunt, Alys Russell, whose childlessness was largely responsible for her separation from the father of Dora Russell's children. But Strachey made no claims for the unique importance or significance of motherhood, and ignored the whole question of family allowances.

Maude Royden did look upon motherhood as 'the joyful exercise of a great creative power'. In writing this in 1917, she was aware that she was disagreeing with 'some of my fellow feminists', but she felt strongly that 'we are on the wrong path when we seek to reduce the burden of motherhood to a mere episode – the birth of the child followed by its upbringing in some Utopian nursery or co-operative creche'.[62] Swanwick and Sharp, in contrast, wrote approvingly of crèches and nurseries, although neither of them denied the importance of motherhood, and it is probable that they both regretted their childlessness. Evelyn Sharp expressed her admiration for the small number of London County Council crèches and nursery schools, but she saw them as supplementary to the care of the mother.[63] Her ideal, as expressed in her novel *Nicolete*, was that women should be able to combine motherhood with creativity, a combination Maude Royden believed to be a rarity.

It seems likely that Helena Swanwick had to make the very choice that Sharp believed should be unnecessary. In a letter to Catherine Marshall, she referred to:

the election we made on our marriage . . . I don't think I knew, thirty years ago, that the sense of loss would go on & on daily with never dulled poignancy. I'm glad I didn't. It seemed *a* decision to take, not 365 x 25 decisions & aches. I didn't in the least realise either that, almost suddenly, when I was nearing 50, the longing and the loss would vanish.[64]

Swanwick may have felt she would be constrained by motherhood: she was certainly determined that the lives of other women should not be limited by having children, nor reduced in society's opinion by choosing not to do so. Her view of motherhood was close to Sharp's, although she believed motherhood to be less central to woman's nature: 'Cramp her nature, limit her activities, and you cramp and limit her love and motherhood.' She accepted the theoretical arguments for family endowment, but she remained wary of the idea precisely because of its association with the ideology of motherhood, and was depressed by enthusiastic, sentimental descriptions of the lives of endowed mothers. Swanwick did not see motherhood as irrelevant to the women's movement: she found 'the importance of motherhood more fully understood and vigorously proclaimed by the women in the movement than by any other women'. She may have had in mind Catherine Marshall, who based her arguments for the need and value of women's contribution to peace on their motherhood.[65]

In 1927 Swanwick wrote a series of three articles entitled 'A Woman's Place'. In the first of these she made the tentative suggestion that men might play a part in looking after the home:

'Some women even think that if men are so very fond of the home, they might themselves take a spell of home work.' She did not develop this theme, but she did argue for 'equal pay for equal value'. In the final article she categorically stated that 'All healthy women should work', and that the 'claim that a man should "keep" his wife . . . is . . . deeply demoralising to both parties'. She argued that women who did housework should be paid for it, or that there should be 'co-operative housekeeping' with men playing their part, albeit as 'cooks, furnace-men, cleaners etc.' She accepted that it was the woman's part to look after the children within this framework. However, she believed that a woman should have the choice about whether she did so, and a wage if she made this option. After the children had grown up, a woman who wished to continue to work at home should be able to do 'part-time work or piece-work or home-work.' She was well aware of the exploitation to which this work was, and is, subject. Her hope was that the nationalisation of industries would make it possible for the introduction of much greater flexibility in working arrangements.[66]

Swanwick's ideas are radical. They are to some extent limited by the ideology of motherhood, but her moral imperative is reserved for work. In the 1920s she was a hard-working journalist and for a time an editor; in giving her work the first priority she was typical of feminists in the 1920s.

INDEPENDENCE: A NEW MORALITY

The need for women to be financially independent of men was recognised, although in different ways, by all the feminists whose ideas have been examined in this chapter. Vera Brittain analysed the change in feminism which took place in the 1920s as a move from the political to the economic sphere, and concluded that the postwar feminist believed that it was her duty to find professional work which would provide her with an income. In the time left over from her work she fitted in sitting on committees or making speeches. Brittain believed that it was important for the prewar feminist to understand that the belief of the postwar feminist that economic independence was a moral obligation was a logical product of the women's movement of the nineteenth and early twentieth centuries. She was also concerned that the postwar feminists remember that the young professional woman would not have existed had not earlier feminists sat on committees and public platforms without remuneration. She expressed her own gratitude in a letter to Evelyn Sharp:

> You have always fought so bravely for all the things I care for most, that at times I felt almost moved to tears by the thought of how much my generation owes to the fighters of yours, and how little gratitude we generally show for it.[67]

A symbolic illustration of Brittain's categorisation of the two generations of feminists occurred when Alison Neilans was asked to join the committee of the NUSEC. She replied that she would need to obtain permission from the Association for Moral and Social Hygiene, her employer, in order to attend daytime meetings. The feminists central to this study do not fall neatly into Brittain's two categories. Both Elizabeth Robins and Evelyn Sharp of the older generation had earned their own living since they were young women. Margaret Rhondda and Eleanor Rathbone were financially independent, although not through their own earnings. Catherine Marshall's financial dependence on her father continued to prove a problem for her in the 1920s as it had before the war. Of the younger women Margery Corbett Ashby and Mary Stocks can be seen as committee women of the prewar mould, although Stocks did have to earn her own living after the early death of her husband in 1937. Eva Hubback was widowed young and dependent mainly on what she could earn. Ray Strachey was not entirely dependent on her own earnings until the 1930s, although she certainly was not financially dependent on her husband, and she believed that: 'Women who are financially dependent on men are not on terms of equality with them.'[68]

Emmeline Pethick Lawrence gave fervent expression to this new morality in a speech delivered in 1927:

> For many women, as well as for many men, their self-chosen work is not only a means of self-support, but a means of self-expression. Work is worship. Love and work are religion. If a man is successful in his love and in his self-chosen work, he is in possession of the fullness of life. The same is true of women.[69]

The new morality for feminists in the 1920s did not place an emphasis on a woman's sexuality but on work as a liberating force in her life. All of the feminists we have met accepted the importance of the role of the mother in the life of the child, and of society, but the ideology of motherhood was contained within the idea that a woman's work was of the utmost importance both to her and to society. Birth control would help a woman to have greater choice about what work she did, and if that choice lay primarily in motherhood, then that job would be better done with fewer children. Marriage and motherhood were personally more important to the younger feminists in this study, but they shared with their older friends and colleagues a strong belief that a woman's potential contribution to society lay beyond her role as wife and mother. As middle-class women they were less clear about the role of working-class women. Those who advocated the spread of information on birth control were trying to make it possible for working-class women to have greater control over their own lives. Those who worked towards the achievement of some payment for working-class mothers wanted domestic labour to be recognised and valued, although they valued other work more highly themselves. They are also open to the charge that they did not transfer their demand for gender equality into the domestic sphere. Evelyn Sharp and Helena Swanwick, who did tentatively advocate such equality, did not put their energy into working for equality in the 1920s. This limitation in feminist aims also placed a constraint on the struggle to achieve equality outside the home to which we now turn.

6 Lobbying for Equality, 1921–25

In the first five years of the 1920s feminists learned that persistence and patience would be needed to achieve any further move in the direction of equality. In this chapter I want to look at the efforts of two of the feminist pressure groups which continued to lobby for equality: the National Union of Societies for Equal Citizenship and the Six Point Group. We have seen in the last chapter that they worked together in pursuit of an equal moral standard: they also pressed towards the even more elusive goal of economic equality. They continued the tradition of the suffrage movement in concentrating their pressure for change on Parliament. Nine of the women whom we are following were involved in this work to a greater or lesser extent. A tenth, Emmeline Pethick Lawrence, was a member of a third feminist pressure group, the Women's Freedom League.[1]

The pattern of the history of these years is complex: feminist activity took place in a fluid and tense political context. Class differences and party allegiances blunted the sharp edge of feminist demands for economic equality, and these demands covered ground which contained the possibility of division between the search for equality and the recognition of women's separate needs. There was uncertainty partly because no organisation was able to hold together large numbers of women: postwar feminists lacked the confidence which the sheer size of the suffrage movement had given its members. The war had also served to undermine the confidence of individual suffragists and arguably of women in general in their own contribution to the political world. For others peace became their political priority.

But there were those who were prepared to put their efforts into the persistent and often unrewarding task of putting pressure on Parliament to change the laws in the direction of equality for women. Eleanor Rathbone, Kathleen Courtney, Margery Corbett Ashby, Mary Stocks and Ray Strachey were all on the executive committee of the NUSEC, and Eva Hubback had become secretary to the Parliamentary Department and Information Bureau of the

National Union in May 1918. Hubback has been a shadowy figure
in the background so far. The war led to her teaching post at
Newnham, and brought her widowhood and the need to earn a
living for herself and her three children. One of them remembered
'disliking the foggy, smoky smell of London which seemed to hang
about Eva's bag of books and her coat on her return in the late
evening, symbolizing grinding work in a city'. The grinding work
of lobbying meant many hours buttonholing members of the House
of Commons, briefing those who supported feminist legislation and
arranging informal meetings to discuss the contents of bills. Hubback
was at the sharp end of the work that she herself described as entering
into 'questions of law and of policy far more subtle and complicated
than in the old suffrage days.'[2]

In October, 1920, Eva Hubback reviewed the gains made for
women through Parliament and found evidence of a:

> reaction which was inevitable after the wave of enthusiasm which
> carried the vote, the right to sit in Parliament, and the right to
> hold all offices and follow all professions, in the amazing space of
> two years.

She was determined both to recognise the current obstacles for
feminists, and their achievements since February 1918. She knew
that the pace of change would slow down, but it was her task, and
one which she embraced with energy and determination, to maintain
the pressure on Parliament. Apart from her work in Parliament she
was responsible for keeping local societies informed, and for dealing
with suggestions from them. She spoke at meetings outside London
to affiliated societies and to other interested organisations. Hubback
had also to keep 'faith in ultimate success', not an easy matter when
bills for equal suffrage, for example, were defeated in session after
session. She believed that the achievement of equal franchise was
essential: 'Those of us who have the vote cannot rest content until
all other adult women share the privileges with men.'[3] The campaign
for equal franchise was not successful until 1928, and in that same year
Hubback left her paid post in the NUSEC, remaining as chairman of
the Parliamentary committee.

Other feminists were not content to work through the well-tried,
but cautious and sometimes cumbersome structures of the NUSEC.
In the first decade of the century the patience of constitutional
suffragists had been challenged by the passion of the suffragettes.

The NUWSS neither rejected nor publicly condemned the actions of their more militant sisters. In the 1920s this pattern was to some extent repeated. In February 1921, a different group of women drew up Six Points, and the Six Point Group was launched. The woman at the centre of this new organisation was Margaret Mackworth, now known as Margaret Haig, Lady Rhondda. On the surface it would seem that in comparison with Eva Hubback, she had been well-cocooned from the worst effects of the war: yet the war had changed her life. Her marriage was dissolved, and then in 1918 her beloved father died. In her autobiography she wrote of the sense of the discontinuity which the war brought, as it cut through the lives of her generation:

> Time had stopped during the war as if we were just waiting for it to be over. It was as if those four years were a gap in which the hours stood still. Yet we who had gone into the war young came out, as it seemed, middle-aged. Time had not stood still, it had galloped, and in that gallop had robbed us of the last years of our youth.
>
> We found ourselves in an utterly changed world . . . We could not, even had we wished, join this new, comparatively sane world on the jagged edges of the one that had broken off five years before – this new one was quite a different place. The war had broken down barriers and customs and conventions. It had left us curiously free.[4]

Rhondda's freedom included great personal wealth inherited from her father. She could have continued to run the family business, but decided that such a life was not one she 'was really best fitted for.' She knew that she had 'succeeded well enough', but that this success was not just the result of personal ability, 'I had succeeded as the usual son succeeds.' Business had been her profession, now she could choose a vocation; 'I had money and freedom and the whole world to choose from . . . ' She chose 'to found a paper' because she wanted 'passionately, urgently, to change customs and influence ideas'. The postwar world seemed likely 'to lead back towards the same abyss' from which it had just precariously clambered, unless new ideas and solutions could be found. 'I wanted to find, to test, and to spread the customs and ideas that could be health-giving and life-saving – that more than anything.'[5]

Rhondda discussed the founding of *Time & Tide* with Elizabeth Robins. Although they had both been members of the WSPU, they did not meet until the month the war ended. Robins and Wilberforce then met Rhondda often in London, and went to stay at Robins's house in Sussex. Here they walked and talked of how Robins might help Rhondda through her wide network of friends and by introductions to potential contributors. According to Wilberforce the aim was to 'produce an independent, unbiased periodical which would be directed by a picked body of distinguished women who had gained some recognition in the public eye, and would give confidence especially to women readers'. Rhondda was well aware that 'the thing had never yet been done by a woman', and the board and staff of *Time & Tide* were all women.[6] The first editor was Helen Archdale, who had been a member of the WSPU, and Elizabeth Robins was a member of the board. The first issue was published in May 1920.

Rhondda evidently saw her new paper as fulfilling a quite different role from that embraced by *Common Cause*. Nor have I found any evidence that *Time & Tide* was seen as in any way a threat to the former, although *Common Cause* had narrowly avoided a financial collapse in the spring, reappearing as *The Woman's Leader and Common Cause*. Although run by women *Time & Tide* did not claim to put forward women's views, and there was a conscious difference of approach between the two papers. *The Woman's Leader* was the organ of the NUSEC: *Time & Tide* aspired to show 'all sides of national life, dealing with them solely on the ground that they are interesting'. The paper aimed to be 'untainted by any suspicion of preconceived views'. The first editorial also stated that it would be possible to lay 'too much stress' on the fact that the paper was run by women, that the significance of this lay in women's need and demand for 'an independent Press'. If one assumes that Rhondda agreed with this first editorial, it is apparent that she saw women as free from party and sectarian ties, and also that she believed that women wanted a paper which would 'treat men and women as equally part of the great human family'.[7]

Time & Tide was launched in the faith and hope that women could act as equals in the political world. Work had given Rhondda herself the key to freedom, and 'the right of entry into the world of free men', but she was reluctantly aware that women in general had not yet gained 'equal political freedom' with men. When she wrote of this time fifteen years later, her recollection was that she had been:

> a little bored at still having to bother with this . . . but since we had not even yet got equality, and I knew that it was an essential tool, I could not very well stop short of taking my share in helping to get it. So I made an effort to get into the House of Lords . . . it would, after all, if one could get there, be a useful enough platform for all sorts of purposes, quite apart from the value of breaking down that particular barrier.[8]

Lady Rhondda did not succeed in her attempt to be allowed to take the seat in the House of Lords which she argued was an inherent part of the title she had inherited from her father. This failure may well have affected her decision to continue to work for equality. She wrote to Elizabeth Robins soon after the House of Lords threw out her first petition that she was 'thinking and thinking of that same problem of the co-ordination of woman-power.' The answer she came to was not to join the NUSEC, and there seems to be no evidence that she thought of such a mundane solution, Instead she 'formed an equality society, the Six Point Group'.[9] She must surely have known that the NUSEC was also working towards six points, and that there was a striking similarity in the two programmes. The demands put forward most consistently by the NUSEC in the early twenties were: 'equal pay for equal work, involving an open field for women in industry and the professions'; 'an equal standard of sex morals as between men and women, involving a reform of the existing divorce law'; legislation which would provide pensions for civilian widows and their children; the equalisation of the franchise and 'the return to Parliament of women candidates pledged to the equality programme'; and 'equal guardianship of children'. The Six Point Group sought specifically for equal pay only for teachers; they claimed 'equal opportunities' in the Civil Service. There was no mention of an 'equal standard of sex morals', but the group sought to obtain 'satisfactory legislation on Child Assault', and 'for the Unmarried Mother and her Child'. At first there was no mention of the equalisation of the franchise. The Six Point Group shared with the NUSEC the objects of equal guardianship for parents and 'satisfactory legislation for the Widowed Mother'.[10]

The Woman's Leader welcomed the formation of the Six Point Group and expressed confidence that it would 'do excellent publicity work'. The paper welcomed constructive criticism of existing women's organisations, accepting that it might be true that 'they are not properly co-ordinated and that their strength is not brought to bear upon the Government in a form which is effective'. It does seem probable that Rhondda saw the NUSEC as too clumsy an instrument for what she had in mind. The report of the formation of the group in *Time & Tide* referred to the 'state of stagnation' which confronted women 'in spite of their newly acquired power'. The report quoted from an article by Cicely Hamilton, a former suffragette who would be a frequent contributor to *Time & Tide*. Hamilton's article sheds some light on the spirit in which the Six Point Group was launched. She maintained that women had entered politics 'at an unfortunate moment; at a moment, that is to say, when the much-demanded vote had declined in value – since representative institutions and all that they stand for had practically ceased to exist'.[11] Cicely Hamilton was in France when the vote was won and was presumably unaware of the efforts of suffragists in the year before partial suffrage was achieved. Her view reflects the impatience of the suffragette with the slow and persistent methods of the suffragist.

Rhondda defined her position as advocating equality rather than special recognition for women's needs, yet it is apparent that the Six Point Group, like the NUSEC, appealed to feminists who understood a woman's contribution to society to be rooted in her role as a mother. The six points of the two groups include both the objective of strict equality, and the issues which concerned women as mothers of children. Maude Royden expressed the views of the feminist who supported the Six Point Group yet who was not content to work only for strict equality. Royden had indeed been attracted to the WSPU before the war, but had rejected militancy. In the postwar world it seems that she found in the new group the spirit of the women's movement as she understood it. *Time & Tide* reported her as saying that:

> The Six Point Group . . . stood for the deepest traditions of the old Woman Suffrage Movement, in some ways they represented the old traditions of the Suffrage Movement before the vote was achieved more faithfully than did any other woman's society today.

The reason she gave for this assertion was that the group 'stood first and foremost for the protection of children, in other words their chief concern was with the race itself'.[12] This was not the sort of justification for the Six Point Group that Rhondda put forward, and it is rooted in an ideology of motherhood which was not accepted by all feminists. Royden's views represent an aspect of feminist thinking in the 1920s which existed alongside the idea of 'equality' in the early part of the decade. In Chapter 4 we saw that there was an awareness of how 'equality' and 'women's interests' might diverge within the NUSEC. In neither organisation was there yet a division between those who would later be seen as 'old' and 'new feminists.'

THE PROTECTION OF CHILDREN

The cause of the assaulted child, together with the needs of the widow and of the unmarried mother, can be grouped under the concept of 'women's questions'; equal guardianship can be seen as fitting into either category. The other two demands of the Six Point Group are more obviously concerned with the question of gender equality. In dividing these issues it is important to remember that in pressing for these reforms, feminists did not at first distinguish between arguments for equality and the recognition of the special needs of women.

The first objective on the Six Point Group's agenda was concerned with 'child assault' and on this question there was wide agreement, concerted action and the limited success we observed in the last chapter. The inclusion of the second aim of securing satisfactory legislation for the unmarried mother had a mixed, and somewhat confused genesis. The article in *Time & Tide* which outlined the group's aims referred to this point as concerned with making both parents equally responsible for the care of the illegitimate child. Yet the responsibility of the father was seen in strictly financial terms; that of the mother as the long-term care of the child. Royden had argued the case for supporting the unmarried mother before the Royal Commission for the Birth Rate in 1918. She believed that most women who had illegitimate children were themselves illegitimate, and often prostitutes. She wanted to break the 'vicious circle by which illegitimacy continually breeds illegitimacy'. Royden was the chairman of a hostel for unmarried mothers, and she believed that the way to break 'the vicious circle' was to give a woman the chance to keep and support her illegitimate child:

> I know from my own experience that there is no incentive in the world that keeps her straight in the future better than the keeping with her of her own child.

At the hostel where Royden was chairman the mothers went out to work while their children were cared for, and she claimed that 'we have hardly had a single case of a girl going wrong a second time'.[13] The pressure to make it financially feasible for the unmarried mother to look after her own child led to an Act passed in 1923 which doubled the amount which a father was supposed to contribute to his illegitimate child's upkeep: the mother of the child could then more easily retain care of it. There was no way in which contributions which were different in kind could be made precisely equal, and there was no challenge to the concept that the mother should care for the child.

On the question of divorce the NUSEC was clear that the existing law condoned adultery by men: for a woman to obtain a divorce, it was necessary for her to provide evidence of other misconduct than adultery, while a man could obtain a divorce solely on that count. According to her daughter, Eva Hubback suggested the idea of the Bill which was put forward by the NUSEC executive committee. The Bill was drafted with legal help and finally became the Matrimonial Causes Amendment Act of 1923 by which infidelity by a husband became grounds for divorce. The process by which the lobby for changes in the Divorce Law succeeded is a paradigm of the way the NUSEC intended to operate. Articles were published in *The Woman's Leader* which argued the need for equal justice in the divorce law; contributors to the paper were urged to write letters to their MPs, and Eva Hubback contacted and kept in touch with those who were prepared to put forward and support a Private Member's Bill. When the Bill went through the House of Commons in June 1923, the division list of those who voted for and against it was published in *The Woman's Leader*.[14]

The same method was used to obtain another objective which was contained in the programmes of both the Six Point Group and the NUSEC: to obtain legislation which would give the mother of children a right to guardianship of her children equal to that of their father. This change in the law had been a desideratum of the women's movement since the 1830s. In the confident period immediately after the war the NUSEC had hoped that the question would appear at once on the Government's legislative programme, and were disappointed when this was not the case. Once the Six Point Group was launched, the two women's organisations cooperated in their efforts to drum up public support for a bill and to lobby Members of Parliament, and Eva Hubback wrote articles on the subject in both *Time & Tide* and *The Woman's Leader*. Private Members' Bills concerned with guardianship were introduced into the House of Commons in 1922 and again in 1923. By the autumn of 1923 frustration with Parliament was beginning to cause some dissension among feminists. The NUSEC's method of working through Private Members' Bills was challenged by Rhondda. In reply Hubback argued that it was unwise to rely too heavily on government legislation.[15] This was an issue which was to provoke considerable discussion in the columns of *Time & Tide*, and its significance lay outside the question of which was the most efficient way of proceeding. It was uncomfortably entwined with the dispute over whether feminists should align themselves with the existing political parties.

'DON'T TALK TO ME OF SISYPHUS'[16]

The failure of the early Bills on equal guardianship was partly caused by political factors apparently outside the context of feminism, although there are connections. Feminist hopes for equality took place within a political context which was unstable; for many people alarmingly so. A total change in gender relations would have been as revolutionary as the sort of changes the political left hoped or feared might take place. Catherine Marshall revealed the insecurity of the period in a letter written to her brother in the spring of 1921. Hal Marshall had suggested to her that the situation contained a volatility like that of August 1914, and Catherine agreed. She believed that the political and economic system was incapable of dealing with the effects of '5 years' war and destruction', and was 'in any case breaking down'. In her view some of those in possession of power wanted violence, and were prepared 'to provoke the Labour people', so that they could use the navy and the police to preserve their control. She wrote that she thought Lloyd George was 'a master at this kind of manoeuvring'. This letter was written the day before 'Black Friday', remembered with bitterness as the day when the miners were deserted by the trade union movement and a threat of widespread strikes withdrawn. As the threat of violence receded so did hopes of change. The government limped through another eighteen months before it fell in October 1922. In the four years since the war ended, reconstruction had become 'a faded mockery' under the combined pressures of economic crisis and fear of revolution.[17] Feminists were not alone in hoping to reform the economic and political structures, nor in the experience of hope turning to fear, or resignation.

The effects of political frustration were apparent in a report of the activities of the Six Point Group written by Elizabeth Robins for *Time & Tide* in January 1923. In those first eighteen months of its existence members of the group had come to a much greater awareness of the obstacles facing such legislation, among them the frustrations of relying on Private Members' Bills, and the fact that 'disqualification on account of sex' was 'still a governing influence in social life'. The group also soon learned that there was still a need to educate people as to the necessity for legislation. Winifred Holtby spoke for the Six Point Group once or twice a week, and she wrote to a friend of the shortage of speakers.[18] In 1923 *Time & Tide* complained that a huge meeting on the subject of child abuse, supported by both the Six Point Group and the NUSEC, had not been reported in the press, save in the *Manchester Guardian*. Both women's organisations were learning that the tide had turned on that early postwar wave of optimism.

There was a new surge of hope for change in December 1923, when another General Election was called. The Conservative government which had been elected in November 1922 was forced to call election after only a year in office. According to *The Woman's Leader* 'this Election has been named the Woman's Election, because the appeals made by every candidate to the housewife, has meant that candidates have been more alive than in any previous Election to the need of satisfying women voters . . . '[19] The appeal to the woman as housewife had a double edge to it of which some feminists were aware, but tactically hoped they might use to further the type of reforms which would benefit many women.

The results of the election seemed to bode well for women's interests. Eight women were elected, three Labour, three Conservative and two Liberal. A minority Labour Government was formed, although the Conservative Party still held most seats. *Time & Tide* expressed cautious hopes of the new government. The paper felt that there was reason for optimism in that, as one sympathetic Labour MP put it: 'whilst this Government is usually spoken of as a minority Government, it is, so far as women's questions are concerned, a majority Government'. The Consultative Committee of Women's Organisations which Lady Astor had established put three crucial demands before the Government. The first of these was equal franchise, and activity directed towards the passage of a government-sponsored equal franchise bill absorbed much of the political energies of feminist activists in the early months of the new government. The failure of these efforts soured relations between the feminist groups and the new government. In her report to the Annual Council of the NUSEC, Eleanor Rathbone documented the union's disappointment in the Labour Government and asked, with acid irony: 'Has a party in office *no* responsibility towards its principles and past professions and pledges? Are its members expected to quaff the waters of lethe before kissing hands?' In April *Time & Tide* commented:

> It would be interesting to know how long a Government pledged to democratic ideals expects to go on receiving enthusiastic support from amongst a body of citizens to whom it continues without explanation of excuse to refuse the full right of citizenship.[20]

Equal guardianship was the second demand put forward by the Consultative Committee. Mrs Wintringham sought government sponsorship of her bill to secure this objective, but a separate government bill was introduced, presenting feminists with a dilemma. The Government Bill did not go as far as the Wintringham Bill, but it was feared that if amendments enlarging its scope were pressed, it might be dropped altogether. A crucial part was played in these discussions by Barbara Aytron Gould, who was an active member of the Labour Party and was doing her best to put pressure on the Government. After considerable debate the NUSEC executive committee agreed to support the Government bill, 'although the Bill does not give all the NUSEC would wish'. Talks then took place between the executive and Margaret Rhondda on what tactics over the issue should be. Her attitude proved to be 'that any bill which did not give complete equal status between mothers and fathers with regard to guardianship should be attacked'.[21]

The debate between feminists continued over the summer with letters from Hubback and Rathbone appearing in *Time & Tide*. They agreed that the bill fell short of achieving equal rights for parents in that there was no machinery provided to put into effect the principle of equality declared in the preamble. However, they believed that the bill would provide relief in some of the most tragic cases. They ended by sharply asserting that the NUSEC was 'in a better position than other organisations to know its strong and weak points, and, further, to estimate the strength of the forces against it and the chances of improving on it'. It was the NUSEC which 'scrutinised every clause and word in the Bill', and 'fought every point inch by inch, in the negotiations that led up to it'. But *Time & Tide* continued 'to believe that the NUSEC is making a grave mistake in accepting the Bill . . . . ', which 'will in fact only serve to stereotype the present position of inequality between mothers and fathers'.[22]

This difference of opinion did not prevent the two organisations from continuing to work together. In July the NUSEC executive endorsed Eva Hubback's action in lobbying members of the House of Lords on the Peeresses Bill, at the request of the Six Point Group. (This bill represented another attempt to allow peeresses such as Lady Rhondda to take their seat in the House of Lords.) Rathbone and Hubback wrote to *Time & Tide* in August, sharing their despair that the 'fruits' of the parliamentary session had been 'nil'. At that stage there was still room for hope that something might be achieved in the autumn session, but these hopes too were dashed when the Labour Government was defeated on a vote of censure and another general election was called in October. In 1925 an Equal Guardian-ship Act similar to the one which had fallen in 1924 did at last reach the statute book. Although it did not satisfy the Six Point Group, it was accepted by the NUSEC as a satisfactory outcome of the long struggle.[23]

Together with the pressure to obtain equal guardianship went efforts for increased financial support for widowed mothers. Pensions for widowed mothers were incorporated into the national contribu-tory insurance scheme in 1925. This was seen as only a limited success by many women's organisations, including the Women's Co-operative Guild, because it did not cover those who had not contributed. Eva Hubback recognised this limitation but rejoiced that some widows would benefit and would lose some of their dread of old age. Despite the incomplete nature of both these measures *The Woman's Leader* judged that the Parliamentary session had been a fruitful one, leaving feminists with the 'unusual sense of some-thing accomplished.' Eleanor Rathbone comforted members of the NUSEC with the knowledge that:

There are thousands and soon will be tens of thousands of women – unhappy wives, widows, tired old working spinsters – who have cause to bless the name of the NUSEC.[24]

The struggle to introduce parliamentary legislation was proving hard. Moreover, measures such as Widows' Pensions or Equal Guardianship seemed to some feminists to be more in the nature of welfare than equality. Writing about the issue of Widows' Pensions in the 1940s Mary Stocks judged that it was part of the tide of social reform which carried 'distressed persons' away from the dependence on the Poor Law and placed them 'in the framework of a social security structure'.[25] Mary Stocks's comments and those of *Time & Tide* suggest that feminists both at the time and later could see that 'women's questions' could be subsumed under 'social questions'. In the early 1920s this seemed to add strength to the struggle both for equality and reform. But the aims of feminists such as Mary Stocks and Eleanor Rathbone could become more clearly identified by others with social reform than with gender equality. The tendency to react against reforming measures was made the more likely as it became increasingly clear that the struggle for equality for women in employment faced even more stubborn opposition.

ECONOMIC EQUALITY: WOMEN'S WORK AND PAY

The employment of women, and the terms and conditions of that employment, had been a central focus for the women's movement since the 1860s.[26] Women in both feminist organisations knew that the issue was a tricky one, because the formidable obstacles to change included gender attitudes as well as the prevailing economic structures. Moreover, it was a period of economic decline and in this context women tended to disappear; many connived at their own disappearance, others refused to be deleted without a struggle.

There were differences of opinion between the feminists whom we are studying as to the level and direction of the commitment which could be given to the question. Ray Strachey had hoped that the employment of women would be central to the work of feminist organisations after the war. Rhondda had demonstrated her commitment to the importance of women's employment when she worked through the Women's Industrial League in 1919. She had cooperated with Strachey at a time when Ray was in some despair at the direction the NUWSS was taking. Eleanor Rathbone and Eva Hubback conceded its vital importance, but they wanted to work on other issues as well. Strachey had urged the NUWSS to make the question of 'industrial work' its 'one big job'. When Rathbone proposed that the Union take action over the Pre-war Practices Act in 1919, Strachey wrote an angry letter to her, pointing out that it was probably too late by then to intervene without the preparatory work on the question which she felt should have been done:

> I don't believe we can at this late moment *efficiently* intervene – we haven't prepared the way or got the necessary confidence from the women workers or the experts; at least, I fear we have not. Even at this last council, with demobilisation thick upon us, the only person to bring up the subject was myself, acting for the London Society, and you yourself put all your weight into the social reforms. I daresay you and the Union have been right: but I do say that it is too late to change the general drift now.[27]

One of the reasons why the NUWSS had apparently neglected the question of employment was that in the heady enthusiasm of the months which followed enfranchisement there was confident expectation that there was no need for political pressure in this area. It was at first assumed that the Disqualification Removal Act would achieve equal pay and opportunities in the civil service, which would in turn lead the way to changes in other areas of work: it was widely accepted that private employers would follow the lead of the Government as employer. Women had achieved a remarkable entry into the Civil Service during the war when the percentage of women employed rose from 21 per cent to 56 per cent. They were engaged in most departments, but they were dissatisfied with their generally low and undoubtedly unequal pay, and they argued strongly for an open recruitment at all levels. In May 1920, there was a debate in the House of Commons on a resolution which proposed that 'women employed in the service of the State, whether in the central Civil Service or in the employ of the local authorities, shall be given equal opportunities and equal pay'. The resolution was passed 'without a single dissenting voice'. In *The Woman's Leader* Eva Hubback reported that all speakers in the debate 'declared that the days of unequal opportunity and unequal reward were over . . . never in the whole course of our experience have we spent so dream-like an evening'. But she added:

> the economic problem is almost tougher in itself than the franchise; the prejudice is as great and the attainment less straightforward. And yet the battle is hardly begun before the House of Commons, without even a division, concedes the whole thing. So much, as we so often say, for the value of enfranchisement.[28]

It was one thing for the House of Commons to 'concede the whole thing' in principle: putting that principle into action revealed the continued resistance to the idea that women should have equal opportunity of employment. Regulations published later that year reserved to men all posts in the Diplomatic and Consular Service. Sympathetic MPs pressed for a debate and this took place in August 1921. As a result of strong support for the woman civil servant's case a pledge was obtained from the Government that all examinations should be open to women, but posts could still be reserved. Moreover, the cause of the woman civil servant, like that of the woman in industry, was undermined by the perceived needs of the returning servicemen. There was a massive recruitment of ex-servicemen at the expense of women into the temporary and unestablished staff in the immediate postwar years, and later into the permanent ranks. A woman on the temporary establishment in 1919 had a 6 per cent chance of being made permanent by 1926, while a man in a similar position had a 48 per cent chance.[29]

Feminists did not give up the struggle. The London Society for Women's Service – with Ray Strachey in the chair throughout the decade – continued to bring pressure to bear when and where they could. Strachey had been involved and concerned with the question of women's employment during the war, working with Pippa Strachey in the Women's Service Bureau of the London Society. The Bureau continued its work after the war; collecting information on jobs that were available; interviewing women who were in search of work; conducting surveys of occupations which might be suitable for women and attempting to persuade employers to take them on. On a small scale this was a valuable contribution to the satisfactory employment of women: on a wider scale it made little impact. The women who came to the Bureau were seeking for clerical rather than industrial jobs. Moreover, the Bureau was under considerable financial strain after the war, and its employment department closed down in January 1922. Its closure may be seen as symbolic of the closing of doors to women which occurred during the period of economic crisis following the immediate postwar boom. By the winter of 1921 – 22 more than two million people were registered as unemployed, and the number fell only slowly during the 1920s. Writing on the question in the early 1930s Strachey concluded that where new trades or new processes had come in, women retained the jobs they had done during the war. This was the case in the electrical trade and in light engineering where women were employed in semi-skilled processes. She was certain that the range of occupations for women had widened, but she also observed that wages 'flopped back to the women's level' of prewar years. Overall participation rates by women did in fact rise during the interwar years, but only slightly.[30]

There was also a widespread commitment to the principle of equal pay among feminists, and Ray Strachey in particular had worked during the war towards its achievement in the engineering trade. Eleanor Rathbone's advocacy of family endowment was expressed as a necessary concommitant to equal pay. Equal pay remained firmly on the agenda of both the Six Point Group and the NUSEC. But it was widely feared that if women were offered the same rates of pay as men they would be unlikely to be employed: there was widely-felt assumption that women workers were not as efficient as men. Maude Royden faced this question squarely:

> I am persuaded that if, when you pay men and women alike, women are driven out, it will be because the work is really better done by men, and in that case it is for the advantage both of men and women, that is for the whole community, that the men should do it.[31]

There were obvious dangers in this argument in that social pressures would operate as much as women's essential attributes to allow discrimination to take place against them. But Royden believed that there were many jobs which women would retain in open competition, and she demonstrated a confidence in women's abilities which was not shared by those who supposedly represented women's industrial interests. The Majority Report of the War Cabinet Committee and Women in Industry had advocated that women should be paid the same piece-rates as men, so that if their output, as anticipated, was lower they would get less pay. This proposal had the support of Janet Campbell, the Senior Medical Officer for Maternity and Child Welfare, Beatrice Webb, who was also on the committee, drew up a Minority Report which advocated a single occupational rate for the job. But her priority was not equality but efficiency: she recognised that her solution would lead to unemployment among women and accepted this because they were inferior workers. She believed that alterations of the wage system depended on the power of the trade union movement, and she was well aware of the weak position of women in trade unions, and of their failure to challenge the principle and practice of unequal pay. So was Eleanor Rathbone. Eleanor Rathbone compared occupation rate with piece rates, and asserted that the acceptance of the latter by women was made under pressure from male trade unionists. Rathbone pointed out that women trade unionists were persuaded to consider the effect on the Labour Movement as a whole of women's rates of pay. She understood how women trade unionists who had 'won a late and precarious footing in the world of unionism are not likely to jeopardise it by questioning a principle which their leaders proclaim is essential'. But she was anxious that women outside the Labour Movement should retain their independence of judgement, so that other restrictions on women's employment should not be accepted 'under the guise of protection'.[32] The whole issue of protective legislation was to become a central issue for feminists as the decade progressed.

One unionised group of women did put up a fight for equal pay. The National Union of Women Teachers was affiliated to the Six Point Group and the efforts of the union to achieve equal pay just after the war were given full coverage and support in *Time & Tide*. The commitment of the NUSEC to the principle of equal pay for teachers and for civil servants was also persistent. In July 1924 the executive committee 'strongly supported' a motion to join a deputation to the Chancellor of the Exchequer to protest against the failure of the Government to implement equal pay in the Civil Service. In September of the same year the executive wrote to the negotiating body on pay for teachers, 'pointing out that to give unequal remuneration for equal work is fundamentally unjust'. At

the NUSEC annual council meeting in 1925 a resolution was passed
which pressed for equal pay with or without the supplement of
family allowances. However, at that same Council Meeting, Eleanor
Rathbone admitted that 'The question of Equal Opportunities and
Pay is even more elusive and difficult' than the search for an 'Equal
Moral Standard'. She reckoned that feminists could not ask for a
bill requiring private employers to engage men and women in equal
numbers at equal salaries, or trades unions to remove the barriers
of sex exclusiveness:

> It is difficult even to find means of bringing public opinion effec-
> tively to bear on such employers and Trades Unions. The actual
> facts relating to these sex privileges and exclusions are hard to
> get at . . . so far, with the exception of the London Society for
> Women's Service, which concentrates almost entirely on this prob-
> lem, there have been few symptoms that our Societies have been
> interesting themselves actively in it. I think we may assume that
> you feel yourselves, as we do at Headquarters, baffled and rather
> helpless in face of forces which tend to limit women's opportunities
> in the professions and to keep them to a definitely inferior status
> in industry.[33]

One of the most baffling aspects of the equal pay question
for some feminists was the attitude of women activists in the
Labour Movement. Women in the Civil Service trade unions
gave evidence to the Royal Commission on the Civil Service
which was directly opposed to that of the NUSEC and the
London Society. In 1927 the Civil Service Clerical Association
refused to cooperate with the London Society in a campaign
on equal pay, citing personal distrust of Ray Strachey as one
of the reasons.[34] The gap between feminist and trade unionist
would widen over the question of protective legislation as we shall
see in the next chapter, and these differences would spill over into
other areas.

It is easy to discount the efforts of women to stake a claim
for equal pay in the early 1920s because they fell so far short
of success. Yet for a few feminists the question of equal pay was
central to their thinking, and for many it was a long-term goal,
although they recognised the strength of the economic and social
forces ranged against them. One of those forces – and it was one
which operated within the women's trade union movement – was
the low self-esteem of most women.

A SENSE OF DIFFERENCE

One witness said in her evidence to the War Cabinet Committee that after the war, 'The residue of women could provide a margin of labour for periods of good trade. If either sex is to be short of employment it had better be the women.' She was not alone among the small number of women in positions of influence in lacking confidence in her own sex. The part played by the war in this crisis of confidence is subtle and complex. Evidence based on the experience of women who worked in munitions factories during the war suggests that they developed greater self-respect and that they found an identity outside their families. Non-combatant guilt, which was felt by both men in positions of political power and by women, helped to drive women out of industrial jobs when the war ended. What is remarkable, considering the force of this guilt, combined with union pressure, is that some women did protest.[35] Enfranchisement was another ambiguous triumph in this context. Women had been given the vote, but only some women, and the messages which came with the giving were mixed. It was widely seen as a reward for war work, yet the women who were not enfranchised were the younger ones, many of whom had worked in the munitions factories. Moreover, this work was seen as something women did for men, or at least for Britain, certainly not for themselves.

Elizabeth Robins recognised the extent and the causes of the betrayal of women's contribution to the war. She described the women who had worked during the war as 'eager battalions – soldiers of civilisation, drilled to heal and build and to sustain'. After the war ended they were ready to 'build and sustain . . . a world never before in such need of hope and help'. Yet they were told to go home and fold their hands:

> You are well-to-do? You can afford to do nothing.
> You are poor? Go back to the kitchen.
> You have never been there before? No matter. Anyone can be a kitchen-maid. Any patriotic person is ready to be a kitchen-maid. Your country needs kitchen-maids.
> You worked at munitions in 'danger buildings'! You broke horses at a Remount Camp! What then? You were praised and paid for designing aeroplane parts! You drove an army lorry over shell-pitted roads at night! Go home, go home!

Robins believed that even after obtaining a limited franchise, women judged themselves by men's standards, and that men still viewed women with contempt. Moreover, she believed that some of the prewar victories had been smudged or obliterated by the postwar catastrophe. She quoted from a letter from Janet Courtney to *The Times* in which Courtney, who had worked in the Civil Service in the 1890s as well as during the war, wrote:

> The strange thing is that in the 'nineties we were not 'experiments'. . . . It has been left to the post-war world to decide that we are experiments – a world that in its short-sightedness is prepared to leave untrained and unused the great labour force upon which it drew in the time of its sorest adversity, and which it well may need again.[36]

Janet Courtney had been one of those who left the Civil Service after the war without protest and in the belief that women's presence there was established. In an autobiography published in 1926 Courtney identified the strengthening of 'masculine prejudice' against giving women equal opportunities, but did not attempt to suggest a cause. She handed over responsibility for finding a solution to the continuing problem to the new generation: 'We, whose best working years were in the pre-War world, can be little more now than lookers-on. There has been so great a change. The struggle and the prizes are for the young.'[37]

Elizabeth Robins – who was three years older than Courtney – felt that working-class women had been let down by those who should have led them: 'A lethargy seems to have fallen on the discouraged guardians of the interests of women.'[38] This judgement was not directed towards the Six Point Group of which Robins was a member, nor could it apply to the NUSEC. The feminist commitment to women's employment interests was there, a commitment with a long tradition. The primary aim of many nineteenth-century feminists had been to secure appropriate employment for women who wished to be employed, and to widen the scope of potential occupations. Women's trade union organisations had developed in order to secure these objectives. A few middle-class feminists were energetic advocates of the widening of employment opportunities for working-class women and they worked towards the establishment of separate unions for women. The Women's Trade Union League inherited the latter objective, but the aim of widening opportunities was gradually eroded. During the war there was an increase in women's membership of trade unions in parallel with the increased numbers of women employed, but this expansion did not protect women from sudden unemployment as men returned to industrial jobs upon demobilisation. The war had indeed served to increase tensions between men and women workers, while at the same time building up the myth that there was no genuine clash of interests. Thus in 1920 the work of the Women's Trade Union League was taken over by the Trades Union Congress. In the same year the National Federation of Women Workers, with the blessing of Mary Macarthur, voted to merge with the National Union of General Workers. The effect of these moves was that the voice of women trade unionists was muted. A union like the NUWT, wishing to fight for equal pay and opportunities, had to fight alone.

One area where middle-class feminists did have power was where they themselves were the employers of working-class women; in domestic service. Moreover, this was the one area of employment where there was more demand than supply in the 1920s. This was a delicate issue for feminists, and one upon which most declined to make any stand. It was another area where solidarity among women was tenuous, because the interests of employer and employee were not always the same. Eleanor Rathbone had pointed out that equal pay was 'the claim put forward by practically all women, except, of course, when they are themselves employing women.' The war had given many former domestic servants a taste for greater freedom, and women resisted the pressures on them to return to domestic service, but their resistance was tempered by their need. Employment for women was not easy to find, and domestic work was one area for which there was training available.[39]

The question received regular attention on the pages of both *The Woman's Leader* and *Time & Tide*, and articles were supporting the right of women to refuse to take domestic work, and criticising the inconsiderate and unreasonable attitude of many mistresses. In 1923 the author of an article in *Time & Tide* challenged the necessity for servants:

> Domestic Servants are not a necessity of life, some two-thirds of the population lives without them as it is, and domestic servants, who are for the most part drawn from this section of the community, are perfectly well aware of the fact.[40]

There was a move towards daily rather than residential domestic work which did at least give the workers a greater chance of regular hours. *The Woman's Leader* published articles in which the author, a former servant, revealed the class-ridden attitudes of employers, and advocated set, regular hours on a daily basis. Another contributor to *The Woman's Leader* seemed to sympathise with the plight of the resident domestic servant and agreed that 'the comfort and efficiency of middle-class families can be bought too dear', but she felt that this was not what was happening. To those who suggested that daily workers were the answer, she pointed out that the hours between six and nine a.m. were when women needed help most, and that these were precisely the hours when 'dailies' would not wish to come.[41]

The NUSEC did protest about the pay of waitresses at the British Empire Exhibition in 1924, and there was support among feminists for some form of organisation to back up the claims of domestic workers. Jessie Stephens, a suffragist from Glasgow, became the secretary to a Domestic Workers' Union which proposed that there should be maximum hours for domestic workers, adequate time off, regular meals and payment for overtime. The issue was uncomfortably linked to the whole question of the valuation put on domesticity and the role of women in the home. A contributor to *The Woman's Leader* advocated a 'National Guild of Homemakers', to include employers and employed, the aim of which would be to call attention 'to the importance of the home in the national interest, and to show the wide interests which have their root in the home.'[42] The same pressure which led this contributor to press for higher value being placed on domestic work was responsible for the widespread acceptance outside feminist circles of the idea that all girls – and no boys – should be given lessons in 'domestic science' at school.

The gulf between the lives of domestic workers and the middle-class women who employed them is apparent in Ray Strachey's letters, in the autobiographical reflections of Mary Stocks and, to a lesser extent, those of Helena Swanwick. When the Stracheys moved in with Oliver's brother James and his wife in 1921, Ray gave one month's notice to the cook who had worked for them for many years. Ray's comment was that the cook's 'heart will break. But she is too expensive for me, and I daresay it is a good plan not to let her become a fixture. There are as good fish in the sea – and if not, I'm sure she would come back like a flash if I ever wanted her.' The following year Ray returned from a day's campaigning to find all her servants in tears. She pointed out in a letter to her mother that at least education prevented that sort of emotional behaviour; as she put it, 'obviates that horror.'[43]

Mary Stocks wrote of what she called 'The Evolution of Domesticity' when looking back from the 1970s at the first decade of this century. By the time she wrote she reckoned that only Spanish or Portugese residential servants were obtainable – for 'money, separate quarters and television'. She was aware that residential domestic service deprived 'large numbers of women from living in homes of their own, in order that they may reside in other people's homes for the daily performance of tedious and repetitive domestic duties which almost all women would gladly avoid, and which most men succeed in avoiding'. But she believed that such a service led to a 'cross-fertilisation of gracious living' which benefited both servants and served: the latter learned to be considerate, the former learned manners.[44]

Helena Swanwick wrote in her autobiography in the early 1930s of her experiences in the 1890s in Manchester. Her views were distinctively judicious. She did not challenge the necessity for servants and recalled that she had difficulty in finding a competent 'general': she found only two over the years, and spoke of them both as friends. Swanwick recognised that the problem might well have been that the life of the lone, living-in servant was 'unattractive', and advocated the training and registration of 'outside workers'. She felt that the reform of domestic service was one that would help both employers and employed, giving competent and reliable help to the former, and regularity and independence to the latter. Swanwick was scathing about 'middle-class women who write to the papers celebrating the merits of domestic service and the folly of women in not crowding into it', and pointed out that they would not do such work themselves, nor 'like their daughters to take it up'. In contrast, Swanwick could imagine herself being 'happy as a day or night worker in domestic service under decent conditions', but not as a resident.[45]

A sense of difference also existed between married and unmarried women. Articles by Leonora Eyles in *Time & Tide* repeated a question which had haunted the Victorian spinster: 'What Are They For?' Eyles herself had earned her living, partly by doing domestic work, brought up her children and cared for an invalid mother, and she is sharply critical of the bored, moneyed unmarried woman. Eyles did not want such women to 'blackleg' by taking jobs, but suggested that they might voluntarily help 'overburdened mothers and vicars'. The spectre of the woman who does not need to earn her living yet works for money also haunted the debates on whether married women should be entitled to work. Feminist organisations claimed the right of married women to work and supported the teachers in their unsuccessful struggle against Local Authority decisions to ban the employment of married women. Where the question was one of protecting the rights of women against men, the issue was relatively clear, but there remained an undercurrent of anxiety about depriving men of work when they had families to support. In an economic climate of cuts in public expenditure the fear of unemployment sapped support for women's rights. In 1921 *The Woman's Leader* reported the decision of Glasgow Corporation to forbid the employment of married women:

> The extraordinary feature of the voting was that the dismissal of married women was strongly supported by members of the Labour Party – a Party understood to hold the view that no employer has any right to inquire into the private life and concerns of his or her employee.[46]

This sharp rebuke warns of the edging part of feminist organisations and the Labour Movement which was such a damaging aspect of the period. Susan Lawrence, an unmarried Labour Councillor in St. Pancras, was reported approvingly by *The Woman's Leader* as supporting the right of women to work. Significantly, it was the charwoman whom she was anxious to protect, not the more middle-class teacher. Eva Hubback, herself a married woman – albeit a widow – working for money, defended the right of the married woman teacher to work:

> It is an insult to any body of adult women not to be allowed, together with their husbands, to decide whether the interests of the home can be most effectively served by the wife doing the domestic work, for which she is not trained, or by her continuing her work as a teacher for which she is trained.[47]

In 1927 the NUSEC was the driving force behind the introduction of a Married Women's Employment Bill which would have ended the marriage bar for all women public employees. But the Civil Service Clerical Association voted by three to one in favour of the marriage bar, and lobbied against the Bill.[48]

WOMEN AND POLITICAL PARTIES

Soon after the end of the war Margery Corbett Ashby's sister, Cicely, wrote to Pippa Strachey to say that she could no longer speak for the London Society of Women's Service:

> The war has brought me over very strongly to Labour and especially to pacifist Labour. My feeling is that I had better not speak very much on non-party platforms.

She clearly did not believe that it would be possible to do both. Women in the Labour Movement did not work easily together with feminists in the 1920s, despite the hopes of those like Catherine Marshall and Helena Swanwick who understood socialism and feminism to be so strongly linked as to be synonymous. In the spring of 1921 Catherine Marshall was being pressed to stand as a Labour candidate for the Penrith and Cockermouth Division of Cumberland. In the end the party decided not to put a candidate forward, perhaps to Marshall's relief, since campaigns were expensive both financially and emotionally.[49] We have seen that she was aware of the problems facing middle-class feminists in cooperating with women whose background was in the Labour Movement, and in particular in trade unions. The discord between these two groups of women was a painful accompaniment, part cause and part effect, of the increasing friction between feminists and the Labour Party which we shall examine in the next chapter.

In the first half of the decade there were still many feminists who hoped that it would be possible to work for feminist aims within the party structures. Helen Fraser, who stood as a Liberal candidate in 1922, 1923 and 1924, wrote in *The Woman's Leader* that independent women in Parliament would not be in a position to put forward policies without a group to back them. She also argued that the party system, while not 'perfect or eternal', represented political realities. More women were needed inside 'the machinery of politics': 'Politics and parties are human concerns, and we need more women playing their part in them.' Helen Fraser was never elected, and she resigned from the Liberal Party in 1925.[50] She found out the hard way how difficult it was for women to be fully accepted into the party structures. Margery Corbett Ashby stood unsuccessfully as a Liberal candidate in every election in the 1920s. The Liberal Party was declining in the 1920s. Women with strong party allegiance to the Conservative and Labour Parties were occasionally elected.

Dorothea Jewson, one of the three women elected as Labour MPs in 1923, had been a member of the WSPU, and *Time & Tide* welcomed her election as it did that of Susan Lawrence and Margaret Bondfield to the same Parliament. *The Woman's Leader* also published an article on the three new Labour women MPs, identifying them as 'closely associated in their work for women in the industrial field', adding on a cautious note:

> though all three are deeply interested in these and all other women's questions, they have all won their election battle on the full programme of the Labour Party.[51]

Time & Tide again gave full coverage to the women who stood at the election in the autumn of 1924. But, as the paper pointed out, no woman was standing in a seat formerly held by her party, so that she would need to swing the vote to get elected.[52] In the event, the total number of women MPs dropped from eight to four. One new woman MP was elected: Ellen Wilkinson for Labour.

Many feminists were unable to adopt the full programme of any party. As her daughter points out, Eva Hubback 'would have made an excellent Member of Parliament . . . But she was not sufficiently strong a party woman to gain nomination.' Eleanor Rathbone and Margaret Rhondda felt that feminists must avoid commitment to a particular party. Rathbone believed that women were being marshalled behind party banners in order 'to prevent their energies being "dissipated" or their minds "confused" by mingling with women of other parties than their own and so discovering the bond between them.' She and other non-party feminists had hoped that women would be wary of promises made by political parties, and would not give their allegiance so totally that the 'vertical cleavage of class' became of more importance than the 'horizontal cleavage of sex'.[53] But for non-party women the first half of the twenties brought the experience of failing to make any political headway while men whom they could see were inferior held positions of power. Eleanor Rathbone stood as an Independent candidate in East Toxteth, Liverpool in 1922 and again in 1923. She was eventually elected in 1929 to represent the English Universities: it is possible that without such an unusual constituency, she might never have been elected.

Strachey shared Rathbone's commitment to stand outside the political parties, but as we have seen they already differed in what they saw as the essential feminist aims. The fact that non-party feminists did not necessarily agree heightened the anxiety about what was seen as the loss of women's independence to political parties. Elizabeth Robins identified lack of confidence as one of the reasons for women's failure to make an impact on the political structures in the 1920s. Ray Strachey had a just sense of her own worth which was rare even among able women of her generation. Brought up in a family of women, she was securely aware that she could rival many of the men she met in political life. She wrote to her step-father:

> A regular buzz of a life I lead, with one complicated semi-political intrigue after another. If it doesn't lead me into the Cabinet in the end it will be strange – for its a perfect preparation.[54]

We have traced Ray's first attempt to launch a political career in 1918. During the following four years she looked for a constituency where she might have a greater chance of success. She did not allow her efforts to dominate her life, coolly assessing the possibility of a Bradford seat. 'I am hesitating about it until I know more of the local situation. It is damnably far from London, and I am in no hurry, as the political situation is changing so quickly.' Her faith in the possibility of women being elected was strengthened in 1921 when she campaigned for Margaret Wintringham. In a letter to Wintringham after her election, Ray wrote: 'It makes the suffrage victory seem real and solid to find women in the remote villages so keen about politics and so thoroughly unprejudiced about women . . . '[55]

But Ray was fully aware that Margaret Wintringham had the advantage of a party affiliation strongly emphasised by her late husband's position as a Liberal MP. At the end of 1921 she was seriously considering standing for Chiswick again, and admitted that she would 'very much like to be in the next House.' A month later she had 'decided not to stand this time anyway. The only way to have any chance is to join a party, as you say, and the only one of the existing parties I could join is the Liberals, and I *hate* them!' Three months later she nearly stood in a by-election in Chertsey, but did not in the end because the chances were slim, and a committed Liberal candidate came forward. In Chertsey the alternative to standing as a Liberal had been to accept the backing of Lord Robert Cecil – with whom Ray was working in the League of Nations Union – as an independent. Ray described Lord Robert as the chief of a 'group of discontented conservatives', who were 'almost indistinguishable from Liberals'.[56]

With Lord Robert Cecil's backing Strachey was able to approach a possible candidature at Chiswick with thorough preparation. In order to 'settle the Chiswick question once and for all', she arranged for a survey to be done, 'a detailed study of a group of specimen streets, by which we shall find out what the ordinary average voter thinks. If it is unfavourable I won't try then at all. If it is favourable an influential local co. will be got together to invite me to stand.' The survey must have been encouraging, for two weeks later she wrote that she was expecting to be formally adopted in Chiswick by the end of July. Her confidence was justified and she enjoyed the campaign as she had her first one. When she was once again defeated, she wrote with determined cheerfulness to her more cynical mother:

> I have returned from the election, and am full of schemes. Those who know about such things are very well pleased with the result, and say it is thoroughly worth nursing – and they will find the cash to do so. It was of course a great bore not to do it all at a blow, but it was too much to hope for.[57]

She told her mother that she had no intention of settling down quietly to write novels, as she had 'got the political fever badly and can't seem to shake it off whatever happens.' Yet during the following year she almost shook it off. Two weeks after the 1922 election she was confessing that she was being encouraged to try again at Chiswick. 'But it's a frightful bore to go on nursing it indefinitely!' In the spring she went on a lecturing tour in the USA, and returned intending to 'keep Chiswick simmering', but with 'a slight sickness of the job' after what she had seen of American politics. In October she decided not to contest the next election, her chief reason being that she did not 'want to be in Parliament as I did a year ago'. Her distaste for the political game lingered until mid-November when she suddenly changed her mind after she was given financial backing by a group of women. She was also given such active support in her campaign that on the eve of the election, her 'only fear now is that I shall really get in!' She was defeated and her response was 'unrelieved relief. I woke up this morning feeling that the holidays had begun. Never to go to Chiswick again is itself a blessing . . .'[58]

When the next election was held a year later Strachey was on holiday in Greece. She felt that this absence taught her 'a very good lesson on the skin deepness of my detachment from politics.' Yet she never stood as a candidate again. Two months after the 1923 election a publisher asked her to write a 'history of the women's movement' and she agreed. Although she did not abandon her commitment either to the League of Nations Union or to the London Society, Ray Strachey became absorbed in her writing and detached from politics. In the summer of 1924 she wrote to Pippa that her hands were so full with her children that she was 'thankful I am not in Parliament.'[59]

In the mid-twenties feminists were being told, then as now, that there were more important matters for the attention of those who were in favour of reform than 'women's issues'. *The Woman's Leader* was aware that in such circumstances it was all the more vital, and requiring 'higher skill, grimmer forbearance' to 'carry on the struggle'.[60] But in the struggle for equality the effects of partial suffrage on the representation of women by women had been disappointing, and the defence of the position of women as wage-earners had proved complex. Equality was an elusive concept; women's interests when defined as in some way different from those of men seemed to have a more tangible appeal.

7 New and Old Feminists

In the spring of each year of the 1920s Eleanor Rathbone gave a presidential address to the Annual Council of the NUSEC. To read these speeches - which were later collected together under the title *Milestones* – is to follow a clearly marked path of feminism in the period. In March 1925, when reflecting on the stage which the National Union had reached and the decisions facing it, she introduced the concept of a 'new' feminism. The ideas contained within this phrase were not new; they had been running parallel to those of 'old' feminism for a generation. What was new and contentious was the open acceptance of the suggestion that individuals and organisations might have to make a choice between them.

Rathbone defended the objectives of new feminism on grounds that seemed to some feminists to undermine the demand for equality with men. Her analysis of equality in her speech led her to propose a redefinition of that concept which, she argued, would enrich the philosophy of feminism and prevent the 'once broad river of the NUSEC' from dwindling until it became 'a trickle', losing itself in the sands. She wanted its members to say:

At last we have done with the boring business of measuring everything that women want, or is offered them by men's standards, to see if it is exactly up to sample. At last we can stop looking at all our problems through men's eyes and discussing them in men's phraseology. We can demand what we want for women, not because it is what men have got, but because it is what women need to fulfil the potentialities of their own natures and to adjust themselves to the circumstances of their own lives.[1]

Other feminists could not agree that the struggle for equality had reached the stage where a shift of emphasis was desirable, nor did they accept Rathbone's redefinition. To many it seemed that such a redefinition constituted an acceptance of a world where gender differences were emphasised to the detriment of freedom and equal opportunities for women. For 'old' feminists, it was the emphasis on gender differences which had resulted in the drawing of a horizontal division between the genders, with men above and women below.[2]

In this chapter I shall look at the intricate patterns of thinking which lay behind what can be a somewhat facile division of feminists into the old and the new. Crucial to the debate were the political structures through which women worked and which were themselves the source of pressures and tensions. Party and class loyalty operating within and outside Parliament made demands on women whose force non-party women recognised and at times openly resented. Among the women who wrote and spoke about the different directions in which feminism was moving were Eva Hubback, Mary Stocks, Margery Corbett Ashby, Maude Royden, Margaret Rhondda and Rathbone herself. The silence of others arose partly from their absorption in their own work where the debate might appear irrelevant, but also from a distrust of theory, particularly where it seemed to divide, rather than unite, feminists. Behind the debate on the meanings of 'equality' and 'feminism', lay a continued determination to work together.

A QUESTION OF DEFINITION

Rathbone's call for the NUSEC to consider new departures was stimulated by the anticipation of legislative successes in the Parliamentary session of 1925 on Divorce, Widows' Pensions, and the Guardianship of Infants. There was agreement among feminists that there was a need for deliberation, reassessment, and a renewed sense of direction. In September 1925, an article in *Time & Tide* echoed Rathbone's words, suggesting that 'the women's movement has reached the stage when it must consider seriously the next step.'[3] In the first half of the 1920s there had been fairly close agreement on feminist priorities: in the second half the Six Point Group and the NUSEC diverged in part, though never wholly, in their objectives. The potential for differences in judgement as to the most effective way to continue the struggle for the emancipation of women had always been there. The question at issue was what the position of women in society should be, and the simple answer given by feminists was 'equality'. But equality seemed to many to require definition. The NUSEC had extended their search for equality when the object of the Union had been expanded to include 'such reforms as are necessary to make it possible for women adequately to discharge their functions as citizens'. This gloss on equality was in part an acknowledgement of the increasing involvement of individuals and

societies of the union in the campaigns to secure family endowment
and birth control advice. Rathbone's address to the NUSEC in 1925
immediately preceded the vote at the Annual Council which led to
the Union's acceptance of the principle of family endowment. In
the early 1920s her defence of this proposal was firmly rooted in
a claim for equality: in the second half of the decade her arguments
were challenged by other feminists.

Time & Tide did not at first criticise the involvement of feminists in the campaigns for family endowment and birth control.
Then towards the end of 1925 the paper began to express some
doubts about the priority given to such 'social reforms' by the
NUSEC. While recognising that the movement was 'faced with
new problems' and was 'beginning to venture along new lines:
Family Endowment, temperance, housing, peace, education, birth
control', the paper pointed out that the movement did not speak
with one voice on such issues, and warned that they should not
be 'hurriedly incorporated' in its programme.[4] The 1925 Annual
Council of the NUSEC had declared its support for birth control
and family endowment, but they were not yet part of its programme
for action. This move was made in 1926, and it was followed by a
tense, fiercely argued debate on the question on the pages of *Time
& Tide*.

In February 1926, the NUSEC amended its immediate programme
in the light of the legislative successes of the previous year. The
new programme placed equal franchise first, followed by the equal
moral standard, the election of more women to Parliament and local
authorities and then the achievement of equal pay and opportunities
in industry and the professions. The sixth and final objective was the
alteration of the law regarding the nationality of married women.[5] It
was the fifth objective which stirred up controversy. The demand for
family endowment and birth control information were bracketed in
this objective under the title 'Status of Wives and Mothers'. *Time and
Tide* responded very rapidly to these changes. Before they had been
reported in *The Woman's Leader*, a special feature on the NUSEC
council in the paper did not yet challenge the idea that the fifth
objective was a feminist one, but did suggest that it was not urgent:

At a moment when all efforts should be concentrated upon
achieving political equality it is regrettable to find one of the
important feminist bodies giving new emphasis to its intention
of dividing its energies into a dozen fields.[6]

Eleanor Rathbone's response to this criticism was published in *Time & Tide* two weeks later. In it she introduced a distinction which I shall look at later between feminism and equality. She also reacted somewhat irritably – as did Eva Hubback later that month – to the suggestion that the NUSEC was spreading itself too thinly and ought to concentrate its efforts on the achievement of equal franchise. She pointed out that the NUSEC had always placed 'the completion of our Franchise' at the top of its agenda, while the Six Point Group had only included it as one of its aims in the previous year. Rathbone added that she did not doubt the sincerity of the group's commitment, and we shall see that the two organisations did work effectively together towards equal franchise during the next two years. The friction underlying this correspondence was that between the NUSEC as an organisation which could claim a long tradition of patient lobbying, and the Six Point Group as a newer, smaller and less disparate body. The old feminists connected with the Six Point Group and *Time & Tide* accused the new feminists of being 'sanguine' in their assessment of success in the struggle for 'liberty and equality of action and status' for women. Yet it was often the old feminist who was impatient. Winifred Holtby declared that she was an old feminist because she disliked all that feminism implied, and wanted an end to the whole business so that she could get on with her own work. Margaret Rhondda shared this impatience to be finished with the 'heap of niggling little laws that needed altering'. It was not, she later confessed, 'really my kind of work: it never had been. I was never really much interested in changing details of laws. I want bigger game than that.'[7]

Eva Hubback had been working on a day-to-day basis to change 'niggling little laws', and her response to both the criticism and the impatience was understandably indignant. She accused Holtby of underestimating 'not only the actual achievements which had been reached . . . ', but also 'the struggle which has resulted in these achievements . . . '. Holtby had observed that there were 'significant signs of a reawakening of Feminism from the six years' lassitude which followed the partial success of 1918'. Hubback retorted: 'There has been no lassitude among organisations such as the NUSEC who are now widening their range to include New Feminism.' While Hubback, Rathbone, Stocks and others saw this extension of its aims as reinvigorating, *Time & Tide* repeatedly warned against the weakening of the 'woman's movement' if it continued:

to spread itself thin over any number of social activities which are in no way concerned with equality, if it continues to allow the energies which ought to be concentrated on achieving equality to be diverted into every fresh reform that happens to take its fancy.[8]

Time & Tide was moving towards a sort of streamlining of feminism. Eleanor Rathbone, partly in response to this move, was concerned to widen the feminist definition of equality. In the letter referred to above and published in *Time & Tide* in Marsh 1926 she wrote:

As I see it, the woman's movement comprises a large number of reforms, all of which are 'feminism', but only some of them 'equality'.

Rathbone warned that even when the reforms concerned with equality had been put into effect, the 'aim of enabling women to be and do their best will not have been accomplished'. On the same day in an article in *The Woman's Leader*, she defined feminism as 'The demand of women that the whole structure and movement of society shall reflect in proportionate degree their experiences, their needs and their aspirations.' Eva Hubback agreed, and asserted that:

All Feminists whether 'new' or 'old' unite in striving to 'restrict to a minimum the department of life where sex differentiation obtains.' But the new Feminist recognises that sex differences – i.e. different needs and a different outlook – must prevail in that most important of women's occupations, maternity.[9]

Time & Tide refused to accept this argument. An article in October 1926 commented favourably on the efforts of women in the Labour movement to get the question on the agenda of the party conference, but firmly states that 'information as to artificial methods of birth control has nothing whatever to do with feminism'. Not all readers of the paper agreed with this judgement, and a letter from Edith How Martyn in the following month challenged it:

I very much enjoy reading *Time & Tide*, but my pleasure would be still greater if you would not carp and criticise the NUSEC for their activities which you do not consider feminist. This is especially regrettable in the case of Birth Control, which is the one thing which puts women on a real sex equality with men.[10]

The division of feminism into the old and the new seemed to many to be, as a writer in *The Woman's Leader* put it, 'largely academic'.[11] Yet in the spring of 1927 a division within the NUSEC took place at the Annual Council Meeting, a division made all the more painful in that *Time & Tide* gave it extensive coverage and offered unqualified support to one side. The split was the result of two issues which came before the council. One of these was the question of protective legislation which we will look at more closely later in this chapter; the other was concerned with the definition of equality. Although the two issues are not clearly separable, the strength of feeling and complexity of thinking on each makes it more intelligible to deal with them separately.

The crucial event at the meeting was the resignation of eleven of the twenty-four newly elected members of the executive committee. No one of them has been central to this book, although Chrystal MacMillan has appeared several times. Those who resigned included the Honorary Secretary, Lady Balfour, and the Honorary Treasurer, Winifred Soddy. The chief spokeswoman for the group was Elizabeth Abbott. The disagreement over the interpretation of equality occurred when an amendment was proposed to a resolution which had clearly placed the achievement of 'real equality of liberties, status and opportunity between men and women', above the 'secondary function' of the Union, which was 'to secure such reforms . . . as are necessary to make it possible for women adequately to discharge their functions as citizens'. The amendment, which was moved by Kathleen Courtney, defined family allowances, the availability of birth control information and support for and involvement in the League of Nations in the first category as equality measures, not as reforms. The amendment was carried by 'a large majority'. The eleven members who had opposed the amendment resigned because they felt that they could not work within the NUSEC in the direction they wished while remaining members of the Executive, 'bound to carry out the policy laid down by the Annual Council'.[12]

The decision of the resigning members to remain within the NUSEC, and the conciliatory tone of the correspondence in *The Woman's Leader* about the split, is indicative of the reluctance of the two groups to emphasise the importance of the resignations. Two articles in which the protagonists presented their views before the Council Meeting were printed in *The Woman's Leader* three weeks before the meeting. Eleanor Rathbone began the presentation of her case with an acknowledgement that 'no two members of the NUSEC or of the other women's societies working for equal citizenship, would put exactly the same interpretation' on the 'formula' contained in the object of the NUSEC. Her argument was that to work for equality in a world constructed by men was to accept that 'men are always, so to speak, the measuring tape for women.' The world which women found themselves in was 'planned, laid out, built over by men to suit their own conceptions and needs.' In this world women's experience of marriage and parenthood was different from men's, so that the interest of women in 'questions such as birth control, family allowances, housing, smoke abatement . . . is both more extensive and more intensive than that of men.'

The main thrust of Elizabeth Abbott's argument lay in her concern over the weakening, as she saw it, of the NUSEC's commitment to equality of pay and opportunities at work. She understood the difference in attitude towards what she saw as 'social reforms' as part of this turning away from a prior and essential commitment to the 'demand for the removal of every arbitrary impediment that hinders the progress, in any realm of life and work, of women'. She argued that 'New Feminism' accepted that women were not and could not be equal, and that it tried to make 'the inequality of women as well-built and secure and comfortable as possible' – according to its own views of comfort and security. Abbott faced the critical issue of maternity and contended:

> 'New Feminism' sees in maternity an eternal disability – just as anti-suffragism saw eternal disability in other generalizations such as 'sex', 'motherhood', 'the home'. The equalitarian knows that it is not maternity in itself which is the disability; it is the horribly low and unequal status of woman; the everlasting conception of her as a means to an end instead of as an end in herself, that makes not only maternity but sometimes every hour of a woman's day a disability.[13]

Mary Stocks offered an answer to Abbott in a later issue of *The Woman's Leader*. She supported Rathbone's contention that there could be no real equality for women if they were merely offered equal opportunities in 'a State whose conception of what kind of liberties and opportunities are necessary, has been determined almost exclusively by men'. She suggested that to fight only for equality in areas defined by men was to accept men's evaluation of what jobs were worth doing. She wanted feminists to challenge the idea that those jobs 'which command social prestige and economic independence, the ability to fight or to engage uninterruptedly in the production of exchangeable wealth', were more important than the care of children.[14]

Elizabeth Abbott spoke at the council meeting and her speech was given warm support by *Time & Tide*. Abbott had implied that the NUSEC's policy was no longer feminist; *Time & Tide* stated this categorically in an article entitled 'A Deep Cleavage'. The article prompted an indignant reply from Eva Hubback; she wrote that the NUSEC 'is becoming accustomed to a regular campaign of misrepresentation in your columns.' While Hubback challenged the accuracy of the article, a letter from Mary Stocks defended the record of the NUSEC – and of Eleanor Rathbone in particular – as an organisation which had 'successfully initiated a number of equalitarian reforms', and had 'kept the flag of equal franchise flying year in year out, and at times when less tenacious suffragists have thought the occasion not yet ripe'. She offered this record as an answer to the accusation that the NUSEC was not feminist. Mary Stocks was a committed exponent of the 'new feminism'. Later that same year she wrote *The Case for Family Endowment* in which she located the argument for endowment firmly 'in its place as a feminist claim for sex equality'. She claimed in a letter to Marie Stopes that the split in the NUSEC 'was bound to come'. In phrases which are reminiscent of Ray Strachey's on the wartime split in the Union, she wrote:

> Well – we have got rid of the pure 'Equalitarians' on the Executive, and though it is rather a drastic purge, I for one am not altogether sorry to be rid of them.[15]

In public Mary Stocks had asked feminists to be more tolerant of nonconformity. This plea was partly stimulated by the need for a united front in the final stages of the struggle to achieve equal franchise. It also reflected the sensitivity of the new feminists to the beliefs, feelings and practices of the societies which constituted the NUSEC. Throughout the 1920s there was a decline in the membership of the NUSEC, and it was inevitable and understandable that the officers of the Union should wish to consider the best way of maintaining the size and commitment of its membership. Suggestions as to different ways to attract new members appear in the leader pages of *The Woman's Leader* and in Eleanor Rathbone's presidential addresses. In 1921 she spoke of the 'complaint we hear so often from the officers of our societies that they find it difficult to sustain the interest of their members in our programme, or to attract new recruits'. In 1925 her advocacy of the new feminism was buttressed by the need to arouse 'enthusiasm and attract new recruits'. In 1926 she suggested that the 'watchword of Equality has lost much of its potency for the younger generation, which has never known the harsher forms of inequality'. Later that year *The Woman's Leader* asked: 'Why is the political pressure exerted by women so weak?' One of the reasons seemed to be that women were not attending the meetings of societies affiliated to the NUSEC. The paper suggested that the societies might be neglecting the ordinary members, and advocated that they hold meetings where members could discuss 'local issues of current concern,' instead of having fixed agendas and 'known' speakers.[16]

The majorities in favour of the extension of the programme support Rathbone's judgement that members of the NUSEC were attracted by a programme which went beyond the demand for legal equality. Elizabeth Abbott felt and spoke with passion about the denial to women of 'the most precious of all things in any State, personal rights and liberties.' On this question the Union was indeed united: the final demonstrations in favour of equal franchise showed that other women shared her passion on that issue. On the other aims to which the old feminists were committed – 'equal rights and conditions and opportunities for the industrial woman' – there was more ambivalence and less clarity of purpose and direction. Active feminists in the 1920s found it hard to accept that the passionate and widespread support for the suffrage movement could dissipate and be defused when they could see that the struggle for equality was not complete. They wanted to recreate the ardour and zeal of the suffrage movement, and to some it seemed that the issues of birth control, family endowment and peace offered something of the same intensity, and anticipation of success. The struggle to improve the pay and conditions of working women did not.

Another explanation for the support for new feminism evident in the voting at the NUSEC Annual Council suggested by *Time & Tide* was a lack of understanding among delegates of 'what lay behind the resolutions'. This somewhat patronising suggestion does not ring true of delegates who had been involved in debates on the issues for many years. They applauded Elizabeth Abbott enthusiastically, but they did not agree with the judgement of those who resigned that 'the decisions of the Council show an increasing tendency to overlook the fundamental object of the Union – equal status with men'. They certainly would have challenged the assertion of *Time & Tide* that 'their vote was in fact a vote against equality'. *Time & Tide* itself was not consistent on the question of whether birth control and family endowment were feminist issues. In an article on the National Conference of Labour Women held in May 1927, the paper offered as evidence of feminism the support given for resolutions on birth control and family endowment.[17]

It is also apparent from letters to *Time & Tide* and *The Woman's Leader* that some members of the Union did not feel the need to make a choice between activities, nor that the choice of new feminism implied a rejection of true feminism. Edith How Martyn wrote to *Time & Tide* about her position on the question:

> As an Equalitarian I find myself agreeing with Mrs. Abbott's definition of Equality . . . .
> As one anxious to realise this equality, I soon find myself ranged as an ardent supporter of Miss Eleanor Rathbone and the NUSEC. Their work is essentially removing the arbitrary impediments that hinder the progress in the lives and work of women. The largest section of women are married women without servants and knowledge of reliable contraceptive measures and a practical system of family endowment with equal guardianship of children will bring that group of women more real equality with men than ever the franchise achieved.
> We want both equality and the new feminism, and can work for both simultaneously. It is well for Societies to specialise and for individuals to choose which they prefer.[18]

Helen Ward emphasised in a letter to *Time & Tide* that the amendment proposed by Courtney was an addition to the original resolution, not a substitute for it. She agreed that there was an 'important point at issue', but argued that it was not 'between "social reformers" and "feminists", but between different groups of feminists themselves.'[19]

A letter from Dorothy Balfour, another of those who resigned, illustrates the narrowness of the gap between the two groups in the NUSEC. But her letter also reveals the doubts in the mind of a young feminist as to the sincerity of the new feminist's commitment to equality. She did not reject, indeed she wrote that she had welcomed, the reforms advocated by the new feminist, but could only accept them – however valuable in themselves – 'in so far as they conduce to the quicker realization of Equality'. She accused new feminists of accepting 'the theory of Equality only in so far as it will help towards the achievement of the particular Social Reforms advocated by its supporters'. Referring to the warnings of 'old hands' that acceptance of such reforms had led to the 'weakening and the final petering out of groups', she declared that she 'would far rather see these valuable reforms swept off the N.U. programme altogether than see the keen edge of our Equality sword blunted by the inclusions of these and other reforms.'[20]

'AS FRAGILE AS A HUMMING BIRD'S EGG'

Disagreement over what was meant by equality led feminists to diverge. They chose separate paths, some convinced that other paths were leading in the wrong direction, but many of them feeling that it was a question of choosing different routes to the same goal. Over the question of the protection of industrial women at work there was again theoretical agreement about eventual aims, but the choice of strategies differed. It was a matter, according to *The Woman's Leader*, 'of interpretation or tactics, rather than of principle'.[21] The issue became contentious partly because of the distrust bred by the controversy over equality, and partly because of the position taken by organisations which represented women who worked in industry. Those who spoke on behalf of women working in industry accepted the principle that any legislation which controlled or restricted conditions at work should apply equally to men and women, but they were often unable to see men and women workers in the same light. They believed that a woman's chief interest lay in her role as wife and mother. In such a role a woman had traditionally required protection.

The question of who could or should speak for industrial women on protective legislation again exposed the lack of confidence and cohesion in feminism on class issues. The division of opinion was not strictly on class lines, for women trade union organisers were often middle-class, but those organisers argued that feminists outside the Labour Movement had no direct knowledge or experience of the needs of industrial women and should not speak for them. Moreover, where the question of protective legislation touched on the wider issue of women's employment and pay opportunities and challenged the position of men, class and gender divisions could coincide explosively.[22]

The debate over protective legislation for women in industry had its roots in the Victorian age. The investigation of children's employment in mines had revealed a use of women's labour which had so shocked Victorians that women were included in the resulting legislation. In practice such laws were not enforced for many years, but the idea had been born that women, like children, should not be exposed to the worst evils of industrial working conditions. The reaction of women to the Mines Act and later legislation depended on a variety of factors: those whose working lives were affected welcomed better conditions but opposed restrictions which prevented them getting jobs. Feminists became involved in debates on the issue from the late 1870s, calling for no restrictive legislation on the basis of sex. Women involved in the trade union movement were more ambivalent: they were acutely aware that conditions at work were so bad that to resist protection for women was to expose them to danger and even death.[23]

During the controversy within the NUSEC, family endowment became linked to the question of protective legislation. There was no direct connection, but the argument that family endowment was a feminist issue suggested to those who did not agree that a whole ideology of protection was involved. This was not in fact the case. Eleanor Rathbone, Mary Stocks and Eva Hubback had all done voluntary work with mothers struggling to make ends meet on a low income and their support for endowment was based on their desire to help such women. They had no similar experience of, or contact with, women in industry. Eleanor Rathbone's ideas had at first challenged the idea of the living wage for the breadwinner – assumed to be a man – which was widely accepted among men and women trade unionists. It later became absorbed by it, as the demand for endowment of motherhood was transformed into the concept of family allowances. Her original formulation had been crucially linked to the question of equal pay, and we have seen that the issue of equal pay was one where feminists found themselves opposed to those who believed that its implementation could drive women out of industrial jobs. Although they accepted the theory of equal pay and were opposed to protective legislation, Rathbone, Hubback and Stocks did not feel strongly or personally on such questions and tended to accept the judgement of others. They felt that they could speak for mothers, and that others – women in the labour movement – would speak for workers.

The war had provided an impetus for middle-class women to think and talk about the question of women's employment. After women had been rapidly moved out of industry the topic became of less apparent political interest. The views of feminists were no longer publicised, and possibly no longer so confidently expressed. None of the women in our study was deeply involved in the controversy. Catherine Marshall had some knowledge and interest in the women working in industry, but she was committed to international affairs by this period. Maude Royden had spoken after the war on the position of women in industry, but afterwards she too no longer felt that she could speak on such topics. Ray Strachey's involvement in the London Society for Women's Service had continued, but this organisation was not involved with the employment in industry. Ray was at the crucial Council meeting, although she confessed to feeling 'detached from these matters'. Chrystal Macmillan was again actively involved, and the woman who was the leader of the campaign against protective legislation was Elizabeth Abbott. She had founded the Open Door Council in 1926 with the express aim that 'a woman shall be free to work and protected as a worker on the same terms as a man'.[24]

The position of the NUSEC on the question of protective legislation was at first unequivocal, with women who would later be divided on the issue working closely together. In the summer of 1924, when the Labour Government proposed to introduce a Factories Bill which would offer shorter working hours to women only, Chrystal Macmillan proposed that letters should be sent to MPs and the Press setting forth 'the opposition of the National Union to legislation which imposes restrictions with regard to the sex of the worker rather than to the nature of the work'. Her motion was seconded by Margery Corbett Ashby. In the following March *Time & Tide* noted approvingly that the Annual Council of the NUSEC had voted decisively on the issue, manifesting 'no compromise, undiluted feminism'. Warnings of a potential controversy had been given by Helen Ward earlier that same month, and she advocated an open discussion of the issue. At the Annual Conference of the NUSEC in the following year a 'special conference at the close of the first day was held on the subject'. Helen Ward spoke against 'sex restrictions'. The main speakers opposing her were not delegates to the conference, but women involved in the trade union movement.

On the following day, 'the Council with no uncertain voice reaffirmed its opinion that legislation for the protection of workers should be based not upon sex but upon the nature of the work'.[25]

Meanwhile Margery Corbett Ashby was active within the Liberal Party in opposing any further restrictions on women's work, although she did accept the need for the protection of pregnant and nursing mothers. On the need for special regulations for pregnant women, the NUSEC felt that it was not:

a feminist issue at all, but merely a question of cruelty to children. If a man had an infant fastened to him by a chain and on the ground that he was a free citizen he went for his usual swim before breakfast on a December morning, he would be found guilty of murder unless the doctors succeeded in getting him off on the score of insanity.[26]

With this caveat the NUSEC remained staunchly opposed to restrictive legislation, as did the London Society for Women's Service. When the Parliamentary session ended, Eva Hubback recorded her disappointment in the lack of success of women's organisations in trying to ensure that the Lead Paint Bill applied to men as well as women. This Bill, which passed into law at the end of the year, enlarged on a clause in the Factories Bill which had been defeated on second reading. It extended an earlier Act of 1920 which had forbidden the employment of women in the preparation of lead-based paints, to exclude women from painting buildings using such paints.[27]

Helen Ward wrote a forceful criticism of the Factories Bill which, she maintained, consolidated the attitude that 'the moment a woman engages in a "gainful occupation" she becomes fragile as a humming bird's egg'. In November another conference was called by the NUSEC to consider the question: 'What is the Real Protection for the Women Worker?' The speakers opposing protection included Elizabeth Abbott, Ray Strachey, Helen Ward and Vera Brittain. A leading article in *The Woman's Leader* published after the conference was firmly opposed to protective legislation, but it did refer to the fact that the Standing Joint Committee of Industrial Women's Organisations had 'asked the Government to amend the Factories Bill in a sense that would impose further restrictions on the work of women'.[28] *Time & Tide* provided an explanation for the attitude of the SJCIWO which showed an understanding of the quandary of those who represented women in industry. The paper suggested that they were suspicious of:

the feminist outlook, because they felt that by opposing special protective legislation they are playing into the hands of the die-hards, who are glad enough of excuses to delay any improvement in factory legislation, and because they fear that a demand for equality would result in depriving them of advantages which some of them have already gained.

The author asserted that in fact protection was likely to be given as a substitute for equal pay.[29]

A case for protection was presented by Ellen Wilkinson to yet another debate on the question. The influence of women such as Wilkinson, who could with some justice claim to speak for working-class women, pushed the NUSEC into compromising their firm position on protective legislation. At the Annual Council of the NUSEC in 1926 Mary Stocks had moved a resolution on restrictive legislation which allowed for the possibility that such legislation 'may be in the best interests' of the workers concerned. In her speech she referred to the support given to protection by women such as Margaret Bondfield and Marion Phillips. *Time & Tide* commented:

> the chief argument of those who supported Mrs. Stocks (among them were Miss Rathbone and Mrs. Ayrton Gould) appeared to be based on the fact that middle-class women had no right to interfere with the concerns of working women.[30]

This was the argument that had been put forward in an attack on feminist attitudes to restrictive legislation in *The Labour Woman*. *Time & Tide* asserted that this argument was fallacious both because the women in the Labour Party 'who would appear to arrogate to themselves the right to speak in the name of the industrial women, are for the most part drawn from exactly the same class as are the leaders of the NUSEC,' and because – outside the Women's Co-operative Guild – there was 'no real woman's movement within the Labour Party'. Mary Stocks's resolution was opposed by Ray Strachey and Helen Ward, and it was lost by a large majority.[31]

The pressure to take note of the views of women in the Labour Movement remained despite this defeat. The resolution which was passed at the Annual Council in 1927 was interpreted by those who subsequently resigned from the executive committee as a dilution of the NUSEC's opposition to protective legislation. A resolution before the council reaffirmed 'its conviction that legislation for the protection of the workers should be based, not upon sex, but upon the nature of the occupation', and directed the Executive Committee to decide in any particular instance of proposed regulation 'whether to work for the extension of the regulation to both sexes or to oppose it for both sexes'. But an amendment proposed by Eleanor Rathbone was passed by 81 votes to 80. It called on the committee to take three factors into account when deciding which option to choose; one of these factors was whether 'the workers affected desire the regulation and are promoting it through their organisations'. Given the views of the industrial women's organisations, it was assumed by those who resigned that this clause was intended to 'whittle down' the Union's commitment. They asserted that:

> To make the wishes of those affected by any law or reform a test of its merits would result in stagnation. That 'the women concerned do not want it' is our old friend, the perennial anti-feminist argument. It has been used against suffrage, against education, against admission to local government, against the fight of married women to control their own property, against every improvement in the status of women.[32]

Eva Hubback refused to accept this interpretation of the amendment. She reacted angrily to the assertion in *Time & Tide* that 'Miss Rathbone's amendment, in the spirit if not in the letter, amounted to a declaration in favour of protective legislation for women.' Hubback's interpretation of the amending clause was that the additional factors, including 'the welfare and wishes of the worker', would be taken into consideration when making a choice between 'whether to work for the extension or for the elimination of any given regulation for both sexes'. It did not in her mind imply that legislation applying only to women would be acceptable. The LSWS executive passed a resolution pressing the NUSEC to hold another Council meeting specifically on the subject of protective legislation, but Ray reported back that the resolution which had led to the division was in fact 'staunchly egalitarian', and therefore a special Council might be 'counterproductive'. Whether the editorial group agreed with this interpretation or not, *Time & Tide* did cease to press the issue, and the controversy died down without any further open hostility. *The Woman's Leader* continued to oppose protection for women workers and gave space to the activities of the Open Door Council. The paper continued to challenge the views of those who were prepared to accept restrictive legislation, even in the short

term. In April 1927 Eva Hubback wrote to *Time & Tide* pointing
out that the NUSEC was promoting two bills which were opposed
to limiting protection in industry to women, and asking for the help
of the paper's readers, and that of the Open Door Council.[33]

Whatever the intention of those who introduced the amendment
to the resolution, the controversy over the 'new feminism' and
protective legislation had damaged the alliance between feminist
organisations. The National Union of Women Teachers disaffiliated
from the NUSEC in July 1926 on the grounds that affiliation 'seemed
to lead to confusion as to the exact position of the NUWT as an
independent organisation,' and that it 'did not find itself in agreement with the Immediate Programme and policy of the NUSEC'.
The NUWT continued to work with the Six Point Group, and
together with the Open Door Council and the Women's Freedom
League, they sponsored the attendance of Elizabeth Abbott at the
International Labour Organisations Conference in the summer of
1928. The NUSEC, to its open disappointment, was not involved
in this cooperative effort.[34]

The rupture which was not healed was a political one and
one which was made more painful by 'class passion' which Vera
Brittain, in an article on the question, deplored, but could not
escape. The association of feminism with middle-class interests and
aspirations has dogged the women's movement from the time when
class became a social and political concept. Feminists resisted such
an interpretation. As *Time & Tide* firmly states:

> It is as ridiculous as it is impossible to segregate women into
> classes and to tell one class that it has no right to take any interest
> in the doings or the restrictions placed on another class . . . . What
> happens to the woman who works with her hands does affect, and
> affect vitally, the woman who works with her head.[35]

There have always been areas where the interests of working-class
women are perceived as shaped more by their class than their
gender. Yet it is in precisely these areas – pay, conditions of
work, the production of wealth – where men have articulated the
needs of the working-class, not women. In the 1920s there were
women in the Labour Movement like Ellen Wilkinson and Marion
Phillips who spoke for their working-class sisters, but they worked
alongside men in their daily lives and were strongly influenced by
their male colleagues. The absorption of the National Federation of
Women Workers and the Women's Trade Union League into the

male-dominated structures of the trade union movement made it that much more difficult for women to draw strength from each other, and to develop their ideas without male influence or interference. An indication of the power of solidarity between women operating to assist the achievement of feminist aims is found in the way women MPs worked together. Women MPs were bonded by their visibility and the provision of separate accommodation in Westminster. There were disagreements and occasions when party loyalty was stronger, but to a significant extent they cooperated with each other. This cooperation took place despite the fact that the party structures outside Westminster militated against women working together towards feminist aims. The attitude and relationship of feminists to political parties was a crucial factor in shaping the contours of the women's movement in the 1920s.

'PUT NOT YOUR TRUST IN PARTIES'

The separation of the NUSEC from women in the Labour Movement was mutually damaging and it was regretted by many women. In 1921 Marion Phillips appealed as Woman's Officer to women in the Labour Party to have nothing to do with those who 'come to them in the guise of friends and ask them to cooperate in regard to certain individual parts of the Labour Party's Programme'. Among these 'undesirable friends' was the NUSEC. In response *The Woman's Leader* defended the value of cooperation between 'women of different views and different experience', and warned that if Labour women were not represented in non-party organisations then 'expressions of anti-labour opinion and misunderstandings of the Labour case within their ranks will go unchallenged'. In another article in the same issue the paper recognised that there was a temptation to avoid 'distracting and contaminating contact with women of other parties, in whose company the Labour woman may feel more conscious of the economic and social differences which divide, than of the feminist affinities which unite'.[36]

The separation of Labour woman from feminist was extended to the Women's Co-operative Guild. In the view of *The Woman's Leader* the Guild was 'perhaps the most significant social factor in the lives of the great mass of married working women . . . . It is an incomparable organization. If any body is qualified by tradition and function to reflect in national life "the woman's point of view", that body is the Co-operative Guild.' Yet the Guild had adopted a policy of withdrawing from affiliation with 'any organizations except those of working-class women in sympathy with the Labour Party, and the Guild branches no longer allow their members to remain on committees of the NUSEC.' The author of the article stoutly refused to be put off by this embargo which, she reckoned, was:

> like a precisely similar embargo imposed on its women by the Labour Party, merely a piece of advice issued from headquarters . . . . Its members may take it or leave it. And to our certain knowledge many of them do, in fact, leave it – with considerable benefit to their own more abundant life and to the non-party organizations whom they elect, in defiance of party orthodoxy, to serve.

The article finished strongly with a call to its readers 'to repudiate all such advice as imposes barriers or sows distrust between the women of classes, creeds or countries'.[37]

Officially the NUSEC was a non-party organisation but many members had strong links with the Labour Movement. A structural link had existed before the war which was formally severed but emotionally retained. The high expectations of the Labour Government elected in 1923 were partly the result of this bond, and there was disappointment when it did not live up to those expectations. Both the Six Point Group and the NUSEC gave support and encouragement to women candidates for election and to women MPs. Members of the Six Point Group gave personal help to candidates, but the support given by the NUSEC was on an institutional and financial level more extensive. Sometimes either the local society or the local party were not entirely happy about cooperation. During the election campaign in the autumn of 1924 problems were reported to the executive over the candidature of Edith Picton Turberville. Dorothy Auld, who was employed in the NUSEC office, worked for her campaign in Stroud, but local affiliated societies were afraid 'that public opinion would label the NUSEC as being Labour in sympathy'. The NUSEC recognised the difficulties facing the woman voter who was:

> not faced with the direct question: do I care so much for my feminist programme that I am ready for its sake to deliver up my country to the chaos of Socialism, or the stagnation of Conservatism – as the case may be? She is far more likely to be faced with the question: would I be glad to see the party whose

general programme I detest minutely strengthened by the addition of a woman whose presence in the House will improve the status of women in all parties and give a very much increased percentage of strength to all the non-party questions in which I, as a woman, am interested?[38]

The Six Point Group kept a much greater distance from all political parties. In 1923 *Time & Tide* had forecast that it was the 'strength of non-party women's organisations rather than the number of women attached to party organisations which is likely to decide the amount of interest taken by the parties in women's questions'. As the decade progressed, the paper became increasingly cynical about the position of women inside the political parties on issues of gender equality. Reporting the annual party conferences in May, 1927, the paper complained:

one subject of vital importance to women is almost completely ignored by all parties – equal pay and equal opportunities for women. Next to equal franchise it is, in fact, the most important question affecting women, and yet the party-women seem hardly aware of its existence.[39]

An explanation for the halfheartedness of Labour women's commitment to feminism was offered in the next month's issue. In a leading article the paper suggested that a failure of the National Conference of Labour Women to move beyond 'immediate concrete causes of underpayment, or injustice', to the long-term evils of protective legislation or unequal pay, was 'inevitable for those who are greatly pressed by the immediate considerations of trade organisation or working life'.[40]

The deteriorating relationship between members of feminist organisations and the Labour Party made it increasingly difficult for women to remain active members of both. In 1924 Barbara Ayrton Gould 'had found herself unable to use non-party help', but had been sent a car and a chauffeur from Liverpool. Earlier that year she had been active in promoting the principle of equal guardianship in the central committees of the Labour Party, but she had not succeeded in persuading it to adopt a more feminist position on the issue. In January 1926, she resigned from the executive of the NUSEC because of 'lack of time to attend meetings'. Yet feminist faith in the Labour Party died slowly. In 1929 Helena Swanwick was shocked when a young man at a Labour Party meeting warned her against trying to 'turn the Labour Movement into a Feminist Movement'. In my innocence I had assumed that the Labour Party did not need 'turning' towards feminism, in any sense of the word; that, indeed, it was the only really feminist political party in this country, and it was this circumstance that led so many old suffragists to join the Labour Party.[41]

A political polarisation was taking place in the 1920s, making it increasingly difficult for non-party feminists to work with those committed to a particular political party. The event which most vividly illustrated this polarisation is the General Strike of May 1926. The Labour Party itself was split on the question at the time, so that the divisions are not clear, but the fear and the anger which the strike aroused made it all the more difficult for non-party or cross-party alliances to survive. The reactions of middle-class feminists to the strike were moderate, pacific – and distressed. The behaviour of both sides provided a further impetus for feminists to distance themselves from party passions and allegiances from which they felt alienated. Maude Royden declared that she was sympathetic to the strikers, but asked naively that 'there be no talk of victory or defeat, but simply of reconciliation.' Helena Swanwick spoke at a meeting of women's organisations chaired by Courtney which called for an end to the strike. Swanwick was a Labour supporter, but she was infuriated by the fact that the strikers included the printers so that the Government newssheet was the main source of information.[42]

Evelyn Sharp believed that 'the capitalists have been preparing for this a very long time.' Once provoked she thought that the strikers were making a revolution with which she sympathised, but saw and understood from a distance. Her attitude is quite different from someone like Ellen Wilkinson who was actively and passionately involved. Interestingly, although Sharp had cut herself off from feminist organisations in the 1920s, her assessment of the strike reveals a feminist perspective. She compared the strike with the suffrage struggle which she understood as a non-violent revolution:

How familiar it all sounds to an old suffragette! But there is this great difference between this fight and the women's – women are much better at passive resistance than men and when finally provoked to violence can be trusted not to take life. Now the men are not nearly so likely to remain passive and their violence is of the kind that will provoke force of the worst kind from the other side.[43]

'IT WAS AN OBSTINATE HILL'TO CLIMB'[44]

For feminists in the 1920s there was no escaping the uncomfortable
conclusion that whether working inside a political party or in
a non-party organisation they could expect no radical changes.
Eleanor Rathbone and Eva Hubback wrote a letter to the House
of Lords on the question of equal franchise in May 1928. In it
they comforted those noble lords who feared that 'because women
outnumber men their enfranchisement would give them political
supremacy', by suggesting they 'consider the way in which eight
million women enfranchised in 1918 have divided themselves up
among the various political parties'. It was apparent, they pointed
out, that 'a woman's party is the very last thing wanted by women
themselves'.[45] A woman's party had been advocated by only a very
few, but many more feminists had hoped that women would make
a much greater impact both within existing political structures, and
through feminist organisations.

The need to reassure members of the House of Lords arose
from the imminent, although belated, attainment of equal franchise.
Efforts to achieve equal franchise for women were made consistently
during the ten years between the 1918 Act and the final victory in
the summer of 1928. After early hopes of rapid success the NUSEC
had settled down to patient, low-key lobbying. The election of
the Labour Government had brought renewed optimism for this
as for other objectives of the Union. Disappointment was acute
when, instead of the government measure which 'we had reason
confidently to expect (were it not that old suffragists have learnt
to expect nothing), we found ourselves confronted with a debate on
a Private Member's Bill . . . '. The Government's half-heartedness
led Rathbone to ask, angrily: 'has a party in office no responsibility
towards its principles and past professions and pledges?'[46]

The return of a Conservative majority at the end of the year
did not augur well for equal franchise. Commenting on the
prospects for 1925 Eva Hubback warned that Equal Franchise
was the reform advocated by the NUSEC which was least likely
to be achieved. She noted that although Baldwin had committed
himself to support for 'equal political rights' during the election
campaign, he was leading a party of which a third at least was
opposed to equal franchise. Fears of a sudden expansion of the
'least experienced and least trustworthy part of the electorate' had
been expressed by Conservative MPs during the 1924 debate, so that

there was a possibility that the extension of the franchise would be limited to women over 25.[47]

Success on other issues in the 1925 session made the NUSEC grimly determined to keep up the pressure. An article on 'The Woman's Programme in 1926' reminded readers that successes were the 'fruits of hard and prolonged grinding labour year in and year out – how hard and how prolonged only those who are behind the scenes can ever know'.[48] These words may well have been directed at the Six Point Group which in 1926 placed 'Equal Political Rights' as the first of its demands. A wide variety of women's organisations emphasised their commitment to the cause of equal franchise in that year. The fifth biennial conference of The Women's International League for Peace and Freedom passed a resolution confirming its commitment to the view that a preliminary step to peace was the achievement of complete citizenship and absolutely equal rights by women. The Women's Freedom League, for whom equal franchise had always been a top priority, organised a meeting in January, which was followed by a 'Mass meeting' held by the NUSEC at which Maude Royden was one of the chief speakers. The Six Point Group held a dinner and reception at the Hyde Park Hotel in March, at which Emmeline Pankhurst was the guest of honour.

The climax of this manifestation of feeling on the issue occurred on 3 July. On that day a demonstration brought together forty women's organisations in a procession from the Embankment to a mass meeting in Hyde Park. The names of the leading speakers – speaking from twelve platforms! – read like a roll-call of suffragists from every political and feminist persuasion. They included Emmeline Pankhurst and Millicent Garrett Fawcett, the women who symbolised the two main branches of the suffrage movement. They were now elderly, and frail: Pankhurst died in 1928 and Fawcett a year later. The solidarity of Labour with feminist women on this issue at least was demonstrated by the presence of Margaret Dondfield and Ellen Wilkinson. Wilkinson argued that it was working-class women in particular who were disenfranchised after the 1918 Act because the continued residence qualification for women affected them more than middle-class women. Finally, Margaret Rhondda and Eleanor Rathbone demonstrated the unity of postwar feminist organisations.[49]

This unity was not totally without strain. Articles in *Time & Tide* suggested that the demonstration of 3 July showed that the women's movement had shaken off 'the political lassitude left by the war-years'. The paper warned against a tendency to 'spread itself thin in widespread social activities', to 'rest on its oars'. The NUSEC was understandably irritated at this advice, and especially the implied dismissal of its efforts since the war. Eleanor Rathbone pointed out that the NUSEC had never neglected equal franchise, but had held regular meetings, published pamphlets, written letters, and put questions to parliamentary candidates in elections. After the success of the 1926 demonstration, an Equal Political Rights Campaign Committee with Margaret Rhondda in the chair was set up to coordinate the activities of the women's organisations. In the spring of 1927 there was wide discussion of the prospect of a further measure of franchise for women. Most of the press comment favoured the idea of giving votes only to women over 25. The NUSEC was committed to votes at 21, but found themselves between the hammer and the anvil once again. Nancy Astor did not want the women's organisations to press for 21 if the government offered 25, and Rathbone was prepared to compromise. She knew that Margaret Rhondda would be opposed to such a compromise, and was prepared to 'get on to her at once . . . and try to make her take the same line'. There was no need for compromise: a government statement was made on 13 April – Eva Hubback's birthday – after a deputation had been to Westminster on 8 March. The Prime Minister promised that there would be legislation in the next session, and that the vote would be given to women over the age of 21.[50]

The imminent prospect of equal franchise seems to have acted as a stimulus to the NUSEC: the Annual Council of 1928 was the largest on record since 1919. Among those who attended was Catherine Marshall. Her presence was a symbol of the reconciliation of the dispersed suffrage movement as suffragists came together to celebrate. In her address Rathbone paid tribute to the militant suffragettes: 'both wings of the suffrage movement had an indispensable contribution to make'. *Time & Tide* was not so generous. An article in the paper in July aroused Rathbone's anger when it claimed that, 'although in Great Britain, Equal Franchise was given in two parts . . . the action of one group was in the final event responsible for the whole reform – that of the militants whom Mrs. Pankhurst led from 1905 to 1914'. In looking at the work done since 1918, the article referred only to 'the past three or four years' and did not mention the NUSEC.[51]

The final debate in the House of Commons was something of a celebration. Ray Strachey attended this debate and commented, in words that echo her feelings in 1918: 'It is incredible that things should have changed so completely in so short a time.' There were ten votes against the bill, but the speakers mainly provided Nancy Astor with an opportunity for witty repartee:

> 'I ask, has man less spirit, less vision?' inquired Sir George Cockerill.
> 'Yes,' replied Lady Astor.[52]

The Bill became law on 2 July 1928. As *Time & Tide* said, it 'marked the end of an epoch'. But feminists were also aware, contrary to the Prime Minister's assertions, that the struggle was far from over. The vote was 'a big step forward,' but:

> What about the exclusion of women from the House of Lords? What about the barring of women from the diplomatic service? What about the dismissal of women on marriage, and equal pay for equal work in the Civil Service? What about the whole body of restrictive legislation? We are a long way from equality of treatment between men and women even so far as actual legal enactments go.[53]

'VICTORY – AND AFTER?'[54]

As the campaign to achieve equal franchise was coming to an end, evidence that there was a long way still to go was reported in both feminist papers. In April 1927, *The Woman's Leader* 'was tempted to reflect with some despair on the continued virulence of the Turk Complex' in the correspondence columns of the *Evening Standard* and the proceedings of the National Association of Schoolmasters. The following year the secretary to the Young Suffragists wrote to *Time & Tide* to protest against the 'extreme anti-feminism of the Bishop of Durham' in the remarks he made about the ordination of women. *The Woman's Leader* linked that issue with the failure of certain medical schools to admit women, and argued that:

> the admission of women to full status in the spheres of religion and medicine are twin reforms having a most special significance in the second quarter of the twentieth century.[55]

Women's position in medicine seemed actually to be regressing as three of the leading London hospitals announced that they were closing their doors to women medical students. It was clear that this was not a time for feminists, as Eleanor Rathbone put it, 'to depart to enjoy a well-earned rest, or to enlist under other banners.' *Time & Tide* agreed that 'the brushing aside of legal inequalities . . . is but a preliminary, though an essential one, to the real task of feminism'. At the end of the year, the NUSEC drew up 'Proposed Lines of Expansion for the NUSEC'. These proposals were an attempt to prevent any further decline in the Union's membership by encouraging societies to extend:

> their activities, local, national and international, to cover all questions on which women as women – independent of their class, party or creed – have an interest to protect, a point of view to express, or a specialized contribution to make to the common store of thought and action.[56]

The idea that women had a point of view, or an interest different from that of men was seen by other feminists as dangerous. Acceptance of difference in perspective could seem to be the acceptance of inequality. Articles in *Time & Tide*, although by no means totally consistent on this point, called on 'the individual' to 'stand out without trappings as a human being'. Part of the fight for women was 'to achieve the point of view of the equal'. The ambiguity of the concept of equality if gender differences are acknowledged has been a constant factor in the philosophy of feminism. Most feminists in the 1920s did not come down firmly on one side or the other. The NUSEC's object was an attempt to combine both points of view, adding to the achievement of 'real equality', 'such reforms as are necessary to make it possible for women adequately to discharge their functions as citizens'. To others there was 'a humble, pious tang' to this addition, 'as though women were still in a state of tutelage, needing special training to fit them for the great privilege of citizenship'.[57] The type of reforms which came under this heading were, in their view, as important for men as for women, and the underlying attitude led to such anomalies as protective legislation.

The experience of women seemed to others indelibly different from that of men. Helen Ward expressed the view of those who wanted:

> to tackle certain complex problems, where direct parallelism is not possible, but because of which much of the degradation and

humiliation suffered by our sex in the past has resulted . . . no feminist can deny that a woman's control over her own body and her right to secure economic stability for herself and her children are matters most cognate to a real equality of citizenship between men and women.[58]

For some feminists a possible difference in perspective between men and women meant that women might be able to offer much more than the special qualifications of motherhood. In 1928 Eleanor Rathbone was about to begin a new career at the age of fifty-seven as a member of Parliament. Her address to the 1929 Annual Council of the NUSEC was her last one. In it she asked the delegates whether the contribution of the women's movement to society need be 'limited to those questions which specially concern women and their children?' She suggested that women were especially likely to respond to human suffering, and that 'the Women's Movement might do well consciously to aim' at a 'changed attitude on the part of society toward human happiness and suffering'.[59]

Rathbone herself had become acutely conscious of one area of intense human suffering when she read of the experiences in marriage and childbirth of Indian women in Katharine Mayo's *Mother India*. As Mary Stocks put it: 'The shock of Mother India had switched her thoughts from home affairs to far horizons.'[60] On those far horizons she would join those women who had already been active in international affairs throughout the 1920s. There the question of whether there was such a thing as 'a woman's point of view' was one which inevitably confronted feminists, especially those whose main concern was peace.

8 International Feminism, 1921–28

Immediately after her success in the 1929 election Eleanor Rathbone went to Berlin as leader of the British delegation to a conference of the International Woman Suffrage Alliance. The NUSEC was affiliated to the Alliance and maintained its links with it throughout the 1920s. The object of the IWSA was amended at its first congress after the war in words which echo the revision of the NUWSS. To the 'promotion of Woman Suffrage' was added 'and such other reforms as are necessary to establish a real equality of liberties, status, and opportunities between men and women.'[1] In the years that followed feminists learned that progress on the international scale was even more arduous and elusive than on the national scene. Some of the issues which were contentious within the Union also led to tensions within the Alliance; in particular, the question of protective legislation. Margery Corbett Ashby found herself in the position of attempting to reconcile conflicting views in both organisations, with many of the same women involved.

The IWSA was not the only organisation through which feminists made an impact on the international scene in the 1920s. The Women's International League for Peace and Freedom, which had been founded at the Hague in 1915, continued to work towards peaceful solutions to international problems. Helena Swanwick and later Kathleen Courtney presided over the British section of the WILPF; Maude Royden was a sporadically active member and Catherine Marshall and Mary Sheepshanks were involved in the League's work in Europe. Swanwick's main concern was the education of the public, and women in particular, about international affairs and towards the end of the decade she became editor of *Foreign Affairs*, the journal of the Union of Democratic Control. Her knowledge of international problems led the Labour Government to send her to Geneva as substitute delegate to the Fifth Assembly of the League of Nations. The League of Nations became the focus for the hopes of many people concerned about international questions in the 1920s. The structure of the League had been widely criticised by the WILPF among other organisations and individuals but it still seemed to offer a chance for reconciliation of international disputes. Ray Strachey worked with the League of Nations Union in the early twenties and Kathleen Courtney was increasingly involved in the LNU, becoming a member of its executive in 1928.

In this chapter I will follow individual women who had been active suffragists into the international arena. Their motives for entering that arena and the activities they undertook varied. By following their individual paths I hope to elucidate the way choices were made by individuals in order to throw some light on the complex general picture of the women's peace movement. The involvement of feminists in international affairs does not require any justification in itself, but it is relevant to consider whether they were involved as feminists, or because their prior commitment was to maintenance of peace. The answer to this question is often unclear – many feminists were ambivalent about the question. Within these constraints the final section of the chapter will look at the links between feminism and the peace movement.

'SLOW AND DISCOURAGING WORK': RAY STRACHEY AND THE LEAGUE OF NATIONS UNION

Ray Strachey's involvement in international affairs in the 1920s was not central to her life, nor to her political commitment, but her background, her American roots and her frequent visits to Europe, especially to her mother's home in Italy, meant that she shared with Margery Corbett Ashby an ease in travelling abroad, and a total absence of insularity. She was politically most deeply concerned about the employment of women, and she took part in the work of the IWSA on this issue. Knowing that the collection of statistics and the exchange of information would bring no rapid results.[2]

We have seen that Strachey was reluctantly drawn into the IWSA Congress in Geneva in 1920 because of Lady Astor. From 1921 she became increasingly involved in activities, including public demonstrations, in favour of the League of Nations. In October she wrote to her mother of her growing interest in the question of disarmament. In November Ray was at a Disarmament Conference in Manchester, and in December she was 'immersed in League of Nations work, and am thick as thieves with Ld Robert whom I see daily'. In the following two years Ray's political career was to some extent shaped by her connection with Lord Robert Cecil who gave her financial support in Chiswick, and with whom she travelled to the USA early in 1923. In the summer of that year she attended the session of the Assembly of the League of Nations, and observed Cecil as leader of the British delegation. She was drawn into activity in the League of Nations Union again in 1927, but found the work 'slow and discouraging'.[3] Her commitment to disarmament and the LNU was undoubtedly sincere, and she found Cecil politically and personally sympathetic. But disarmament and the labyrinthine complexities of League politics were questions which required single-minded devotion and commitment in the long term.

'THE PAIN OF MANKIND': EVELYN SHARP

Evelyn Sharp's engagement in the international arena provides a contrast to that of Strachey, reflecting the variety of choices made by feminists. Many women continued their traditional role as healers and carers after the war in the devastated areas. The Save the Children Fund, which had emerged from the Fight the Famine Council, continued to bring relief throughout the 1920s, and many women were involved both as relief workers and in putting pressure on governments to increase their assistance to those who were suffering. The Fight the Famine Council had early links with the Women's International League, but the League eased away from the connection, determined to be a political and not a philanthropic organisation. Some feminists saw the involvement of women in relief work as counterproductive to the fight for equality; other did not want to abandon the role of women as carers, understanding such relief work as a way of demonstrating their opposition to war and militarism. Kathleen Courtney and her friends Hilda Clark and Edith Pye were involved in relief work and active in the WILPF.

Evelyn Sharp had left the WILPF because she no longer saw any necessity for separatist women's organisations. Her choice of direction was to continue the political struggle by moving closer to the Labour Party, and by working as a journalist for the left-wing press. Much of her writing in the early 1920s was on the international situation, and especially on the effects of the war on civilian populations, which she observed as an eyewitness in Vienna and Germany. In 1922 her political sympathies coincided with her wish to relieve 'the pain of mankind' when she went to bear witness to the suffering of the Russian people in the aftermath of the Civil War. She spent two weeks in Buzuluk, where she was one of three women at the Quaker relief centre. Buzuluk, was in the middle of the famine area where people were dying at the rate of one hundred a day, many of the bodies piling up unburied. She was told that she would 'get used to seeing people drop dead'. But she knew that 'It is that fatal propensity to "get used" to things that no-one should see unmoved that causes most of the cruelty in the world to go on.' She later travelled round the famine area by sledge before returning to England.[4]

Relief work might not be central to the lives of other former suffragists, but just after Sharp returned from Russia a deputation from women's organisations went to Downing Street and pressed the government to give financial assistance to the relief work in Russia. Evelyn Sharp joined the deputation, which included Catherine Marshall representing the WILPF, and Eleanor Rathbone for the NUSEC. After the deputation a meeting was held with Helena Swanwick in the chair; among the speakers were Marshall and Emmeline Pethick Lawrence. Sharp then wrote articles for the press and spoke to audiences all over the country. When one of her audience commented that Sharp had given a more favourable impression of the Soviet Government than had the British newspapers, she pointed out that 'the Soviet Government had behaved as every Government behaves when people do what it wants them to do, and that only those who put themselves in conflict with their rulers ever know the extent of their power to impress'. She added wryly of her questioner: 'She did not seem to have had any experience of finding herself in conflict with the British Government.'[5]

'A WILLING SPIRIT': CATHERINE MARSHALL AND THE WOMEN'S INTERNATIONAL LEAGUE FOR PEACE AND FREEDOM

Evelyn Sharp understood the problems of relief in their political context: so did Catherine Marshall. Marshall served as a representative of the League of Nations on the International Relief Commission convened by the Red Cross to tackle the famine in Russia. As a suffragist Catherine Marshall had not challenged authority directly, as had Sharp, and even in the No Conscription Fellowship she had worked through influence and persuasion rather than confrontation. In the 1920s she continued to seek to influence events by direct contact with those in power. After the Zurich Congress the WILPF had established its headquarters in Geneva and Marshall went to work there in November 1920, in order to help the secretary during the first Assembly of the League. At first she was neither enthusiastic nor optimistic about her task, but when she left in March 1921, she declared:

> I am personally convinced by my own experience there, contrary to my expectation, that a very great deal can be done . . . . This Assembly is where our hope lies.

Marshall pressed the WILPF to 'create public opinion, organise public opinion' and use it to put pressure on 'the political machinery'.[6] Other members of the WILPF were not yet prepared to work closely alongside a League which had been created by a peace settlement they condemned. At a Congress at the Hague a resolution was passed which called for a 'New Peace based on a new International Assembly'. But the Congress also initiated more immediate action of the sort which Marshall advocated. She was one of the envoys sent to seek personal interviews with statesmen in the hope of persuading them to press for a reasonable settlement of the reparations demanded of Germany. The British Government was prepared to withdraw any further claims, but the French refused to do so and sent troops into the Ruhr in January 1923, to enforce continued payment of reparations. The German response was to offer passive resistance with the effect of disrupting trade and industry and returning their own country to the postwar conditions of poverty and starvation. In Germany in 1923 Catherine Marshall's path crossed with Evelyn Sharp's again. They were both in sympathy with the stand taken by the Germans, and Marshall published a letter to the 'Pacifists and Passive Resisters in the Ruhr,' in which she wrote that the WILPF decision to send:

> two of its members to go and live in the Ruhr and work with you . . . was a gesture not only of sympathy with you in what you are suffering, but of deep affection, gratitude and faith . . . . You have shown to the world the great example that force can be defeated by a refusal to resort to force.[7]

Sharp was sent by the *Daily Herald* to write a series of articles on the French occupation. The passport authorities were reluctant to grant her the necessary visa because she was a woman and the conditions there were so 'unsettled'. This did not deter her in the least. Moreover, when she found that the newspaper correspondents had been given a room in a private hotel owned by the arms manufacturers, Krupps, she moved out into a hospital run by nuns where she insisted on being given the same meagre diet as the staff. The superintendant of the hospital 'in her anxiety that I should miss no detail for my paper, fetched me to the bedside of every victim of hunger and cold who was carried in from the streets'.[8]

Meanwhile Marshall had been forced to take a rest before the envoys finished their work. The other envoys wrote to her in sympathy, one of them pointing out that she had 'done much too much for a healthy woman and certainly you must have felt exhausted after what you have done for a – let us say – convalescent woman'. In the 1920s Catherine was never able to work as hard as she wished or she felt the situation demanded. She had been in a state of exhaustion before the journey through Europe, 'snowed under with work of all kinds and urgent family business . . . I am working till after midnight every day.' After the death of her father she and her mother moved from Keswick to London and the move took place soon after she returned from Europe. Catherine was happy to be settled in London, but the move from their 'beloved home' was an emotional as well as a physical strain, and after it was over, she was 'very tired' and 'in constant pain'. The pain in her back from which she suffered was only relieved by frequent hot baths; she could walk very little and had to avoid going up and down stairs if at all possible. Travelling was especially painful, so that her desire to work for the WILPF in the international arena was often impossible, and this she found very difficult to accept. She wrote to the WILPF secretary in Geneva: 'If only the flesh were not so weak where the spirit is so willing.'[9]

'I AM NOT AFRAID TO SPEAK AS A WOMAN': HELENA SWANWICK IN THE LEAGUE OF NATIONS

Catherine Marshall was again appointed as referent to the League of Nations Assembly by the WILPF in 1926. While she and the international secretary to the WILPF attempted to bring pressure on members of the League from the outside, women's organisations worked together to get more women inside the structures of the League. Both the NUSEC and the IWSA were committed to making the League 'a real force in regulating international relationships.' At the Annual Council meeting in 1920 the last of the six points containing the objectives of the NUSEC was: 'An active propaganda in support of a democratic League of Nations and of the practical application of the principles of equal opportunity for men and women within it.' In 1920 the IWSA proposed that there should be an annual conference summoned by the League 'for the purpose of considering questions relating to the welfare and status of women', with delegates from member countries and from international women's organisations. The result of this demand was the establishment of a Council for Representation of Women in the League of Nations. This body fought steadily, with limited success, for increased representation of women in the structures of the League. Other organisations were more interested in getting women to support the League, rather than the League to support women. Lord Robert Cecil published an appeal to women to give their support to the League in June 1921, and the Union demonstrated its commitment by organising a demonstration.

Millicent Garrett Fawcett led a procession from the Embankment – 'at a run', according to Ray Strachey. Ray herself then 'hounded' Cecil from platform to platform as he delivered nine speeches in succession. In the following year, the NUSEC sent a contingent to join a demonstration celebrating League of Nations Day.[10]

The only body in the League where more than a token woman was to be found was the Advisory Committee on the Traffic in Women and Children. This committee had a very low status, and was regarded by many with distrust because of its potential for 'interference' in internal affairs. Women's organisations did not dismiss it in the same terms, for the IWSA in particular was deeply concerned with issues considered by the committee: for example the age of consent and the question of prostitution, including the continued buying and selling of young girls. Nevertheless, they were determined that women should also be recognised as eligible and appropriate for the higher-status bodies such as the Mandates Commission, for which Elizabeth Abbott was unsuccessfully proposed by the NUSEC. Lack of confidence is reflected in the view expressed by Kathleen Courtney that lack of expertise hampered the appointment of women to expert committees. Helena Swanwick was also sensitive to the problem of women's organisations pressing for the appointment of women and then being unable to 'name any woman really suitable for the position'. Her remedy was: 'Train Women!'[11]

Helena Swanwick was aware of the pitfalls and possibilities of the appointment of women to prestigious positions. The other capacity in which a woman could and did play a part in the League was as a national delegate to the yearly Assembly. In 1924 Swanwick was approached by the Labour Government to go to the Fifty Assembly as a substitute delegate. (Each delegation was composed of three full and five substitute delegates.) This request was especially remarkable in that the Fifth Assembly of the League of Nations was seen by its participants as crucially important. The national delegations included authoritative representatives such as politicians who held or were likely to hold office. The British delegation was led by Ramsay MacDonald, the Prime Minister. Swanwick's reaction reflected her knowledge of the limitations and ambiguities of the job she was offered. She did not doubt her own knowledge, nor her ability as a public speaker, but she was 'intimidated by the notion of having to find my feet among diplomats and officials of all sorts.' She knew that it was possible simply to rely on being 'piloted by clever permanent officials', but she was too astute to think that there was any point in going if that was to be her role.

Swanwick did not lack the necessary confidence to accept, although she was 'immensely surprised', and her 'first feeling was fear'. She knew she could rely on her educational background and her experience as a suffragist. Yet she hesitated before moving into the political structures which she believed should be open to women. Part of her hesitation arose from her absorption in her own work: many active feminists no longer had the spare energy and frustration of the educated women in the pre-war period. She also hesitated about leaving her elderly and ailing husband; Fred, however, encouraged her to go, and she threw herself into the necessary preparations during the month before she left for Geneva. These preparations not only involved reading a mass of bulky reports, but collecting copy for her weekly gardening articles in the *Manchester Guardian* and the *Observer*, completing all reviews and other articles she had in hand, and, since she never bought clothes and hated doing so, making herself two evening dresses and four day dresses. On top of this there were regular meetings, and the completion of the book she was writing on the Union of Democratic Control.[12]

On arriving in Geneva, Swanwick was not surprised to be assigned to the general area covered by the 'Fifth Committee, a sort of ragbag of miseries and forlorn hopes . . . . A woman, it appeared, was assumed to be well-informed about Opium, Refugees, Protection of

Children, Relief after Earthquakes, Prison Reform, Municipal Co-operation, Alcoholism, Traffic in Women.' She was asked to be a Rapporteur for the committee on refugees, which gave her a moment of acute panic, quickly dispelled by the amount of work facing her in getting to grips with the subject. She was moved to speak in committee when a proposer of a resolution appealed to the women on the committee 'to leave to men the task of stating practical objections and let your mother-hearts be moved by suffering'. Swanwick challenged this distinction, and argued 'that it would be injurious to our work that we should be presumed to be sentimentalists who passed a number of resolutions without any serious intention of implementing them'. She did not feel that the incident was important, nor that she had wielded any influence, but she was ironically amused that this was the only time she was mentioned in the newspapers – with the exception of the *Manchester Guardian* – and that the report focused on her disagreement with the French delegate, who was also a woman: disagreements between male delegates were not reported in the terms 'men delegates fall out'.[13]

On another occasion she found herself being criticised by a speaker for a report she did not know she had written: it had been issued by the permanent officials without her knowledge. Her realisation of the reality and extent of civil service influence made her appreciate to the full how effectively the marriage bar and other exclusive devices acted to reduce women's opportunities for power. An opportunity for her to wield some influence came when other women delegates asked her if she would 'say a few words' about the main contentious issue in the full Assembly: the Geneva Protocol. This proposal had been the fruit of hard and unusually effective informal work during the Assembly. Its purpose was to close what was referred to as 'a gap' in the Covenant which seemed to some to make it necessary to tighten up procedures for the arbitration of disputes. The Protocol bound signatories to come to the Council of the League for arbitration of a dispute, and to help any member state which was attacked by any aggressor who rejected arbitration. It also arranged for the holding of a conference on Disarmament. When the Assembly met to discuss the Protocol, the atmosphere was one of exhilaration at the speed with which it had been drawn up and the extent of support apparent for it. Swanwick had not been carried away by the general euphoria. She had doubts about the workability of the Protocol, and did not feel that it represented a move away from acceptance of the use of force. She later wrote that she found the whole experience of the

Assembly a disturbing one, in that it revealed to her the full extent of the hyprocrisy and cynicism of international diplomats, 'with their age-old belief in compulsive force'. Yet she was anxious that nothing she said would endanger the expressed aims of the Protocol. As a result she felt that she had:

> given many of my audience the idea that I was supporting the whole of it . . . . It is one of life's little ironies that I have got more credit for this short little speech than for many much better ones that I have made, and that a good deal of that credit was due to my audience misunderstanding me.[14]

Among Swanwick's papers is a newspaper cutting which described her speech in these glowing, and patronising terms: 'The complete mastery of a highly technical subject which she displayed to the astonished audience perhaps did better service than any speech made by a woman delegate before or since.' Swanwick crossed out this passage and wrote beside it: 'NONSENSE'. The irony on which Swanwick does not comment is that the attention given to the speech was partly the result of her gender, yet she was opposed to the idea that she could speak for women in general, since she denied the existence of a woman's point of view. In her opening words to the Assembly Swanwick declared:

> it would be immodest in the extreme for one woman to attempt to speak for all women. It is a danger that every woman in this hall knows, that a woman, who speaks, always runs the risk of people saying that she speaks for all her sex. We differ, gentlemen, as much as you do – no more![15]

Yet Swanwick went on in her speech to say that 'she was not afraid to speak as a woman.' She claimed that there was a sense in which women had a specific responsibility for the future, and a particular understanding of the suffering which led them to plead for reconciliation.[16]

Swanwick had recognised her position as representing the interests of women at the League to the extent of supporting a meeting organised by the WILPF to 'consult the leaders of various women's organisations on matters likely to come before her during the Assembly'. Present at that meeting were Eva Hubback, Mary Stocks, Eleanor Rathbone and Evelyn Sharp. The meeting took place at the International House in Gower Street, London. The house had been established as a meeting place for women from different organisations and different countries at the end of 1921. In Geneva the Maison Internationale, the WILPF headquarters, served the same purpose. It was a beautiful house, old – also 'insanitary' and foul-smelling according to Mary Sheepshanks – with fourteen rooms and one bathroom. It was such a success as a focus for women visiting Geneva, that the WILPF later moved their office to prevent it becoming 'a tourist bureau for travellers', and to allow the secretary – Mary Sheepshanks at that time – to take some time off, 'curling up on a couche, reading a novel or climbing a mountain'.[17]

Perhaps the climax in the life of the Maison Internationale in the 1920s occurred during the meeting of the League of Nations Assembly in 1926. Mary Sheepshanks, Kathleen Courtney, Hilda Clark and Catherine Marshall lived at the house; Evelyn Sharp went there to celebrate Jane Addams's birthday and met Helena Swanwick, but to her regret missed Catherine. A joint lunch was held there for the WILPF and the larger and more conservative International Woman Suffrage Alliance at which Helena Swanwick and Margery Corbett Ashby spoke.[18] The lunch was a symbol of the agreement on many issues of these two women who had not worked together since 1914. The IWSA was a suffrage organisation whose concerns did not at first include the search for peace. It was drawn into the women's peace movement as the issues of peace and disarmament moved into the centre of the political stage in the second half of the 1920s.

'A TRIENNIAL ADVERTISEMENT OF FEMINISM': MARGERY CORBETT ASHBY AND THE INTERNATIONAL WOMAN SUFFRAGE ALLIANCE

The Assembly of the League met in the autumn of 1926; in the summer Margery Corbett Ashby had presided over the Paris Congress of the International Woman Suffrage Alliance. A delegate to the Congress commented admiringly on her ability to:

> say the right thing in four languages. And this she can do with a measure of personal charm, guilelessness of manner, and social grace, such as Providence with a laudable sense of fairness, seldom sees fit to bestow upon a person already well-gifted with sound intelligence and serious political interest.[19]

Margery Corbett Ashby had been involved with the IWSA from

its earliest days. She was well placed to give her time and energy to the alliance: she was an excellent linguist and had travelled in Europe since she was a child. She had the enthusiastic backing of her mother, and her parents gave her financial help, offering to pay her travelling expenses in Europe. Later, like Ray Strachey, she was given a car to ease her travel problems in Britain. She also borrowed her mother's clothes on occasion. Marie Corbett was enormously proud of Margery's achievements. 'The amount of things you do and the efficient way you do them all mark you as one of, say, three women in the world.' She also worried constantly about 'the amount of things' Margery did, especially when she herself was not there to keep an eye on her daughter and grandson. She wrote from a trip to South Africa:

> I will have benefitted from our absence, you on the contrary will be thinner with a more frequent cough and tired expression than ever.[20]

Her mother's help and encouragement certainly made it easier for Corbett Ashby to leave her home and travel extensively abroad in the 1920s. This privileged and supportive background gave her a stability and a confidence which made it possible for her to enjoy the challenge and the stimulation of the travel and the work she did. In a letter to her husband and son she wrote:

> I think of you both the whole time and miss you dreadfully. It seems wrong somehow to leave all the wealth of love you both shower on me and which makes me the happiest woman in the world. Yet on the other hand interesting work comes along and I am reluctant to lose the chance of seeing and learning new things from new people. I suppose like all of us I want to eat my cake and have it too.[21]

Apart from her skills as a linguist, her confidence, and her symbolic importance as a young mother, Corbett Ashby's contribution to the IWSA lay in her awareness of the need to recognise the practical limitations of the organisation. When others in the organisation wanted to press for women to be represented on the Disarmament Commission of the League of Nations. Margery wrote plaintively to her mother that this was 'rather tiresome', and wished 'that we had a little more sense of humour and common sense. I do feel weary of impractical persons . . . '.[22]

There were limitations to the influence of the IWSA. It was not a rich organisation, and had constantly to appeal to its supporters for funds. The executive body was a Board whose meetings were not well attended, for the very good reason that its members had to travel long distances. Much of its work had inevitably to be concentrated in the congresses which were held once in three years. These conferences demanded a great deal of energy to organise and run. The problem of expressing conference agreement in a common language was tricky. In 1923 arguments arose over whether *avant tout* could be translated accurately as 'principally'.[23] On the other hand the congress did offer an opportunity to women from the forty member countries to get together to discuss and to publicise issues of common interest. The wide differences in culture represented by the member countries presented a challenge, but also a powerful symbol of the common struggle of women.

At the Rome conference in 1923 Margery Corbett Ashby was elected President, replacing Carrie Chapman Catt from the USA. As President Corbett Ashby was determined to visit as many member countries of the IWSA as possible. Between 1924 and 1928 she visited all the member countries in Western and Eastern Europe, and went to the USA. 1924 and 1925 seem to have been exceptionally busy years. In 1924 she travelled all over Europe, facing the politically delicate problem of visiting both France and Germany after the tension of the French occupation of the Ruhr valley in 1923. In June she was back in London and presided at a session of a conference held by the International Council of Women.[24] In the summer she was adopted as a parliamentary candidate for Watford and fought the election in October. In the spring of 1925 she went to the USA, but by June of that year she was back in London to help launch a Commonwealth group in support of the League of Nations. In July she travelled to Switzerland for an IWSA Board meeting at which preparations were made for the next congress. In the autumn she was ill, having to undergo an operation, but was back in Paris in December for another board meeting.[25]

By her presence Margery Corbett Ashby provided a personal link between national and international women's organisations. This may not in itself have moved the cause of women very much further forward, yet there were undeniable psychological gains in giving feminists the sense that the struggle was taking place in an international context. To give this sense of connection was one of the aims of the IWSA. A report on the Paris Congress claimed: 'Each Congress brings the feminists societies throughout the world closer to a unit which must necessarily have a far-reaching effect on the policy of nations'.[26]

Just as the search for equality in Britain proved more complex and frustrating as the 1920s progressed, so the IWSA found it increasingly difficult to hold together its heterogeneous membership. In 1923 Corbett Ashby enlarged on her summary of the programme by identifying 'two urgent reforms needing special attention': the need to recognise women's right to work under the same conditions as men, and the establishment of an equal moral standard.[27] The achievement of these aims proved so elusive on a national scale that feminists turned to other concerns. The same pattern was repeated in the IWSA.

In resolutions passed at the Rome Congress the IWSA committed itself to seek for equal pay for women and the right to work with no restrictions; the claim for a 'motherhood allowance' was placed within the resolution demanding an enhanced economic status for wives. The demand for equality of opportunity was again adopted in the resolutions agreed at the Paris Conference in 1926, as was the demand for 'Family Allowances'. However, the optimism of the early 1920s had by then become a sober realisation of the immense obstacles to economic equality. When the IWSA Board met in the summer of 1924, it advocated a defensive position on economic questions:

In the view of the present economic depression, it was decided that all affiliated societies should be urged to work rather for the maintenance of such reforms as have already been won, than for the further extension of economic rights. Not that the women's demand should be one jot abated, but when on every hand women are being crowded out from the professions in which they have difficulty in ensuring a footing, it is of the greatest urgency that women's organisations everywhere should keep a careful watch to see that the waves of reaction do not little by little wash away hard-won privileges.[28]

At the Paris Conference the debate on restrictive legislation for women in industry revealed a 'sharp cleavage', and the resolution adopted called for no regulations to 'be imposed on women contrary to the wishes of the women concerned.' This was the formula which was partially responsible for the resignation of half the executive of the NUSEC in the following year. The IWSA had been faced with the same problem of a lack of confidence in its right to speak on behalf on women in industry. A meeting of the board in the spring of 1924 had discussed 'whether it would be desirable to try and secure closer co-operation with women's industrial organisations, nationally or internationally, for the discussion of questions touching on the economic position of women'. In the month following the report of this meeting in *Jus Suffragii*, an article appeared in the paper by the Assistant Professor of Industrial Medicine at Harvard in support of protective legislation for women. This was the beginning of a restrained debate on the question in the pages of the paper.[29]

The debate on the question of protective legislation illustrates the operation of international feminist links in the 1920s. In Britain this contentious issue was finally contained within a framework of basic agreement, but there is no doubt that the arguments on the question and the strong feelings aroused added to the stresses which weakened the force of feminism in the mid-twenties. In the United States the debate had led to a clearer and earlier division of the women's movement. There were strong personal links between American and British feminists, and knowledge of the American debate influenced those in the NUSEC who were becoming critical of the direction in which it was going. The delegates to the IWSA Paris Conference included all those whose voices were heard in the debates within the NUSEC: Chrystal Macmillan, Elizabeth Abbott, Helen Ward, Margaret Rhondda, Mary Stocks and Eleanor Rathbone.

One woman who strengthened the links between American and British feminists and who was influential on both sides of the Atlantic was Crystal Eastman. Eastman and her two young children lived alternately in England and the United States from 1922 until her death in 1928.[30] Eastman knew many English feminists well. She had attended the conference of the IWSA in 1913 and met there Emmeline Pethick Lawrence who remained a close friend. Later she came to know Margaret Rhondda. At first Eastman recorded the agreement of all feminist organisations in England in opposition to protective legislation. In 1926 she attended the Annual Council of the NUSEC, and praised the rejection of the resolution proposed by Mary Stocks which would have modified the Union's opposition to such legislation. Only after the confusion over the issue at the Annual Council of the NUSEC in 1927 did Eastman develop a thesis which argued that English feminists had always been divided between true feminists and social reformers: they had worked together because they all recognised the need for complete enfranchisement. Eastman now argued that the British women's movement had produced a compromise over feminism while in the States there had been a 'complete realignment of forces.'[31] All women in the United States could vote after 1918 and the split in the American women's movement opened up in 1923 at the seventy-fifty anniversary of the first Equal Rights meeting. There the National Woman's Party challenged the acceptance by leading American feminists, including Jane Addams, of the desirability of protective legislation for women. This challenge became a threat when the National Woman's Party began a campaign for an Equal Rights Amendment to the United States Constitution. The intention of the amendment was to make any legislation limited to women retrospectively unconstitutional. The Equal Rights Amendment was seen by its advocates as crucially important, so that the division in opinion was correspondingly fundamental.[32]

In 1926 the National Woman's Party applied to join the IWSA and the application was discussed at the IWSA meeting in Paris in 1926. The report sent in diary form to *The Woman's Leader* from 'Our Paris Correspondent' suggests that she was somewhat bemused by the recommendation of the IWSA Board that the National Woman's Party application should be refused. She observed that the recommendation 'was the outcome of long, tangled deliberation.' and that of the seven speakers on the question, five spoke against the recommendation of the Board: 'And it must be confessed that the marked ability, good taste, and wisdom with which the representatives of the Women's National Party argued her case, did much to kindle such sympathy.' Yet the final voting was 123 to 49 against allowing the National Woman's Party to join. According to Crystal Eastman, nine of the twelve British delegates voted with the minority, in support of the National Woman's Party. Chrystal Macmillan spoke strongly in favour of the admission, but Eleanor Rathbone asked the delegates to trust to the wisdom of their Board.[33] There is no doubt that the influence there of Carrie Chapman Catt on the Board was crucial. She was the leader of the increasingly conservative and cautious League of Women Voters – one of the founders of the IWSA – whose relations with the NWP were not good.

Margaret Rhondda saw the action of the IWSA in terms of the rejection of passionate feminism. She condemned the official reason for the refusal of the application – the press and publicity campaign of the NWP – as a ruse. The Six Point Group withdrew their own application to affiliate to the IWSA, an application which had already been accepted. Rhondda distinguished between feminists and social reformers who wanted the vote only as a means of achieving reforms, and asserted:

> every woman's organization recognizes that reformers are far more common than feminists, that the passion to look after your fellow man, and especially woman, to do good to her in your way is far more common than the desire to put into every one's hand the power to look after themselves . . . .[34]

Rhondda would carry this analysis into the division in the NUSEC early the following year. The division of opinion on protective legislation was not clearly defined and to some extent the vote on the question, as in the NUSEC, was the effect rather than the cause of a split.

Elizabeth Abbott had set up the Open Door Council to press for the removal of restrictions on women's right to work. The Open Door International, with Chrystal Macmillan in the chair, was set up in 1929 after the Alliance had 'refused to commit itself wholeheartedly to a policy of opposition to all forms of differentiated labour legislation'. The resolutions of the 1929 Congress of the Alliance did not condemn protective legislation outright, but 'recognised that the standpoint (of the member countries) differs widely', and proposed holding a conference on the question at the next Congress. The question of protective legislation became for individuals in the IWSA, as it had for the NUSEC, a hallmark of the distinction between two different perspectives on feminism. For Margaret Rhondda, Crystal Eastman, Elizabeth Abbott and Chrystal Macmillan, to compromise on this issue was to compromise on the essential nature of equality. Yet the division took place, as had the division in the NUSEC, without delegates being fully aware of the significance of the event, or agreeing that there was indeed any need to divide. *The Woman's Leader* Paris Correspondent is an interesting witness to the way opinion shifted on the issue of protective legislation almost without her noticing. She wrote her report in diary form, and early on in the conference reported that the committee dealing with the question had maintained its 'unqualified opposition to restrictive legislation for women workers'. She did add that 'the representatives of Germany and America expressed feminist heresies similar to those cherished by the leading women in the British Labour Party', but understood these to be minority views. Two days later she reported the debate on the question and was clearly startled when:

> the policy of uncompromising opposition to all restrictions women's work received a wholly unexpected check when a resolution embodying this policy was lost by a very narrow majority.

The proceedings of the IWSA Congress provided the Paris Correspondent with food for thought about the purposes of the organisation, and she shared these with the readers of *The Woman's Leader* later that same month. She identified the organisation's need for a united front, and suggested that the result was that the full proceedings of the Congress were tedious, and delegates asked themselves: 'Why Am I here? Isn't it all a fabulous waste of time?' The situation was different in committees where differences of opinion were openly expressed; she suggested that committee work should be extended, and full conference proceedings attenuated. She also suggested that there should be a division between the enfranchised and the unenfranchised at committee level. Crystal Eastman had suggested such a division of the entire Alliance in 1923, observing: 'Women who have suffrage still to win . . . grow impatient on listening to the prolonged discussion on advanced economic legislation contemplated for countries where the vote is an old story.'[36]

Other delegates to the IWSA Congresses defended them vigorously. Helen Fraser was anxious that the enfranchised countries continue to lend support and encouragement to those where women could not yet vote. Kathleen Courtney responded to the issues raised on the question of making the IWSA Congress more effective. She wanted to avoid the sense of unreality and the 'atmosphere of anxiety' which accompanied the debates on controversial issues. Courtney advocated 'departing altogether from the old methods established by men for international congresses, and running an international congress on their own lines'. Her main suggestion was that the IWSA 'avoid any attempt to pass resolutions on controversial subjects, but discuss these in the hope of understanding each other's point of view'. Courtney had no doubts about the intrinsic value of the IWSA. She was aware of the work which went on in the years between. However cautious they might be about exposing the disagreement between women on contentious issues, supporters and critics of the IWSA acknowledged the value of research into those issues. The four committees collected material from all member countries by means of questionnaires, personal research and with the aid of the organisations affiliated to the Alliance. Ray Strachey was responsible for an extensive report on 'The Employment Position of Women in Different Countries' which was presented to the 'Right to Work' committee at the Rome Congress.[37]

One committee which continued to work without open disagreement arising from its resolutions was that on the equal moral standard. The IWSA consistently pressed for the same objectives as the NUSEC: the raising of the age of consent, the removal of laws and regulations specifically directed towards prostitutes, and government action to make available sex instruction. The efforts of the Alliance were not strikingly successful, and state regulation of prostitution, for example, continued to operate in several member countries. Yet the persistence with which these demands were made helped to keep alive the ideal of an equal moral standard. Chrystal MacMillan also used the forum of the IWSA to fight the cause of women who were forced to take the nationality of their husbands.

In the words of *Time & Tide* the IWSA continued after the Paris Congress to 'potter along as it has in the past'. The name was changed to the International Alliance of Women for Suffrage and Equal Citizenship (IAWSEC) but its nature remained for the present unchanged. *Time & Tide* felt that an opportunity had been missed to bring new life into the organisation, but judged that 'it will not die on that account, though it may cease to grow . . . '. The paper was less patronising in its final comment that 'The Alliance whatever its limitations, has a long, useful life before it and much good work to do which it, and it alone, can accomplish.'[38] Such faith was necessary for it was all too easy to be cynical. 'Our Paris Correspondent' was aware that delegates wondered:

> What becomes of our resolutions, however adequately drafted or intelligently discussed, when we have passed them? Is the whole paraphernalia of the Women's International of no more real account than a triennial advertisement of Feminism in a country which needs a peg for publicity? And, if so, is the game worth a candle?

She did not try to answer those difficult questions directly, unwilling to attempt to weigh 'the imponderable'. Yet in the final image she offered of the work of the Congress she gives us a vivid sense of what was the genuine, if elusive, value of the IWSA. She described how those who attended were:

> likely to carry away with them certain additions to the abundance of their lives: mental pictures of others who are fighting the same battle under widely various conditions, embryonic friendships made in cafés and corridors, and having their origins in the deliberations of committees, a more constant view of progress, a more tolerant comprehension of difficulty.[39]

At the Paris Congress the IWSA made a significant move towards involvement in the women's peace movement when it established a new committee 'to study how women can best help to secure peace.' Kathleen Courtney was one of those who welcomed this move.

PILGRIM FOR PEACE, 1925 – 28: KATHLEEN COURTNEY

Margery Corbett Ashby was a much admired and hardworking presidential figure; Helena Swanwick was an authoritative thinker, writer and speaker; Kathleen Courtney, like Catherine Marshall, was often invisible, but always extraordinarily influential behind the scenes. She used her influence in the NUSEC during the 1920s to keep international questions on the agenda. In 1926 she played a key role in organising a public demonstration of women's commitment to international peace.

The publicity given to the Geneva Protocol meant that the question of arbitration was widely discussed after the League of Nations Assembly in 1924. Helena Swanwick wrote a pamphlet on the subject, and the British section of the WILPF began to plan a campaign in support of compulsory arbitration in 1925. At a meeting in London Courtney 'expressed the belief that this was the psychological moment when women should express their views on Arbitration and Disarmament'. Maude Royden suggested that it would be wise to have 'one slogan and one punch' and to 'concentrate on the question of arbitration'. Helen Ward suggested a pilgrimage, and Emmeline Pethick Lawrence advocated some definite political action such as a deputation to Parliament. A joint council representing twenty-eight women's and peace organisations, including the League of Nations Union, began to plan a 'peace pilgrimage'. Its objects were to bring pressure to bear on the Government to support moves which were being made to strengthen the clauses of the Covenant of the League which were concerned with arbitration, and to press for a World Disarmament Conference. These were the aims of the Geneva Protocol, but Kathleen Courtney was determined to steer clear of the party conflict to which the Protocol had given rise. She had spoken in the debate on the Protocol which had taken place at the NUSEC Annual Council in 1925, when discussion of the issue became heated, and 'dangerously near party politics'.[40] Support for the principles of arbitration and disarmament was neatly encapsulated in the slogan which was chosen for the pilgrimage, and which appeared on the banners: 'Law not War'.

In May 1926, pilgrims set out to walk along seven main routes to London. A thousand meetings were held in towns and villages which they passed through. On 11 June *The Woman's Leader* reported that the pilgrimage was 'successful beyond the hopes of its originators . . . ' By 19 June 10 000 women had reached London and they assembled at four rallying points in Hyde Park. They were joined by thousands more women who watched the processions of marchers, each headed by a woman 'in a Madonna-blue cloak on a white horse'. Then came speeches from twenty-two platforms, and the speakers included Emmeline Pethick Lawrence, Margery Corbett Ashby, Helena Swanwick and Hilda Clark. Maude Royden spoke at a rally in Bristol, and Kathleen Courtney in Manchester.[41]

A deputation from the Pilgrimage Council, including Helena Swanwick and Maude Royden, was received by the foreign secretary on 6 July. He expressed support for the principles of arbitration and disarmament, but gave no pledge of action. The efforts of the British section of the WILPF to press for compulsory arbitration did not stop with the Peace Pilgrimage of 1926. In December 1927, 'pilgrims' went out from London and Manchester into the country in cars, delivering leaflets and speaking to anyone who would listen. In 1928 a joint campaign was organised with an American group, initiated by Carrie Chapman Catt.[42] Kathleen Courtney again played a leading role, and she now began to work alongside the League of Nations Union. From 1928 she was on the executive of that body in which she increasingly saw the best hope of influencing governments to establish structures and laws which would make it possible to avoid war.

FEMINISM AND PACIFISM

In her old age Kathleen Courtney talked about how and why she left WILPF. She commented that she did not see 'how you can be a pacifist, unless you are prepared to make it a whole way of life – and I do find pacifists very unpacific people'.[43] She was totally committed to the peaceful settlement of international disputes and wanted to study 'the cause and cure of war', but she was not a pacifist. She had been one of the organisers of the Hague Conference at which the WILPF was launched, and she had been anxious that the message from that conference should not be simply 'Stop the War'. Helena

Swanwick was also determined that her commitment to peace should not be misunderstood. In *Women and War* she had made a clear connection between feminism and pacifism, both of which asserted the use of reason and 'public right' against the use of physical force. She was concerned in the 1920s to make it possible for women to make effective use of their experience as women in a world which was 'still so overwhelmingly manly'. She understood pacifism, not as a protest against war, but as a process of working towards peace. 'I never "preached peace", peace in a vacuum; peace as an abstraction. I conceived of peace as a condition created by a rational conduct of international relations.' She knew that it was all too easy to 'rouse a general sentiment for peace', and much more difficult to consider the 'problems which if left unsolved may lead to war'. She believed that 'women's great function intellectually was to be interpreters'. She saw this as no small task, involving as it did the need 'to make people understand each other not only with their intellect but their emotions'. It was on the emotional plane that there was the greatest difficulty, and it was here that women had the most to offer.[44]

Catherine Marshall, like Swanwick, rejected the idea that there was such a thing as a collective 'women's point of view', but she too believed that women could offer a different perspective from men in international affairs, and that this perspective was diammetrically opposed to militarism. She argued that women had always been opposed to war but that it was only after the emergence of an organised women's movement that it was possible 'to give expression to the passion of horror in women's hearts, to be fired by it to co-operative action'. The horror had its roots in women's realisation that 'every man is a mother's son'. The common experience of motherhood is a theme which recurs in Marshall's analysis; for her 'the common motherhood of woman cut[s] across national barriers and class barriers alike.' Because of their commitment as mothers to preserve rather than to destroy, she argued that 'women, if they turn their minds in that direction, are more likely than men to find some other way of settling international disputes than by an appeal to force'.[45]

During the war these three feminists had been founder members of the WIL, but they worked in different ways in opposition to militarism. After the war they came together again in the WILPF, but there remained distinctions in their attitudes, and they still worked in different ways. Catherine Marshall's efforts can justifiably be called 'a sort of alternative female diplomacy'.[46] Helena Swanwick continued to work in the WILPF towards the greater involvement of women in international affairs, and in cooperation with both men and women in the UDC towards the democratic control of international relations. Kathleen Courtney's activities covered an even wider spectrum. She worked within the NUSEC on a variety of issues, including family endowment, but the focus of her activity was increasingly on international affairs, within both the IWSA and the WILPF. Of the three, all of whom believed in the efficacy of pressure group activity, she was the most skilled and persistent practitioner of the difficult art of working within a group towards political goals. Her main goal from the 1920s on was to achieve security in Europe in order to avoid war, but she was also concerned with the effects of war on individuals, refugees in particular. Unlike Swanwick and Marshall she did not offer any theory of the causes of war, and in her journalism she did not take any firm stand on the connections between feminism and pacifism. Significantly, she avoided giving her own view when she stated 'it has always been held by some advocates of the enfranchisement of women that there was a close connection between women's demand for the vote and their attitude towards international peace.'[47]

Margery Corbett Ashby was equally reticent on the question. During the war her attitude was inevitably influenced by the fact that her husband was fighting. When the question arose of whether the IWSA should concern itself with peace, her attitude is not entirely clear. This is partly because she was in the position of mediator from the chair when the issue became contentious. The IWSA was founded as a suffrage organisation, and in the early 1920s it endeavoured to work towards the completion of women's enfranchisement and, like the NUSEC, pursued the elusive concept of equality. Just as members of the Union became increasingly involved in other issues, so the Alliance was pushed by its own membership into a concern with international affairs, and in particular with the League of Nations. In 1914 the IWSA had refused to take part in the conference at the Hague: in 1926, the situation was very different. Europe was not at war, so that patriotic fervour could not militate against women working towards peace.

Hints of the problems which lay ahead arose in 1922 when a committee was formed to discuss and to raise funds for the IWSA congress to be held in the following year. At a meeting of the committee Maude Royden suggested that peace should be on the agenda in Rome. Others argued that raising the issue would 'wreck the conference', and Elizabeth Abbott asserted that it was the role of the IWSA 'not to stand for peace, but to demand that perfect equality and freedom without which they could not, effectively "stand for" anything'. In her message to the Congress Margery Corbett Ashby avoided this difficult area, declaring that the IWSA stood for peace, and that 'peace must rest on understanding and common work for a single aim gives us that understanding'.[48] She still then saw the work of the IWSA beyond suffrage to be concerned with economic and moral inequalities. The second resolution adopted at Rome pressed 'for the use of judicial methods in place of force', but the IWSA did not begin to be seriously involved in activities directed towards peace until 1926. In that year the division of opinion on the question of protective legislation coincided with arguments on the peace issue. It is no coincidence that these debates occurred at a time when there was a division in the NUSEC over protective legislation and the meaning of equality. Some of the same women who were angry at what they understood as a dilution of commitment to equality in the NUSEC, felt that the IWSA was being drawn from the struggle for equality to work for peace.

In 1926 the IWSA established a new committee with the aim of studying 'how women can best help to secure peace'. Kathleen Courtney welcomed the new Peace Study Committee. She reported on its first conference which was held in Amsterdam in the autumn of 1927, commenting on how the association of peace with feminism had divided feminists in 1915:

> The whirligig of time does indeed bring in his revenges. It was in 1915 that a number of members of the Executive of the NUWSS felt obliged to resign because they found themselves in a minority in holding that the ideas underlying the claim for the enfranchisement of women were closely bound up with the ideals of peace, and because they wanted the Union to study the cause and the cure of war.[49]

Her confidence that there was general acceptance of the connection between the two questions was not justified. In January 1928 an article in *Jus Suffragii* suggested the IAWSEC had excluded the only 'true blue feminists' in the USA – the National Woman's Party – and accused it of becoming interested only in 'Social Reform and Peace.' In a response which her protagonist described as having 'treated me with disarming gentleness and courtesy'. Corbett Ashby pointed out that the decision to move into new areas of work had been made 'by democratic process'. She avoided any explicit statement of her own views on the links between feminism and working for peace. It was left to her predecessor as president, Carrie Chapman Catt, to argue the case for such a connection. Catt was working alongside Kathleen Courtney in a joint peace campaign. She had taken part in the Woman's Peace Congress in New York in 1915 at which the Woman's Peace Party had been launched, but had hesitated to use her influence to sway the IWSA to support the Hague Congress in the spring of that year, and later the suffrage organisation which she led agreed to offer their services to the government when the United States became involved in the war. But she, like Millicent Garrett Fawcett, did not believe that women were in any way responsible for that war, and in the mid-1920s they both supported the association of women's organisations with the peace movement. Catt asserted that:

> there never would have been a feministic movement had war not controlled the peoples of the entire world. Since war reduced women to subservience, it is not unnatural that voting women should recognize their ancient enemy and want to join the movement for its abolition.[50]

Catt's argument was part of a philosophy of gender difference which was seen by some to lie behind the ideas of the 'new feminists'. Yet it is no more possible to divide feminists into distinct groups on peace than on 'equality'. The attitude of members of the Six Point Group and contributors to *Time & Tide* reflect the complexity of feminist groupings on peace in the 1920s. In 1926 the paper was concerned about the tendency of 'the women's movement . . . to be diverted into every fresh reform that happens to take its fancy'; one of those reforms was 'peace by arbitration'. The paper's view was that 'preliminary to any step towards peace' was the achievement for women of 'complete citizenship and absolutely equal rights and opportunities of service with men in their own country'. In 1928 Helen Archdale, the first editor, rejected the association of feminism and peace, and compared an organisation such as the NUSEC and the IAWSEC to 'a huge, rather damp blanket keeping women under, hindering those who wish to rise, but enveloping comfortably those who are content to be depressed'. Yet Maude Royden, who supported the Six Point Group, toured the United States speaking for the WILPF. Emmeline Pethick Lawrence was a member of both the

WILPF and the strictly equalitarian and 'old feminist' Open Door council.[51]

Elizabeth Robins was closely associated with *Time & Tide* and the Six Point Group, and her commitment to the idea that the search for peace was an essential element of feminism was apparent in *Ancilla's Share*. Robins's argument was that men's contempt of women was partly based on fear. She also believed that fear was at the root of 'man's will-to-war'; a fear 'which seeks assuagement by inspiring a yet greater fear . . . '. She linked opposition to enfranchisement with the 'domination of other human beings by violence'. These ideas are similar to those of Swanwick and Royden, and Robins wrote admiringly of the work of the WILPF. She was prepared to admit that not all women were pacifists, nor all men 'war-mongers', but she did believe that 'Wars will cease when woman's will-to-peace is given equal hearing and equal authority in council with man's will-to-war.'[52] Crystal Eastman was also associated with the Six Point Group and she was a founder of the Woman's Peace Party in the United States.

Towards the end of the 1920s the search for peace through disarmament became the dominant issue for many feminists, although there was no general agreement that feminism necessarily entailed pacifism. It is not possible to draw clear lines which delineate the attitudes on the relevance of working for peace to the feminist struggle. Three women who were as closely associated as Courtney, Swanwick and Marshall, and whose ideas were in basic agreement, worked in different ways and their attitudes and ideas were not identical. There was a spectrum of feminist views on peace in the 1920s, but the differences were not such as to prevent many women whose views on the precise nature of feminism were different from working together. In June 1929 Margery Corbett Ashby and Eleaner Rathbone were at the IAWSEC Congress in Berlin which passed a resolution declaring that it was 'the duty of women of all nations to work for friendly international relations, to demand the substitution of judicial methods for those of force . . . '. During that summer the British section of the WILPF was active in the General Election which brought Rathbone into Parliament. Kathleen Courtney presided over a mass meeting of women on the eve of the dissolution. Writing of the results of the election Emmeline Pethick Lawrence declared that the crusade 'to secure the return to Parliament of men and women pledged to support arbitration and disarmament and to make peace a reality', had been successful. She wanted to make her readers realise that these changes represented 'a real growth of the peace spirit', and that this growth had been 'quickened' by the enfranchisement of women. She believed that 'Women can kill the war tradition if they will.'[53]

Conclusion

The feminist commitment of the fourteen women on whom this book has focused burst forth into a variety of activities which have not been contained within these pages. As the suffragist whose words were quoted in the introduction warned, the objectives of the women's movement in the period after the war were diverse, and lacked the apparent coherence of the suffrage campaigns. No two of the fourteen chose the same path, yet only one, Evelyn Sharp, can be said to have moved away from feminism. Maude Royden believed that it was no longer possible 'for me to make feminism my first claim.' Yet her work in the church was inevitably concerned with the recognition of the validity of women's spirituality. The peace movement is not exclusively or essentially feminist, but Helena Swanwick, Catherine Marshall, Kathleen Courtney, Emmeline Pethick Lawrence, Maude Royden, Margery Corbett Ashby and Mary Sheepshanks understood their commitment to peace to be rooted in their feminism. They all continued to be active in international affairs in the 1930s.

The First World War provided the impetus for those who worked for peace in the interwar period. The pressures of war had divided the forces of the NUWSS, but the exigencies of the international situation rather than that division drew feminists into the peace movement: it was not a case of feminists abandoning the cause. Emmeline Pethick Lawrence was active in the WILPF and acted as president of the Women's Freedom League from 1926 until 1935. Kathleen Courtney was willing to work through the NUSEC in pursuit of equality, but she was drawn inexorably into working for peace by the urgent need to help establish international structures which could make peace a reality. In the 1930s the threat of fascism would be added to threats to peace in Europe and thus made the need to work in those areas even more pressing.

The pursuit of equality was seen to be less urgent than the pursuit of peace – and found to be even more intractable. The clarity of the aims which the Six Point Group and the NUSEC presented to their members disguised the formidable social and economic forces which propped up gender inequalities. It was all too clear by the end of the 1920s that the search for equality would not respond to a short, sharp campaign, but would need many more years of persistent work. Women who sought equality were often demonstrating in their personal lives the need and importance of economic independence, and they had only a limited time available for public work. They gave this time in their different ways, and there is no doubt that they contributed to the gradual move towards economic equality which is as yet incomplete.

Differences in political understanding, based to some extent on class, put a considerable strain on feminist solidarity in the 1920s. In order to succeed in the established political structures feminists found that they had to be good party women. This was especially true of the Labour Party which tended to see women's demands for economic equality as a diversion and sometimes as a threat to the solidarity of the Labour Movement. Perhaps the way to understand this uneasy relationship is to see the women in the Labour Movement as part of a wider women's movement which was not always or exclusively feminist. The definition of feminism cannot be exact, but its use by women in the 1920s does suggest a boundary between women in organisations like the NUSEC and the Six Point Group and those in the Labour Movement. One of the crucial distinctions was the recognition by feminist groups of the need for continued separatism. The solidarity of the suffrage struggle had its genesis in the strength which women gain from working with each other. However committed women were to feminist aims, once they left separate women's organisations it was easy for them to lose confidence.

A lack of confidence was apparent in an article on the new voter which appeared in *The Woman's Leader* in the summer of 1928.[1] The author was clearly a seasoned canvasser and she welcomed the prospect of 'discussing the affairs of State' with an 'attractive capped and aproned Phyllis'. She was also anxious that before Phyllis became 'the prey of the party politician', she should 'have some background in what we may call non-party politics'. Part of this background information would be on 'the problems which at the present time should be the special concern of the women of this country'. The author was perplexed as to how Phyllis was to be reached in order to be given this information. There were on offer a NUSEC summer school in Oxford and the Junior Council of the London Society for National Service (as Strachey had persuaded the LSWS to rename itself.) Partly because of its determination to reach Phyllis, the NUSEC was reorganised in the late twenties and re-emerged in the thirties as the Townswomen's Guilds. The impetus for this development had come from Eva Hubback's feeling that the NUSEC could learn from the Women's Institutes how to bring much larger groups of women together. Margery Corbett Ashby was largely responsible for the success of the development, while Hubback herself directed the continuation of the political work of the NUSEC in a separate organisation, the National Council for Equal Citizenship. The task facing this body was elusive, and the number of active women was reduced. The social and educational draw of the Guilds proved attractive to much larger numbers of women than the formidable task of pressing for economic equality.[2] Yet feminist organisations continued in existence after 1928 despite pressures to disperse. Until 1981 the Six Point Group was a small but persistent voice reminding feminists of the areas in which equality had not been achieved.

The pressure to disperse acted on the individual suffragist. In September 1927, Eva Hubback resigned her paid post with the NUSEC to become Principal of Morley College. Although she remained an active feminist her absorption in a new and challenging job meant that she was inevitably less effective. Mary Stocks had been living in Manchester since 1924, coming down to London between Tuesday and Friday in the fourth week of each month. She became increasingly involved in local activities, including the WEA, voluntary social work and the birth control clinic. In 1930 she was appointed a JP and became a self-confessed 'statutory woman'. She ascribed the evolution of this species to the limited number of 'able and public spirited women' known to those responsible for placing the token woman on to commissions and committees; 'the few they did know about were used over and over again'. If such women were feminist this was an almost foolproof way of preventing them from being effective as feminists. Margery Corbett Ashby's absorption into the Townswomen's Guilds operated in a similar way; the continuity of her own feminism was at least partially smothered by her public image. Emmeline Pethick Lawrence's commitment to feminism did not cease, but her voice was to some extent muted by the decision she and Fred made that he should be the one to pursue a parliamentary career.[3]

For Margaret Rhondda the achievement of equal franchise was the climax of her political and feminist activity. She knew that equality had not been won in 1918 and so she had remained active. The Six Point Group was committed to equality of pay and opportunities at work and it was far from reaching these objectives in 1928. Rhondda may have been able to see that there was a long, slow haul ahead and the note of impatience detectable in *Time & Tide* may reflect her increasing restlessness with 'the abolition of various inequalities in the laws'. Later she admitted that:

> when, in 1928, the vote came on equal terms, one felt free to drop the business.
>
> It was a blessed relief to feel that one had not got to trouble with things of that sort any more. They are essential, of course. They must be done. And I like and respect the women who do them – indeed, the chief attraction of the work to me was that, in the course of doing it, one came across some extraordinarily fine people. Some of the nicest people I have ever known were, and are, doing that work – but it was not really my kind of work, it never had been. I was never really interested in changing the details of laws. I want bigger game than that.[4]

Eleanor Rathbone was prepared to continue to work towards changes in the law, and she was the one woman of the fourteen to achieve a position of political prominence. As an MP she consistently supported the political rights of women, especially in the international arena. Ray Strachey worked with Rathbone on the enfranchisement of Indian women. She continued her work for women's employment, and was active with Pippa in the Women's Employment Federation which grew out of the London Society. She continued to write on feminism despite the fact that the reduction of her private income in the depression meant that she took on a paid post as Nancy Astor's secretary in 1931.[5]

As an Independent MP Rathbone worked very much alone, but her influence and her presence as what we might term a role model should not be underestimated. It is important to remember that the influence of individual women could be exerted in ways which are elusive and yet powerful. A letter from Emmeline Pethick Lawrence to Evelyn Sharp gives a hint at the sort of power which the historian cannot easily grasp:

> I have sometimes tried to give you a hint of how I see you – simply because I couldn't help it. Beauty, when you see it, compels that love which passes beyond person and becomes worship of life. Creative attainment in the plane of spiritual ideas demands austerity both of character and conditions of life — Today when I saw you at the 1917 Club with Mrs. Buxton, I seemed to realize it

more than ever – she creative in her home and her children – and you creative of the spiritual idea which if understood and accepted is potent to revolutionize the world.[6]

The recognition of the personal in politics is one way in which feminism has sought to revolutionise the world. The identification of birth control as a political issue by feminists in the interwar period is an example of such a recognition, and of the difficulties inherent in such a change. Naomi Mitchison wrote of the desire of her generation to combine the 'inside and the outside life' in politics in a letter to her aunt. Elizabeth Haldane was a staunch suffragist and a 'statutory woman' of the interwar period: Mitchison accused her aunt's generation of saying of women:

either that we really ran the outside things from the inside (the hand that rocks the cradle rules the world) or that the outside things weren't really important.[7]

Naomi Mitchison could see that the generation of postwar feminists to which she belonged was a disappointment to the prewar suffragist. She believed that the damage done to her generation by the war was underestimated:

The first wave of disturbance was the one at the time, and now we're in the second, after the period of calm and exhaustion immediately following the thing . . . . You have still a balance for your life: all that incredible pre-war period when things seemed in the main still settled, just moving solidly and calmly like a glacier towards all sorts of progress. But we have had the bottom of things knocked out completely, we have been sent reeling into chaos and it seems to us that none of your standards are either fixed or necessarily good because in the end they resulted in this smash up. We have to learn to try and make a world for ourselves, basing it as far as possible on love and awareness, mental and bodily, because it seems to us that all the repressions and formulae, all the cutting off of part of experience, which perhaps looked sensible and even right in those calm years, have not worked.[8]

The war dislocated women's lives and exaggerated the discontinuity between different generations. Before the war Elizabeth Robins had seen the 'woman question' clearly; after the war she found 'that clearness breathed upon, till one lost sight for a while of what one had seen and learned.'9 Individual suffragists persevered, pursuing and extending the objectives of Victorian and Edwardian feminism. A new generation of postwar feminists would find their own way to revolutionise the world.

Appendix:
Fourteen Feminists

(Dame) Margery Corbett Ashby (*1882–1981*) Eldest daughter of socially concerned and politically active parents; father a landowner, briefly a Liberal MP; mother a feminist and a Poor Law Guardian. Educated by her parents and governesses, then at Newnham College, Cambridge. Became a suffragist at Cambridge – briefly paid secretary to the NUWSS – active in IWSA.
First World War Husband in the army – birth of their only son – some voluntary relief work.
1920s Active in the NUSEC and President IWSA. Stood as a Liberal candidate eight times – remained a politically active feminist into her eighties.

(Dame) Kathleen Courtney (*1878–1974*) Daughter of an army officer. Educated at Malvern School and Lady Margaret Hall, Oxford. Voluntary social worker in Lambeth and then worked in the office of the Oxford University Extension delegacy. Heavily involved in suffrage work in Manchester and then secretary of NUWSS.
First World War Founder-member of WILPF – key role in negotiations leading up to enfranchisement.
1920s Active in NUSEC and WILPF. Involved in peace movement until her nineties.

Eva Hubback (*1886–1949*) Wealthy, philanthropic, Jewish family. Educated at St Felix, Suffolk, and Newnham. Fabian at Cambridge. Voluntary social work and elected Poor Law Guardian. NUWSS, but not heavily involved. Married Bill Hubback, lecturer and civil servant. Three children born before Bill died in the war.
First World War Eva temporary lecturer at Newnham.
1920s Paid parliamentary secretary to NUSEC.
1928 Principal of Morley College – politically active feminist until her sudden death.

Catherine Marshall (*1880–1964*) Daughter of a housemaster at Harrow. Educated at St Leonards School, St Andrews. Active in Liberal politics, then totally absorbed in suffrage movement. Parliamentary secretary to the NUWSS. Active in promoting links between suffrage and labour movements.
First World War Secretary of WILPF – left because of demands of the No-Conscription Fellowship.
1917 Overwork led to breakdown. Never fully recovered her health.
1920s Active in WILPF.

Emmeline Pethick Lawrence (*1867–1954*) Wealthy family, father a JP and passionately opposed to injustice. Inadequately eductated at private schools. Worked and lived in West London Mission. With Mary Neal, formed Esperance Social Guild. Married Fred Lawrence, wealthy Liberal lawyer. Together gave vital support to WSPU.
1913 Asked to leave WSPU – helped form United Suffragists.
First World War Present at formation of WILPF at the Hague.
1920s Member, later President WFL, supported WILPF.

Eleanor Rathbone (*1878–1946*) Wealthy and public-spirited Liverpool - family. Father social reformer and Liberal MP. Educated privately and at Somerville, Oxford. Voluntary social, political and educational work in Liverpool.
1897 Secretary to the Liverpool Suffrage Society. On NUWSS executive committee.
1909 Elected first woman councillor in Liverpool.
First World War Relief work.
1920s President of NUSEC, led campaign for family endowment.
1929 Elected independent MP and remained in Parliament until her sudden death.

Margaret Haig, Lady Rhondda (*1883–1958*) Only daughter of Welsh land- and mine-owner and Liberal MP. Educated at St Leonards School, St Andrews, and Somerville, Oxford. Married Humphrey Mackworth – worked for her father. Militantly active in WSPU.
First World War Continued to work with her father; almost drowned in the *Lusitania*.
1920s Founded Six Point Group and *Time & Tide*.

Elizabeth Robins (*1862–1952*) An American – became an actor against the wishes of her family. Married an actor who committed suicide. Came to Europe – chose to settle in London. The struggle to make a living and to put on Ibsen's plays made her a feminist. Began to write novels. Admired the Pankhursts. Inspiring speaker and member of the WSPU board. Established her home, Backsettown in Sussex, as a rest home for suffragettes and other women to whom she gave support.
First World War Worked as a volunteer in a hospital library – continued to write.
1920s Member of Six Point Group; wrote *Ancilla's Share*, a powerful claim for the need to continue the feminist struggle.

Maude Royden (*1876–1956*) Daughter of Liverpool shipowner and Conservative MP. Educated at Cheltenham Ladies College and Lady Margaret Hall, Oxford. Voluntary work in Liverpool – parish work with Rev. Hudson Shaw – lectured and preached in London. Joined NUWSS – member of executive.
First World War Member of WILPF – preached in the City.
1920s Supported Six Point Group and spoke for the WILPF in the US – very active in the Church of England until her death.

Evelyn Sharp (*1869–1955*) Large, middle-class, somewhat impoverished, family. Educated at Strathallan House, girls' school in London. Wrote in secret at home – ran away to London to earn her own living by writing and teaching. Militantly active in WSPU and then joined United Suffragists.
First World War Continued suffrage work – active in final stages of pressure to enfranchise women in 1918.
1920s Refused to support separate women's organisations. Wrote in support of Labour Movement and worked as volunteer for Quaker relief in Europe.

Mary Sheepshanks (*1878–1958*) Eldest daughter of an impoverished cleric in Liverpool. Educated at Liverpool High School and at Newnham, Cambridge. Worked in University Settlement in Southwark, then in Stepney.
1897 Vice-Principal Morley College. Active in NUWSS and IWSA.
First World War Editor of IWSA journal – member of WILPF.
1920s Active in WILPF – politically active into her seventies.

(Dame) Mary Stocks (*1891–1975*) Daughter of London doctor. Educated at St Paul's and LSE. Voluntary work for school care committee. Joined NUWSS. Married John Stocks, lecturer at Oxford – three children.
First World War Taught at Cambridge and for WEA.
1920s Active in NUSEC and in campaigns for birth control and family endowment. Later became known public figure.

Ray Strachey (*1887–1940*) Daughter of Mary Pearsall Smith, American. Brought up largely by feminist grandmother. Educated Kensington High School and Newnham, Cambridge. Active in NUWSS from student days. Wrote a novel and a biography – travelled. Married Oliver Strachey – two children.
First World War Active in women's employment work.
1920s Active in London Society for Women's Service. Stood three times as an independent candidate. Politically active until her sudden death.

Helena Swanwick (*1864–1939*) Daughter of artist from German-speaking Denmark. Educated at Notting Hill High School and Newnham, Cambridge. Taught and wrote. Married Fred Swanwick, lecturer – moved to Manchester. Joined NUWSS – edited *The Cause* in London.
First World War Chairman of British Section, WILPF.
1920s Active in WILPF and wrote on foreign affairs.

Notes

Letters from Ray Strachey(RS) come from her daughter's collection/Smith Archives, Oxford.

Letters to Catherine Marshall(CEM) are from the papers held at the Cumbrian Record Office. I am deeply grateful to Jo Vellacott for the work she did sorting through and organising the Marshall papers. The task was huge and the result immensely helpful to anyone consulting the papers.

Letters to and from Evelyn Sharp(ES) are from the papers held at the Bodleian Library.

Letters to and from Margery Corbett Ashby (MCA) are from the papers held at the Fawcett Library.

Letters to Marie Stopes are from the Stopes Collection in the British Library.

The Women's International League for Peace and Freedom papers referred to are those in the British Library of Political and Economic Science unless otherwise stated.

1 Introduction

1. Evelyn Sharp, *Unfinished Adventure* (John Lane, Bodley Head, 1933), p. 4.
2. Cicely Hamilton, *Life Errant* (J.M. Dent, London, 1935), p.67.
3. Ray Strachey (RS) to Mary Berenson (MB), 11 February 1918.
4. Eva McNaghten to Catherine Marshall (CEM), 12 February 1918; 4/80.
5. *The Woman's Leader* (WL), 12 March 1920.
6. Dale Spender, *There's Always Been a Women's Movement This Century* (Pandora Press, London 1983).
7. Ray Strachey, *The Cause* (Virago, London, 1978).
8. Liz Stanley, *Feminism and Friendship* (Studies in Sexual Politics No. 8, University of Manchester).
9. Maude Royden's and Mary Sheepshanks's autobiographical chapters are in the Fawcett Library. Margery Corbett Ashby's Memoirs are in the possession of her son, Dr Michael Ashby.
10. Linda Anderson, *Vera Brittain: Not I But My Generation*, paper delivered to History Workshop 21, Newcastle, November 1987. Helena Swanwick, *I Have Been Young* (Victor Gollancz, London, 1935).
11. Emmeline Pethick Lawrence, *My Part in a Changing World* (Victor Gollancz, London, 1938), Preface.
12. Sharp, *Unfinished Adventure*, p.9. Elizabeth Robins, *Both Sides of the Curtain* (Heineman, London, 1940).
13. Margaret Rhondda, *This Was My World* (Macmillan, London, 1933) pp.v,vi,x,xi,xiii.
14. Mary Stocks, *My Commonplace Book* (Peter Davies, London, 1970), Prologue.

2 Coming Together

1. RS to MB, 10 July 1908.
2. Grant, McCutcheon and Sanders, *St Leonards: 1877– 1927* (OUP, Oxford, 1927) p. 115.
3. CEM to Julia Grant, 17 February 1903; 2/20.
4. Margaret McKerrow to CEM, 14 August 1899; 2/16.
5. Ibid., 30 October 1899; 2/15. Frank Marshall to CEM, 22 February 1899; 2/16. McKerrow to CEM, 22 January 1906; 2/23.
6. McKerrow to CEM, ibid.
7. Ibid.
8. Frank Marshall to CEM, 9 June 1912; 2/30.
9. Marshall papers; 3/48, 49, 50.
10. Frank Marshall to CEM, 1 January 1913; 2/31.
11. Marshall Papers; 3/26, 29, 32, 33.
12. CEM to Charles Trevelyan, 26 September 1913, Trevelyan papers, Newcastle University Library; 32/59.
13. Ethel Snowden, *A Political Pilgrim in Europe* (Cassell, London, 1921), p. 81. Swanwick to CEM, 4 March 1918; 4/80.
14. Vera Brittain, *Testament of Experience* (Victor Gollancz, London, 1957), p. 226. Swanwick, *I Have Been Young*, pp. 19, 48.
15. Swanwick, *I Have Been Young*, pp. 58, 82.
16. Ibid., pp. 144, 495, 162.
17. Ibid. p. 173.
18. Ibid. p. 223.
19. Ibid. p. 184. Francesca Wilson, *Kathleen Courtney* typescript biography, p. 7, Lady Margaret Hall Library, Oxford.
20. Margot Asquith, *Myself When Young* (Muller, London, 1938), p. 376.
21. Royden to Courtney, quoted in Wilson, *Kathleen Courtney*, op. cit., p. 22.
22. Royden to Courtney, 6 October, February 1902; LMH Library.
23. Royden to Courtney, 2 August 1902; LMH Library.
24. Swanwick, *I Have Been Young*, p. 235.
25. Maude Royden, *Bid Me Discourse*, autobiographical chapters, Fawcett Library. Courtney to CEM, 7 June 1914; 3/29.
26. Information on Rathbone's life comes from Mary Stocks's biography: *Eleanor Rathbone* (Gollancz, London, 1949).
27. Rathbone to CEM, 30 October 1915; 13/48.
28. Information on Sheepshanks's life comes from Sybil Oldfield, *Spinsters of This Parish* (Virago, London, 1984).
29. Sheepshanks to Bertrand Russell, quoted in Oldfield *Spinsters*, pp. 137–42.
30. Hilda Clark was training to become a doctor. Alice worked in the family shoe firm in Street, and then worked at the LSE and wrote a book on women in the seventeenth century.
31. Letters from Sheepshanks to CEM; 3/26. Anne Wiltshire, *Most Dangerous Women* (Pandora, London, 1985) Chapter 1.
32. Sharp, *Unfinished Adventure*, pp. 151, 18.
33. Ibid., pp. 33, 39.
34. Sharp, *Holiday Diary*, 29 June, 1921.

35. Sharp, *Unfinished Adventure*, p. 52, 54.
36. Ibid., p. 64.
37. The National Union of Women Workers with Women and Children was founded in 1895 to coordinate the activities of women voluntary workers. After the war there was an unsuccessful attempt to unite the NUWW with the NUWSS. It was then renamed the National Council of Women.
38. Sharp, *Unfinished Adventure*, p. 130.
39. Ibid., p. 132.
40. Hugh Brown to Sharp, 2 April 1908.
41. Nurse Brown to Sharp, 2 January 1908.
42. Jane Sharp to Sharp, 3 June 1909.
43. Ibid., 25 July 1913.
44. Sharp, *Unfinished Adventure*, p. 147.
45. Hertha Ayrton, a physicist, and her daughter Barbara who opened their house to suffragettes released from prison.
46. Information on Robins's life comes from Jane Marcus's Ph.D. thesis, Northwestern University, 1973 and from Joanne Gates, *Stitches in a Critical Time*, typescript, 1986.
47. Robins, *The Convert* (The Women's Press, London, 1980).
48. Swanwick, *I Have Been Young*, p. 191.
49. Pethick Lawrence, *My Part in a Changing World*, pp. 50, 65, 70, 78, 79.
50. Ibid., pp 86, 96.
51. Ibid., p. 124.
52. Ibid., pp. 285, 146, 176, 225, 295.
53. Sharp to Pethick Lawrence, 1 August 1914, Pethick Lawrence papers, Trinity; 6/269.
54. Liz Stanley has pointed out that it has become a convention when writing about the WSPU to assume that it was synonymous with the Pankhursts and that there is evidence which challenges this assumption: Liz Stanley and Ann Morley, *The Life, Times, Friends and Death of Emily Wilding Davison* (The Women's Press, London, 1988).
55. Rhondda, *This Was My World*, pp. 119, vii.
56. Ibid., pp. 77, 80, 81, 82.
57. Ibid., p. 108.
58. Ibid., pp. 108, 111, 118, 120, 212.
59. Ibid., pp. 220, 235.
60. Mary Agnes Hamilton, *Remembering My Good Friends* (Jonathan Cape, London, 1944), p. 551. Corbett Ashby, 'Why I am a Liberal Candidate', 1918. Hamilton, op. cit., p. 52.
61. Swanwick, *I Have Been Young*, p. 193.
62. RS to MB, 17 December 1907, 29 June 1909.
63. Jane Harrison was a student and then a tutor at Newnham. In 1909 she published a letter describing her conversion to support for suffrage, entitled 'Homo Sum'.
64. Barbara Strachey, *Remarkable Relations* (Gollancz, London, 1980), p. 238. I am indebted to this book for information on Ray and her family.

65.   Ibid., p. 259.
66.   RS to MB, 20 June, 29 July 1914.
67.   Diana Hopkinson, *Family Inheritance, A Life of Eva Hubback* (Staples Press, London 1954), p. 42. I am indebted to this book for information on Eva Hubback's life.
68.   Ibid., p. 54.
69.   Mary Stocks, Woman's Hour, 13 October 1952; typescript in the Fawcett Library.
70.   Stocks, *My Commonplace Book*, p. 2. Information on Stocks's life comes from this source.
71.   Ibid., p. 74.

3 Suffragists and the War

1.   Swanwick, *I Have Been Young*, pp. 233, 239.
2.   Quoted in Anne Wiltsher, *Most Dangerous Women* (Pandora, London, 1985); Swanwick, *I Have Been Young*, p. 241.
3.   Marshall papers; 3/37.
4.   Stocks, *Eleanor Rathbone*, p. 73.
5.   Pethick Lawrence, *My Part in a Changing World*, p. 305.
6.   Sheepshanks, Autobiography, p. 56.
7.   *Jus Suffragii (Jus)*, 1 November 1915. Courtney to Chrystal MacMillan, 15 June 1915, Marshall Papers; 3/46. Millicent Garrett Fawcett, Address to NUWSS, 22 January 1915, Marshall Papers; 3/44.
8.   Swanwick, *I Have Been Young*, pp. 241, 247; *Women and War* (UDC, London, 1915), pp. 9–14.
9.   Courtney to CEM, 13 October 1914; 3/37. Swanwick to CEM, 22 March 1915; 3/45.
10.   NUWSS/EC 15 October 1914, Marshall papers; 3/37.
11.   Maude Royden, 'War and the Women's Movement', in C.R. Buxton, (ed.) *Towards a Lasting Settlement* (Allen & Unwin, London, 1915), pages not numbered.
12.   NUWSS/EC Meeting, op. cit.
13.   NUWSS Council Meeting 12 November 1914, Marshall Papers, 3/39, Courtney to CEM, 24 November 1914; 3/39.
14.   Rathbone to CEM, 14 November 1914; 3/39. Mary Stocks, Election Address, February 4–6, 1915, Marshall papers; 3/44. Millicent Garrett Fawcett to Helena Auerback, IAV papers, Amsterdam.
15.   Draft letter, CEM to Garrett Fawcett, 28 November 1914; 3/39.
16.   Isabella Ford to Garrett Fawcett, October 1914, Autograph Collection, Fawcett Library; K/28.
17.   Swanwick to Garrett Fawcett, 19 December 1914, ibid., IL/49.
18.   RS to MB, 9, 18 December 1914, 6 February 1915.
19.   CEM to Ethel Williams, 2 February 1915; 3/43.
20.   Frank Marshall to CEM, November 1914; 2/32. CEM, speech to Newcastle Suffrage Society, January 1915; 3/43. CEM to Stocks, 2 February 1915; 3/44.
21.   CEM to Strachey, 3 February 1914; 3/44.

22. Jane Harrison to Gilbert Murray, August 1914, quoted in Jessie Stewart, *Jane E. Harrison* (Merlin Press, London, 1959), p. 147.
23. Irene Cooper Willis, *England's Holy War* (Knopf, New York, 1928).
24. Stocks, *My Commonplace Book*, p. 117.
25. Jane Harrison to Gilbert Murray, November 1914, quoted in Stewart, *Jane E. Harrison*, op. cit., p. 154. Helena Swanwick, *Women and War*, p. 8.
26. Rhondda, *This Was My World*, p. 274.
27. MCA to Marie Corbett, 19, 21 September 1914.
28. Ibid., 19 December 1914.
29. Margaret Hills to CEM, 3 November 1917; 2/35.
30. Stocks, *My Commonplace Book*, p. 115.
31. Jane Harrison to Gilbert Murray, August 1914, September 1914; Jane Harrison, *War and Reaction*, quoted in Stewart, *Jane E. Harrison*, op. cit. pp. 147, 149.
32. Garrett Fawcett to Auerbach, 4 November 1916, IAV papers, Amsterdam. Courtney to CEM, 15 June 1915; 3/49.
33. RS to MB, 6 February 1915. NUWSS Council 4–6 February 1915, Marshall papers; 3/44. Frank Marshall to CEM, 5 March 1915; 2/33.
34. Frank Marshall to CEM, ibid.
35. Garrett Fawcett to CEM, 6 March 1915; Alice Clark to CEM, 29, 30 March 1915; 3/45.
36. Swanwick to CEM, 22, 24 March 1915; 3/45.
37. RS to MB, 19 April 1915. Garrett Fawcett to Auerbach, 16 March 1915, IAV papers.
38. Garrett Fawcett to Carrie Chapman Catt, 15 December 1914, quoted in Oldfield, *Spinsters of This Parish*, p. 190.
39. NUWSS/EC Minutes, 18 March 1915.
40. British Committee of the Women's International Congress. *Towards Permanent Peace*: A Record of the Women's International Congress, Fawcett Library, London.
41. Ibid.
42. WIL Annual Reports.
43. Catherine Webb, *Woman with the Basket* (WCG, London, 1927), p. 170.
44. RS to MB, 29 April 1915. Swanwick, *I Have Been Young*, pp. 285–90.
45. Braybon, *Women Workers in the First World War* (Croom Helm, London, 1980), p. 54.
46. Barbara Hammond gave this evidence from the experience of a friend in a letter to Lawrence Hammond, 2 December 1915, Hammond papers, Bodleian. RS to MB, 28 June, 10 March, 22 June 1915. File on Society of Women Welders, Fawcett Library; 3/26. Barbara Drake, *Women in Trade Unions* (Virago, London, 1984), pp. 82–3.
47. RS to MB 13 August, 21 September, 1914. Courtney to Chrystal MacMillan, 15 June 1915, Marshall papers; 3/46. Swanwick to CEM, 2 Nov. 1916; 2/34. Wilson, Kathleen Courtney, p. 27.
48. Octavia Wilberforce, autobiography, p. 11. Dedication by Robins in *Camilla* (Hodder & Stoughton, London, 1918). May Sinclair, *Impressions of the War in Belgium* (Hutchinson, London, 1927). Rhondda, *This Was My World*, Ch. xvi.

49. RS to MB, 26 August 1918. Sharp, *Unfinished Adventure*, p. 159.
50. Wilson, Kathleen Courtney p. 30. Courtney to her family, 9 May 1916, Fawcett Library; CI, 1–4.
51. RS to MB, 20 June, 7 December 1915.
52. Marshall papers; 3/49, 3/50.
53. Sharp, *Unfinished Adventure*, pp. 157–63.
54. Ibid., pp. 164–6. A Few Suffragists to Sharp, 16 November 1916.
55. NUWSS/EC Minutes 3 December 1915, 3 February 1916, Marshall papers; 3/49, 50.
56. Ibid., 26 March 1916; 3/50. RS to MB, 12, 15 August 1916.
57. Sharp, *Unfinished Adventure*, p. 169. ILP, City of London Branch, to CEM, 15 March 1917. NUWSS/EC Minutes, 12 February 1917, Fawcett Library. Stocks *Eleanor Rathbone*, p. 83.
58. RS to MB 11 February 1917. CEM to Fawcett, 7 November 1917; 3/50, 51.
59. Fawcett to CEM, 18 February 1918; 3/52. NUWSS/EC Minutes, 1918, Fawcett Library.
60. Swanwick to CEM, 5 August 1916; 4/78.
61. John Mennell to CEM, 6 November 1917; 4/26.
62. For a study of the relationship between Marshall and Russell, see Jo Vellacott, *Bertrand Russell and the Pacifists in the First World War* (Harvester, Sussex, 1980). Russell to CEM, 7 November 1916; 4/12.
63. Swanwick to CEM, 28 March 1917, CEM to Swanwick, 29 March 1917; 3/51. Marshall Papers, 4/20, 21.
64. Desmond to CEM, 28 November 1916; 4/12. Caroline Marshall to CEM, 26 September 1916, Royden to CEM, 10 August 1916; 2/34. CEM, notes for a letter to Miss Ellis, February 1918; 4/29. CEM to Clifford Allen, 7 November 1916; 4/12.
65. CEM to Russell, 9 September 1917, CEM to Miss Rinder, 13 September 1917; 4/24.
66. Swanwick to CEM, 11 November 1917; 4/26.
67. CEM, notes for a letter to Miss Ellis, letter, op. cit.
68. Ibid. Swanwick to Allen, 11 August 1918; 4/30.
69. Courtney to CEM, 5 March 1918; 3/53.
70. Swanwick to Allen, op cit., Eva Kyle to CEM, n.d., Helen Ward to CEM, 28 September 1918; 4/30.
71. Royden to Courtney, 16 January 1918, Fawcett Library; HI, 1–8.
72. Strachey, op. cit., pp. 273 4. RS to MD, 9 May 1916.

4 Time of Hope, 1918–20

1. CEM, Proposals for a Women Citizens Association, March 1918; 3/5. CEM to Swanwick, 29 March 1917; 3/51.
2. Jill Liddington, 'The Women's Peace Crusade', in Dorothy Thompson (ed.), *Over Our Dead Bodies: Women Against the Bomb* (Virago, London, 1983). Swanwick to CEM, 4 March 1918; 4/80.

3. WIL/EC Minutes, 1918.
4. WIL Objects, Marshall papers; 4/77. Programme for WIL Population Conferences, ibid; 4/80.
5. Proposals for a Women Citizens Association, op. cit.
6. *Common Cause*, 15 February 1918.
7. Courtney to CEM, 5 March 1918; 3/52. Helen Ward to CEM, 28 September 1918; 4/30.
8. *Common Cause*, 21, 28 June 1918.
9. NUWSS/EC Minutes, January 1918, Fawcett Library. RS to MB, 10 March 1918.
10. Eleanor Rathbone, *Economic Journal*, 1917, and 'The Remuneration of Women' in Victor Gollancz (ed.), *The Making of Women, Oxford Essays on Feminism* (Gollancz, London, 1917).
11. Helen Ward to CEM, 28 September 1918; 4/30.
12. Stocks, *My Commonplace Book*, pp. 123–4.
13. Catherine Webb, *The Woman with the Basket*, p. 130. NUWSS Annual Council Report, 1916, Marshall Papers; 3/50.
14. Eleanor Rathbone, *The Disinherited Family* (Falling Wall Press, Bristol, 1986), p. 177. Marion Phillips (ed.) *Women in the Labour Party* (Headley Bros, London, 1918) pp. 30–31, 20, 24.
15. *Common Cause*, 7 Sept. 1918.
16. RS to MB, 14 Oct. 1918.
17. Jill Liddington, *The Life and Times of a Respectable Rebel* (Virago, London, 1984), pp. 295–8.
18. Pethick Lawrence, *My Part in a Changing World*, p. 322. Election Literature on Women Candidates, 1918, Marshall papers; 4/80. Kate Courtney, Diary, 4 Dec. 1918 (British Library of Political and Economic Science, London School of Economics.) *Common Cause*, 20 December 1918.
19. MCA to Brian Ashby, 16 Nov. 1918. RS to MB, 31 July 1918.
20. RS to MB, 31 July 1918.
21. Ibid., 23 October 1918. RS to family, 5 Nov. 1918. Edith How Martyn, *The Need for Women Members of Parliament* (Women's Freedom League, London, n.d.)
22. Constance Gore-Booth to Eva Gore-Booth, undated, in *Prison Letters of Countess Markievicz* (Virago, London, 1987) pp. 205–6.
23. RS to MB, 24 February 1918. Dan Mason to CEM, 1918; 5/1.
24. Sharp, *Unfinished Adventure*, p. 199. MCA to Brian Ashby, 16 November 1918.
25. RS to MB, 19 Jan. 1919. Swanwick to CEM, 28 March 1917; 3/51. Swanwick, *I Have Been Young*, p. 308. *Daily Herald*, 11 January 1919.
26. Swanwick, *I Have Been Young*, p. 307. RS to MB, 3 November 1918.
27. MCA to Brian Ashby, 11 November 1918.
28. Stocks, *My Commonplace Book*, p. 125. Kate Courtney, Diary, 4 December 1918. WIL/EC Minutes, 1918.
29. Pethick Lawrence, *My Part in a Changing World*, p. 325. WIL/EC Minutes, 4 March 1920.
30. Sharp, *Unfinished Adventure*, p. 199.

31. Swanwick, *I Have Been Young*, p. 318.
32. Ethel Williams, *Towards Peace and Freedom* (WIL, London, 1919), pp. 6 –7, 17–19.
33. Millicent Garrett Fawcett, Diary, 12 February 1919, Fawcett Papers; 90/175. RS to Pippa Strachey, 8 February 1919, Autograph collection, Fawcett Library; 8E.
34. Margery Fry to Eva Hubback, 10 April 1919, Fawcett Papers; 90/196.
35. MCA to Millicent Garrett Fawcett, 4 April, 10 May 1919, ibid; 90/194, 198.
36. RS to MB, 2, 16, June 1920.
37. MCA to Brian Ashby, 13 June 1920. WIL/EC Minutes, 4 March 1920. Maude Royden, Sermon, (Church of the League Militant, 1920), Royden Papers, Fawcett Library; 379.
38. Ethel Snowden, *A Political Pilgrim in Europe*, pp. 75–6.
39. WIL/EC Minutes, 13 September 1919.
40. *Common Cause*, 21 February, 14 March, 1919, 23 August, 13 September, 1920.
41. NUWSS/EC Minutes 22 Nov. 1917. *Common Cause*, 24 March 1918. LSWS, Report of General Meeting, 25 February 1919, Fawcett Library. RS to MB, 10 March 1919.
42. WIL/EC Minutes, 2 January 1919, 3, 18 September, 19 February 1919.
43. Swanwick to CEM, 20 February 1920; 4/82.
44. WIL Council Meeting, 22 October 1918. Swanwick to CEM, 5 February 1918; 4/81.
45. *Common Cause*, 10 October 1919.
46. NUWSS/EC Minutes, 6 December 1917, Fawcett Library.
47. Report of WIL Conference, 4 May 1920, Marshall Papers; 4/82. Guild Socialism was a movement within the Labour Movement in the first quarter of the twentieth century advocating the transformation of trade unions into producers' guilds which would control each branch of industry.
48. *Common Cause*, 4 April 1920.
49. WIL/EC Minutes, 7 Oct. 1920. Henry Nevinson to CEM, 12 August 1920; 5/3.
50. CEM to Arthur Henderson, 6 May 1920; 5/2.
51. Courtney to CEM, 5 March 1918; 3/52. CEM to Henderson, op. cit.
52. *WL*, 14 Dec. 1923.
53. *Common Cause*, 15 Dec. 1919. *WL*, 14 Dec. 1923.
54. RS to MB, 6, 20 Nov. 1919.
55. RS to MB, 1 Dec. 1919, 14 Feb. 1920.
56. RS to MB, 7 April, 6 June 1919.
57. *WL*, 12 March 1920.
58. RS to MB, 10 March 1919. *Common Cause*, 25 April 1919. RS to MB, 20 March 1919.
59. Middleton Papers, Labour Party Archives; WOR/1–32. Drake, *Women in Trade Unions*, pp. 107–8. Braybon, *Women Workers in the First World War*, p. 198. *Common Cause*, 1 March, 6 June,

22 August 1919. RS to E. Rathbone, 5 April 1919, LSWS Papers, Fawcett Library; 327.
60. Braybon, *Women Workers*, op. cit., pp. 201, 169.
61. 3 August 1915, Marshall Papers; 3/47.
62. LSWS Papers, Fawcett Library; 327.

5 A New Morality?

1. *Common Cause*, 26 April 1918.
2. Caroline Marshall to CEM, 8 December 1918.
3. In *The Spinster and Her Enemies, Feminism and Sexuality 1880–1930* (Pandora, London, 1985), Sheila Jeffreys has challenged the association of sexual liberation with feminism.
4. Stocks, *My Commonplace Book*, p. 162. Naomi Mitchison, *You May Well Ask* (Fontana, London, 1979). pp. 69–70.
5. Maude Royden, *Sex and Commonsense* (Hurst & Blackett, London, 1922, 1947), pp. 118, 160.
6. Ibid., pp. 155, 175.
7. Maude Royden, *A Threefold Cord* (Victor Gollancz, London, 1947), pp. 39, 43, 103. Royden to Pethick Lawrence, 14 November 1947, Pethick Lawrence Papers; 3/173.
8. Sheila Rowbotham & Jeffrey Weeks, *Socialism and the New Life* (Pluto, London, 1977), p. 169. Maude Royden, 'Modern Love', in Victor Gollancz (ed.), *The Making of Women, Oxford Essays on Feminism*. pp. 62, 122.
9. Royden, *Sex and Commonsense*, p. 171. Elizabeth Robins, *Ancilla's Share* (Hyperion Press, Inc., Westport, Connecticut, 1976), pp. 171, 49, 99. H.G. Wells quoted in *Time & Tide (T&T)*, 19 September 1924. For a modern analysis of Robins as a 'frigid' woman, see Jane Marcus, op. cit.
10. Robins, *Both Sides of the Curtain*, p. 170.
11. Octavia Wilberforce, typescript autobiography, pp. 258–9, Fawcett Library.
12. *T&T*, 27 June 1924.
13. Rhondda, *This Was My World*, pp. 37–8, 47, 126–7.
14. Swanwick, *I Have Been Young*, pp. 83, 121–3.
15. Swanwick, *The Future of the Women's Movement* (G. Bell, London 1913), p. 106, *I Have Been Young*, pp. 109–110, 272.
16. Pethick Lawrence Papers; 7/33.
17. Sharp, Holiday Diary, 12 June 1921.
18. *Daily Herald*, 24 October 1919.
19. Sharp, *Unfinished Adventure*, p. 158.
20. Mary Stocks to Marie Stopes, 17 Nov. 1928.
21. Strachey, *Remarkable Relations*, p. 258.
22. Brian Harrison, *Prudent Revolutionaries* (Clarendon, Oxford, 1987), p. 161: information from an interview with Miss Irene Hilton, 24 February 1977.

23. Hopkinson, *Family Inheritance*, p. 105. Stocks, *Eleanor Rathbone*, p. 120.

24. Swanwick to CEM, 5 February 1918; 4/80. Eva McNaghten to CEM, 3 February 1918; 4/80.

25. Wilberforce, autobiography, p. 271.

26. Rhondda, *This Was My World*, p. 299. Theodora Bosanquet, 1881–1961, was secretary to Henry James from 1907 to 1916. She worked in the Ministry of Food during the First World War, and from 1920 to 1935 she was executive secretary to the International Federation of University Women.

27. Information on Kathleen Courtney from Miss Furlong, her cousin. Mary Sheepshanks to CEM, 8 November 1919; 2/38. Oldfield, *Spinsters of this Parish*, p 216. Mary Sheepshanks, autobiography, p. 58.

28. Louisa Garrett Anderson to Evelyn Sharp, undated. Sharp, diary, 1, 2 Nov. 1942.

29. Sharp, *Unfinished Adventure*, pp. 32–3.

30. Vera Brittain, *Testament of Friendship* (Virago, London, 1980) , p. 2. Carroll Smith-Rosenberg in *Disorderly Conduct* (OUP, Oxford, 1985) discusses the reasons why feminists in the 1920s failed to respond to the attack by Havelock Ellis and others on their loving relationships with other women.

31. Rhondda, *This Was My World*, p. 37.

32. Swanwick, *The Future of the Women's Movement*, p. 115. Royden, *Sex and Commonsense*, p. 34.

33. Mrs Bruce, speaking at the first meeting of the Moral Reform Union, quoted in Jeffreys, *The Spinster and Her Enemies*, p. 34.

34. *Common Cause*, 7 June, 14 July, 1918.

35. Quoted in Jeffreys, op. cit., p. 84.

36. *WL*, 5 Nov. 1920, 13 March 1925, 25 March 1927. *T&T* 1 Jan. 1926.

37. Alison Neilans, 'Changes in Sex Morality', in Ray Strachey (ed.), *Our Freedom and Its Results* (Hogarth Press, London, 1936), pp. 201, 206 – 9. *T&T*, 17 July, 2 Oct. 1925.

38. Neilans, 'Changes in Sex Morality', pp. 219, 222.

39. Ibid., pp. 221, 176, 228.

40. Marie Stopes, *Wise Parenthood* (Putnam's, London, 1918), Introduction.

41. Emmeline Pethick Lawrence to Stopes, 21 January, 4 October, 1922. Fred Pethick Lawrence to Stopes, 21 April 1930.

42. Stocks to Stopes, 9 May 1925. Dora Russell, *The Tamarisk Tree* (Virago, London, 1971), pp. 169, 172. Dora Russell to Stopes, 2 May 1924. Stocks to Stopes, 25 Oct. 1926.

43. Stocks to Stopes, 16 May 1923.

44. Ibid. *WL*, 24 April, 6 May 1921.

45. Stocks to Stopes, 14 Feb. 1924. Stocks, *My Commonplace Book*, p. 162.

46. Stocks, *My Commonplace Book*, p. 162. *T&T*, 16 February 1923, 30 May, 6 June 1924, 19 April 1925.

47. Stocks, *My Commonplace Book*, op. cit., p. 160. *T&T*, 6 June 1925.
48. Naomi Mitchison, *Birth Control* (Faber & Faber, London, n.d.), pp. 6, 9, 27. Mitchison, *You May Well Ask*, pp. 69, 24. *T&T*, 22 June 1928.
49. Stocks to Stopes, 14 March 1925.
50. Russell, *The Tamarisk Tree*, p. 175. Margaret Llewellyn Davies, (ed.), *Maternity: Letters from Working Women* (Virago, London, 1978).
51. Stocks to Stopes, 17 Sept. 1924. Stocks, *Eleanor Rathbone*, p. 315. Stocks to Stopes, 14 March 1925.
52. *WL*, 11, 18 February 1921. NUSEC/EC Minutes 11 November 1920, Fawcett Library.
53. *WL*, 18 March 1921.
54. *WL*, 17 March 1922.
55. *WL*, 15 September, 13 October 1922.
56. *T&T*, 25 December 1925. *WL*, 10 July, 30 January, 1925.
57. *WL*, 6 Feb. 1925. Eleanor Rathbone, *The Disinherited Family* (Falling Wall Press, Bristol, 1986), p. 325.
58. *WL*, 4 March 1921. Rathbone, *Disinherited Family*, pp. 234, 250.
59. Rathbone, *Disinherited Family*, pp. 136, 155, 178, 179, 192–4.
60. Ibid., pp. 178, 177. Hopkinson, *Family Inheritance*, p. 97.
61. Harrison, *Prudent Revolutionaries*, p. 191.
62. Royden, 'Modern Love', p. 51. See also Maude Royden, *Women and the Next Civilisation* (Unwin, Woking, 1941).
63. Evelyn Sharp. *The London Child* (John Lane, London, 1927).
64. Swanwick to CEM, n.d. ?1917; 2/35.
65. Swanwick, *The Future of the Women's Movement*, pp. 22, 84. For Marshall on motherhood, see Chapter 8, p. 212.
66. *T&T*, 4, 11, 18 Nov. 1927.
67. Vera Brittain. 'Committees versus Professions' (1929) in Berry & Bishop (eds), *Testament of a Generation* (Virago, London, 1985), pp. 106–7. Vera Brittain to Sharp, 16 June 1933.
68. David Rubinstein argues in *Before the Suffragettes* (Harvester, London, 1986) that economic independence was crucial for feminists in the 1890s. *WL*, 25 Feb. 1921.
69. *The Vote*, 30 April 1927.

6 Lobbying for Equality, 1921–25

1. The Women's Freedom League continued as an active pressure group in the period covered by this study. It was especially active in promoting equal franchise and equal pay, and also advocated an equal moral standard. It was arguably less powerful than the other two groups, but it was a valuable focus for feminist activity. Some of the minutes of the executive committee of the WFL and microfilm copies of its paper, *The Vote*, are in the Fawcett Library.
2. Hopkinson, *Family Inheritance*, pp. 97, 89.

238 *Notes*

3.　*WL*, 15 Oct. 1920. Hopkinson, *Family Inheritance*, op. cit., pp. 87, 91.
4.　Rhondda, *This Was My World*, p. 294.
5.　Ibid., pp. 298, 301–2.
6.　Wilberforce, autobiography, p. 251. Rhondda, *This Was My World*, p. 303.
7.　Wilberforce, autobiography, pp. 253–4. *T&T*, 14 May 1920.
8.　Rhondda, *This Was My World*, p. 298.
9.　Rhondda to Robins, 8 May 1919, quoted in Wilberforce, autobiography, p. 254. Rhondda, *This Was My World*, p. 299.
10.　Six Points were drawn up each year for the 'immediate programme' which was discussed at the Annual Councils of the NUSEC. *T&T*, 25 February 1921.
11.　*WL*, 25 February, 1921. *T&T*, 25 February 1921.
12.　*T&T*, 15 June 1923.
13.　Evidence before the Royal Commission on the Birth Rate.
14.　Hopkinson, *Family Inheritance*, p. 95. *WL*, 15 April 1921, 23 February 1922, 15 June 1923.
15.　*WL*, 19 August 1921. *T&T*, 7 Sept. 1923.
16.　Eleanor Rathbone, *Milestones: Annual Presidential Addresses to the NUSEC*, (Liverpool, 1929), 26 March 1924.
17.　CEM to Hal Marshall, 14 April 1921. A.J.P.Taylor, *English History, 1914–1945* (Clarendon Press, Oxford, 1965), p. 188.
18.　*T&T*, 19 Jan. 1923. Winifred Holtby, *Letters to a Friend* (Collins, London, 1937), 20 May 1922.
19.　*WL*, 7 December 1923.
20.　*T&T*, 25 January, 29 February, 1924. Rathbone, *Milestones*, 24 March 1924. *T&T*, 11 April 1924.
21.　NUSEC/EC Minutes 8, 22 May 1924.
22.　*T&T*, 20 June 1924.
23.　*T&T*, 8 August 1924. Rathbone, *Milestones*, 24 February 1926. *T&T*, 24 July 1925.
24.　*WL*, 10 July 1925. Hopkinson, *Family Inheritance*, p. 96. *WL*, 14 August 1925. Rathbone, *Milestones*, 24 February 1926.
25.　Stocks, *Eleanor Rathbone*, p. 112.
26.　For a survey of the concern of Victorian feminists with employment question, see Phillippa Levine, *Victorian Feminism*, 1850–1900 (Hutchinson, London, 1987), Chapters 4 & 5.
27.　Rhondda to Strachey, 1 April 1919, Strachey to Rathbone, 5 April 1919, Fawcett Library, 326.
28.　Meta Zimmeck. 'Strategies and Strategems for the Employment of Women in the British Civil Service, 1919–1939', *The Historical Journal*, 27, 4 (1984), pp. 901–24. *WL*, 28 May 1920.
29.　Zimmeck, 'Strategies', op. cit.
30.　LSWS papers, Fawcett Library; 124, 327. Ray Strachey, 'Changes in Employment', in Strachey (ed.), *Our Freedom and Its Results*, p. 131.
31.　Maude Royden, 'The Future of Women in Industry', talk given at Whitefield's Men's Own, 22 June 1919, Fawcett Library; CP 21.
32.　Beatrice Webb, *Diary 1912–1924*, Margaret Cole (ed.) (Longmans,

London, 1952), 8 Dec. 1918, 11 February 1919. *WL*, 18 February 1921.

33. *T&T*, 21 May, 1920, 19 January 1923. Rathbone, *Milestones*, 11 March 1925.
34. Report of Meeting, 5 January 1927, LSWS papers, Fawcett Library; 135.
35. Barbara Drake, quoted in Jane Lewis, *Women in England* (Wheatsheaf, Sussex, 1984), p. 203. Braybon, *Women Workers in the First World War*, pp. 206–208. Sarah Boston, *Women Workers and the Trade Union Movement* (Davis-Poynter, London, 1980), pp. 137–9.
36. Robins, *Ancilla's Share*, p. 226, 234.
37. Janet Courtney, *Recollected in Tranquillity* (Heinemann, London, 1926), pp. 271–5.
38. Robins, *Ancilla's Share*, p. 234.
39. Eleanor Rathbone, 'The Remuneration of Women', in Gollancz, (ed.), *The Making of Women: Oxford Essays on Feminism*, p. 106. Braybon, *Women Workers in the First World War*, pp. 186–8.
40. *T&T*, 22 June 1923.
41. *WL*, 6, 13 May, 18 March 1921.
42. *T&T*, 13 April 1923. *WL*, 20 May 1921.
43. RS to Alys Russell, August 1921. RS to MB, 5 December 1922.
44. Stocks, *My Commonplace Book*, pp. 12–13.
45. Swanwick, *I Have Been Young*, pp. 150–2.
46. *T&T*, 5 January, 2 February 1923. *WL*, 23 September 1921. See also Alison Oram, 'Serving Two masters? The introduction of a marriage bar in teaching in the 1920s', in Feminist History Group, *The Sexual Dynamics of History* (Pluto Press, London, 1983).
47. *WL*, 29 October 1921, 2 February 1923.
48. Harold Smith, 'Sex vs. Class; British Feminists and the Labour Movement, 1919–1929', *The Historian* (1980), p. 30.
49. Cicely Corbett Fisher to Pippa Strachey, 13 May 1919, LSWS papers, Fawcett Library; 326. Marshall papers; 4/4.
50. *WL*, 15 June 1923. Cuttings in the Fawcett Library from *The Times*, 10 May 1924, *Daily Express*, 28 February 1925.
51. *T&T*, 14 December 1923, *WL*, 14 December 1923.
52. *T&T*, 16 October 1924.
53. Hopkinson, *Family Inheritance*, p. 94. Rathbone, *Disinherited Family*, p. 194.
54. RS to Bernard Berenson, 15 May 1921.
55. RS to MB, 14 March 1920. RS to Margaret Wintringham, 24 Sept. 1921.
56. RS to MB, 14 December 1921, 12 March 1922, 18 February 1922, 10 January 1922.
57. RS to MB, 3, 17 July, 18 October, 18 November 1922.
58. RS to MB, 24 November, 5 December, 1922, 8 May, 16 November, 7 December, 1923.
59. RS to MB, 13 November, 26 February, 1924. RS to Pippa Strachey, 10 August 1924, Fawcett, Autograph Collection; 6c/276.
60. *WL*, 2 March 1923.

7 New and Old Feminists

1. Rathbone, *Milestones*, 11 March 1925.
2. *T&T*, 6 August 1926.
3. *T&T*, 18 September 1925.
4. Ibid.
5. In the 1920s the NUSEC, and especially Chrystal Macmillan, pressed for the law to be changed so that a woman did not automatically have to assume the nationality of her husband.
6. *T&T*, 6 Aug. 1926.
7. Ibid. Rhondda, *This Was My World*, p. 299.
8. *T&T*, 13, 6 August, 9, 16 July 1926.
9. *T&T*, 12 March 1926. *WL*, 12 March 1926. *T&T*, 13 Aug. 1926.
10. *T&T*, 15 October, 16 November 1926.
11. *WL*, 31 December 1926.
12. Letters from resigning EC members, *WL*, 11 March 1927.
13. *WL*, 11 February 1927.
14. *WL*, 25 February 1927.
15. *T&T*, 18 March, 1927. Mary Stocks, *The Case for Family Endowment* (London Publishing Co., 1927), p. 38. Stocks to Stopes, 14 March 1927.
16. *WL*, 25 February 1918. Rathbone, *Milestones*, 8 March 1921, 11 March 1925, 24 February 1926. *WL*, 10 September 1926.
17. *T&T*, 11, 4 March, 20 May 1927.
18. *T&T*, 4 March 1927.
19. *T&T*, 1 April 1927.
20. *WL*, 25 February 1927.
21. *WL*, 23 March 1928.
22. Levine, *Victorian Feminism*, pp. 118–24.
23. Ellen F. Mappen, 'Strategies for Change: Social Feminists' Approaches to the Problems of Women's Work', in Angela John (ed.), *Unequal Opportunities in Women's Employment in England* (Basil Blackwell, Oxford, 1986).
24. RS to MB, 3 February 1927. Jane Lewis, *Women in England*, p. 104.
25. NUSEC/EC Minutes, 24 July 1924. *T&T*, 20, 6 March 1925. *WL*, 5 March 1926.
26. *T&T*, 16 July 1926. *WL*, 23 March 1928.
27. *WL*, 26 November 1926.
28. *WL*, 3 September, 3 December, 1926.
29. *T&T*, 3 December, 1926.
30. *T&T*, 4 February, 5 March, 1926.
31. Harold Smith, 'Sex vs. Class', p. 34. *T&T*, 5 March 1926.
32. *WL*, 11 March 1927. *T&T*, 25 March 1927.
33. *T&T*, 11, 18 March 1927. LSWS Minutes, 22 March 1927, Fawcett Library; 138. *WL*, 25 November 1927, 18 May 1928. *T&T*, 22 April 1927.
34. NUSEC/EC Minutes 4 July 1928, Fawcett Library.
35. *Manchester Guardian*, 8 December 1927. *T&T*, 5 March 1926.
36. Title from Rathbone's 'Milestone' speech, 20 March 1924. *WL*, 2 March 1923.

37. *WL*, 30 January 1925.
38. *WL*, 2 January 1925. *T&T*, 16 May 1924. NUSEC/EC Minutes, 25 Sept. 1924, Fawcett Library. *WL*, 31 Oct. 1925.
39. *T&T*, 15 June 1923, 13 May 1927.
40. *T&T*, 20 May 1927.
41. NUSEC/EC Minutes, 23 October 1924. *New Leader*, 2 April 1929.
42. *WL*, 14, 21 May 1926.
43. Sharp, Diary, 3 May 1926.
44. Rathbone, *Milestones*, 6 March 1929.
45. *WL*, 25 May 1928.
46. Rathbone, *Milestones*, 26 March 1924.
47. *WL*, 21 November 1924. Elizabeth Vallance, *Women in the House* (Athlone Press, London, 1979), p. 122.
48. *WL*, 29 January 1926.
49. *T&T*, 9 July 1926. Crystal Eastman, 'British Women Fire the First Gun in Their Second Suffrage Battle', *Equal Rights* (27 March 1926), in Blanche Wiesen Cook, *Crystal Eastman on Women & Revolution* (OUP, Oxford, 1978), p. 178.
50. *T&T*, 9 July 1926, 18 February 1927, 12 November 1926. Rathbone to Hubback, quoted in Hopkinson, *Family Inheritance*, p. 91. *WL*, 30 December 1927. Hopkinson, *Family Inheritance*, p. 94.
51. Rathbone, *Milestones*, 7 March 1928. *T&T*, 6, 20 July 1928.
52. RS to MB, April 1928. Vallance, *Women in the House*, p. 123.
53. *T&T*, 6 April 1928.
54. Rathbone, *Milestones*, 6 March 1929.
55. *WL*, 29 April 1927. *T&T*, 13 April 1928. *WL*, 13 April 1927.
56. Rathbone, *Milestones*, 6 March 1929. *T&T*, 6 April 1928. Proposed Lines of Expansion for the N.U.S.E.C., December 1928, Fawcett Library.
57. *T&T*, 6 April, 6 July 1928, 18 March 1927.
58. *T&T*, 1 April 1927.
59. Rathbone, *Milestones*, 6 March 1929.
60. Stocks, *Eleanor Rathbone*, p. 129.

8 International Feminism, 1921–28

1. *Jus Suffragii (Jus)*, July 1920.
2. *Jus*, March 1923.
3. RS to MB, 8 December 1921, 12 May 1927.
4. Sharp, Diary, 4 June 1920, 19 January 1922.
5. Sharp, *Unfinished Adventure*, p. 267.
6. Marshall, Report on the Famine Areas, March 1921, WILPF papers, BLPES; 4/7.
7. WILPF papers, BLPES; 4/9.
8. Sharp, *Unfinished Adventure*, p. 285.
9. Aletta Jacobs to CEM, 25 September 1923, CEM to Vilma Glucklich, 3 November 1923, CEM to Lisa Gustave Heyman, 11 August 1923, CEM to Glucklich, 18 August 1923, WILPF papers, BLPES; 4/9.

10. NUSEC/EC Minutes, 25 March 1920, Fawcett library. *WL*, 19 March 1920. *Jus*, July 1920. NUSEC/EC Minutes 4 March 1920. RS to MB, 26 June 1921. *Jus*, July 1922.

11. NUSEC/EC Minutes, Fawcett Library, 11 January 1923. *WL*, 30 December 1927. Swanwick, *I Have Been Young*, p.414.

12. Swanwick, *I Have Been Young*, pp. 383–4.

13. Ibid., pp. 398–9.

14. Ibid., pp. 412, 404.

15. WILPF papers, BLPES; 5/3. Swanwick, *I Have Been Young*, pp. 404–5.

16. Swanwick, *I Have Been Young*, p. 405.

17. WIL Yearly Report, 1924, WILPF papers, BLPES; 2/1. *Pax International*, December 1925, November 1927.

18. Sharp, Diary, 6 September 1926.

19. *WL*, 4 June 1926.

20. Marie Corbett to MCA, 1921, 12 February, 12 May 1924.

21. MCA to Brian Ashby, 23 March 1925.

22. MCA to Marie Corbett, 27 February 1922.

23. *WL*, 1 June 1923.

24. See note 37, Chapter 2 for the genesis of the NCW.

25. *Jus*, April, June, July, August/September 1924, April, June, August, September, October, December 1925.

26. *Jus*, July 1926.

27. *WL*, 1 June 1923.

28. *Jus*, Aug./Sept. 1924.

29. *Jus*, July 1926. *WL*, 4 June, 1926. *Jus*, April, May, 1924.

30. Cook, *Crystal Eastman on Women & Revolution*, Introduction.

31. *Equal Rights*, 23 October 1925, 27 March 1926, 4 June 1927, in Cook, *Crystal Eastman*, op. cit., pp. 170, 182, 226–7.

32. Ibid., p. 30.

33. *WL*, 4 June 1926. *Equal Rights*, 26 June 1926, in Cook, op. cit, p. 206.

34. *The World*, 27 June 1926, in Cook, op. cit. p. 193.

35. *Pax*, August 1929. *Jus*, July 1929. *WL*, 4 June 1926.

36. *WL*, 26 June 1926. *The New Republic*, 27 June 1926 in Cook, *Crystal Eastman*, op. cit., p. 135.

37. *WL*, 2 July 1926. *Jus*, March 1923.

38. *T&T*, 11 June 1926.

39. *WL*, 18 June 1926.

40. *Pax International* (*Pax*), February, March 1926. *WL*, 10 July 1925.

41. *WL*, 11, 25 June 1926.

42. *Pax*, December 1927. *WL*, 24 February 1928.

43. Courtney, interviewed by Mary Stott, *Manchester Guardian*, 11 March 1968.

44. Swanwick, *I Have Been Young*, pp. 414, 434. Speech at WILPF Congress, Dublin, July 1926, quoted in *Pax*, Aug./Sept. 1926.

45. CEM to Madeleine Doty, June 1929, quoted in Gertrude Bussey and Margaret Tims, *Women's International League for Peace and Freedom* (George Allen & Unwin, London 1965), p. 75. CEM, 'Women and War', 22 March 1915, 'The Future of Women in Politics', in Margaret

Kamester and Jo Vellacott (eds), *Militarism versus Feminism* (Virago, London, 1987), pp. 40, 50, 38.

46.   Jane Lewis on Jo Vellacott, 'Feminist Consciousness and the First World War', in Ruth Roach Pierson (ed.), *Women and Peace: Theoretical, Historical and Practical Perspectives* (Croom Helm, London, 1987), p. 129.
47.   *WL*, 30 December 1927.
48.   *Jus*, November 1922, June 1923.
49.   *WL*, 30 December 1927.
50.   *Jus*, April 1927, May 1928.
51.   *T&T*, 9, 23 July 1926. *Jus*, June 1928. *WL*, 18 May 1928.
52.   Robins, *Ancilla's Share*, pp. 301–2.
53.   *Jus*, July 1929. *Pax*, Aug. 1929.

Conclusion

1.   *WL*, 8 June 1928.
2.   Mary Stott, *Organization Woman: The Story of the National Union of Townswomen's Guilds* (Heinemann, London, 1978), p. 11.
3.   NUSEC/EC 27 September 1927. Stocks to Stopes, 15 October 1926. Stocks, *My Commonplace Book*, p. 165. Pethick Lawrence, *My Part in a Changing World*, p. 337.
4.   Rhondda, *This Was My World*, p. 299.
5.   For the work of Rathbone and Strachey in the 1930s see Brian Harrison, *Prudent Revolutionaries*, Chapters 4 and 6.
6.   Pethick Lawrence to Sharp, ?1927.
7.   Naomi Mitchison to Elizabeth Haldane, n.d., Haldane papers, National Library of Scotland; Acc. 9186(1).
8.   Ibid., 1928; 6033 f295.
9.   Elizabeth Robins, *Both Sides of the Curtain*, p. 170.

Index